THE BONE DOCTOR'S CONCERTO

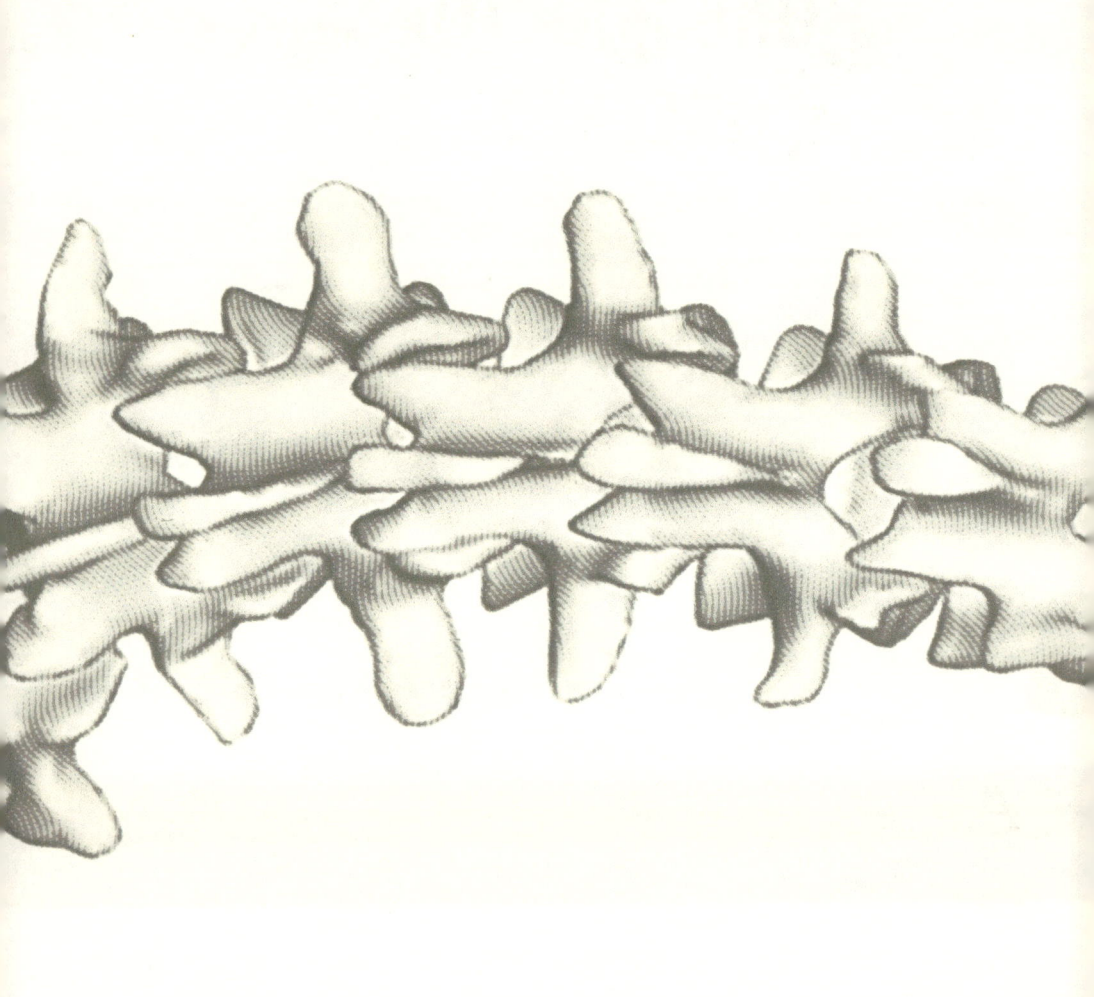

THE BONE DOCTOR'S CONCERTO

Music, Surgery, and the Pieces in Between

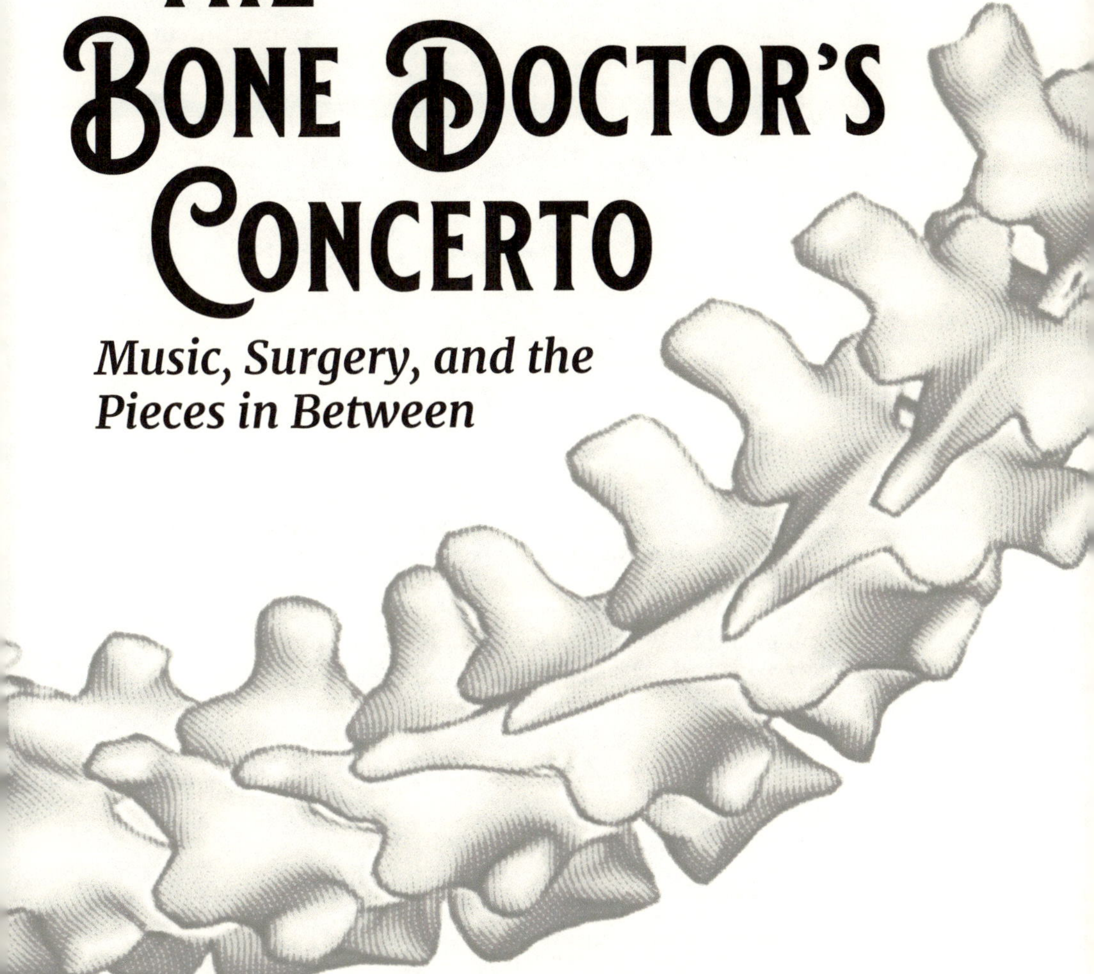

Alvin H. Crawford, MD
With a foreword by G. Dean MacEwen, MD

About the University of Cincinnati Press

The University of Cincinnati Press is committed to publishing rigorous, peer-reviewed, leading scholarship accessibly to stimulate dialog among the academy, public intellectuals, and lay practitioners. The Press endeavors to erase disciplinary boundaries in order to cast fresh light on common problems in our global community. Building on the university's long-standing tradition of social responsibility to the citizens of Cincinnati, the state of Ohio, and the world, the Press publishes books on topics that expose and resolve disparities at every level of society and have local, national, and global impact.

University of Cincinnati Press
Cincinnati 45221
Copyright © 2023

All rights reserved. No part of this book may be reproduced or utilized in any form or by any means, electronic or mechanical, or by any information storage and retrieval system, without written permission from the publisher. Requests for permission to reproduce material from this work should be sent to the University of Cincinnati Press, Langsam Library, 2911 Woodside Drive, Cincinnati, Ohio 45221

ucincinnatipress.uc.edu

Library of Congress Control Number: 2023941911

ISBN 979-8-88550-000-5 (hardback)
ISBN 979-8-88550-001-2 (e-book, PDF)
ISBN 979-8-88550-002-9 (e-book, EPUB)

Designed and produced for UC Press by Alisa Strauss

Production Intern, Jared Brancatelli

Typeset in Baskerville 120 Pro, Libre Baskerville, and Blackriver

Printed in the United States of America

First Printing

Dedication

To my strongest advocate when I was growing up, my mother, who early on said I could move mountains, and talked me into believing that I could.

Mothers are a special type of humanity. Mine was always there for me through thick and thin, success and failure, sickness and health. She was my best friend, the linchpin of the family, and a comfort when I was down. She believed in me, and was caring, supportive, enlightening, loyal, kind, and loving—a nurturing mistress of calm. She was not, however, one to spare the rod.

As a single parent, my mother was fierce in regard to her children, insisting they were well educated, had good manners, developed and used whatever skills they had, became dedicated citizens, and voted, and we loved her for the sacrifices she made for us. Her favorite proverb was: "If a task was once begun, never leave it 'til it's done. Be the labor great or small, do it well or not at all."

TABLE OF CONTENTS

Foreword, by G. Dean MacEwen, MD	ix
Prologue	xi
Introduction	1
In the Beginning	5
As Good as It Gets	18
Music at Tennessee State	23
The Qualified Applicant	27
University of Tennessee College of Medicine	32
The Invisible Man	38
In the Navy Now	46
Boston to San Diego	52
Europe on Five Dollars a Day	73
Henry Ford Hospital and Beyond	78
Pediatric Orthopaedics at Children's Hospital	84
That Dr. Crawford	93
Naval Reserve Activity	101

Advances in Spinal Sugery	105
The "Cincinnati Incision"	112
International Patients	115
Mission Surgery Experiences	123
Global Relationships	132
Ohio National Insurance	163
It Is What It Is and Other Truths	170
The Sink Test	188
Fourth Act: Sabbatical	192
Forth Act: Clinic	199
It Ain't Over until the Tall Man in the White Coat Plays Saxophone	204
Those I've Met (and Almost Met) Along the Way...	207
Epilogue	219
Acknowledgments	228
Endnotes	233
Bibliography	235

FOREWORD

My professional experience with Alvin Crawford began in 1974 when he was one of many orthopaedic fellows to come through the Pediatric Orthopaedic-Spine Fellowship program at the Alfred I. duPont Institute, which is now known as the Alfred I. duPont Hospital for Children in Wilmington, Delaware. Alvin's fellowship evolved out of his interest in doing research there, and I was in charge at that time. He was going to be the first African American fellow at the hospital. We met in person in San Diego where Alvin was serving in the Navy, practicing pediatric orthopaedic medicine at the naval hospital there. I happened to be visiting family in the San Diego area and we arranged to meet in person. Well, the first thing I noticed was that Alvin had a long, black beard. My supervisor at the Institute was a Southern gentleman and he was the doctor in charge. I told Al that Dr. Shands didn't care for beards. So, I advised him that if he wanted to do well there, he should shave it off. And he did. He shaved it off and didn't grow it back. That really cemented our relationship. We never had a cross word at that time or at any time.

It was my practice to assign a project to each of the fellows in the residency program. Since Alvin seemed very special (and had a lot of energy), I saved up a particular project for him on neurofibromatosis. Alvin hesitated at first. But with my strong encouragement, he went ahead and completed it, and the study and treatment of neurofibromatosis became one of the strengths of his career from then on. He's very interested in education, has been involved in many peer reviews and papers, and contributed material for textbooks. Alvin is recognized internationally because of his work in the pediatric orthopaedics field; he has traveled around the world and interacted with doctors and patients in countries all over the globe, particularly in relation to his special knowledge on neurofibromatosis. Alvin was, and is, able to take on many projects simultaneously, which is why I assigned him the study of neurofibromatosis. I felt that he could be very special in that field, and he was. Subsequently, Alvin developed expertise in treating scoliosis and became the first African American president of the prestigious Scoliosis Research Society.

Alvin was one of the best participants in our fellowship programs, which included several hundred doctors over the years. He was excellent with patients, taking very good care of people, and they appreciated his attention in return.

I've followed his career over the years, and he's been very successful. Alvin is still working and is an outstanding orthopaedic surgeon.

G. Dean MacEwen, MD

G. Dean MacEwen, MD served as the second medical director of the Alfred I. duPont Institute from 1969 to 1986. He was the successor to Alfred R. Shands Jr., MD, the first medical director of the Institute. Dr. MacEwen is a pioneer in the treatment of scoliosis and hip dysplasia and helped develop the "Wilmington brace," used worldwide in the correction of scoliosis. During his tenure at the duPont Institute, Dr. MacEwen was instrumental in the training of orthopaedic residents and doctors (including Alvin H. Crawford), and considers the education of doctors to be one of his most satisfying accomplishments.

PROLOGUE

"Who does he think he is?"

Not long ago, I had a surgical case at the new University of Cincinnati West Chester Hospital. I wasn't familiar with the operating room's facilities, so I asked a volunteer at the front desk for directions. One of the volunteers overheard me and after greeting me said, "You're Dr. Crawford, aren't you?"

I said, "Yes, I am."

She continued. "I remember you. Many years ago, I worked in development at Cincinnati Children's and then I went over to HR. I remember when you were being interviewed for the director of pediatric orthopaedics position. They had so much fun with your application. Boy, they talked about you for a long time."

"They?" I remember thinking. This is interesting.

So I asked her, "What did they say?"

Before I continue, here's a brief prelude. I am passionate about tennis. My doubles partner Jose Gonzales Usutu, a Harvard medical student, and I won the 1971 Hub City Open Tennis Tournament in Boston. I also played tennis in the navy as often as I could, wherever I was stationed, and continued to play after I left the service. In 1975, I won the Southern West Coast All-Service Junior Veteran's tournament. When I was working out of Henry Ford Hospital in Detroit, before I came to Cincinnati in 1977, I played a lot of tennis in and around that area, both for recreation and in tournament competition. When I interviewed at

Cincinnati Children's Hospital, one of my hosts took me over to Triangle Park, a municipal park located near the hospital. Conveniently, the park had several tennis courts. I told the folks who were recruiting me that I'd need a shower installed in my office in case I played tennis in the morning prior to clinic or after surgery. Their response wasn't quite what I expected.

They said, "What?"

I reiterated my request. "I'm going to need a shower in or adjacent to my office, so that after tennis I can clean up."

The volunteer said that there were lengthy discussions in HR concerning my request and even though she'd been retired for many years, she vividly remembered the conversations that took place. Later chapters will delve into this, but I did indeed get my shower. The question around HR about me and my unorthodox preemployment request included, "Who does he think he is?"

And I thought: good question.

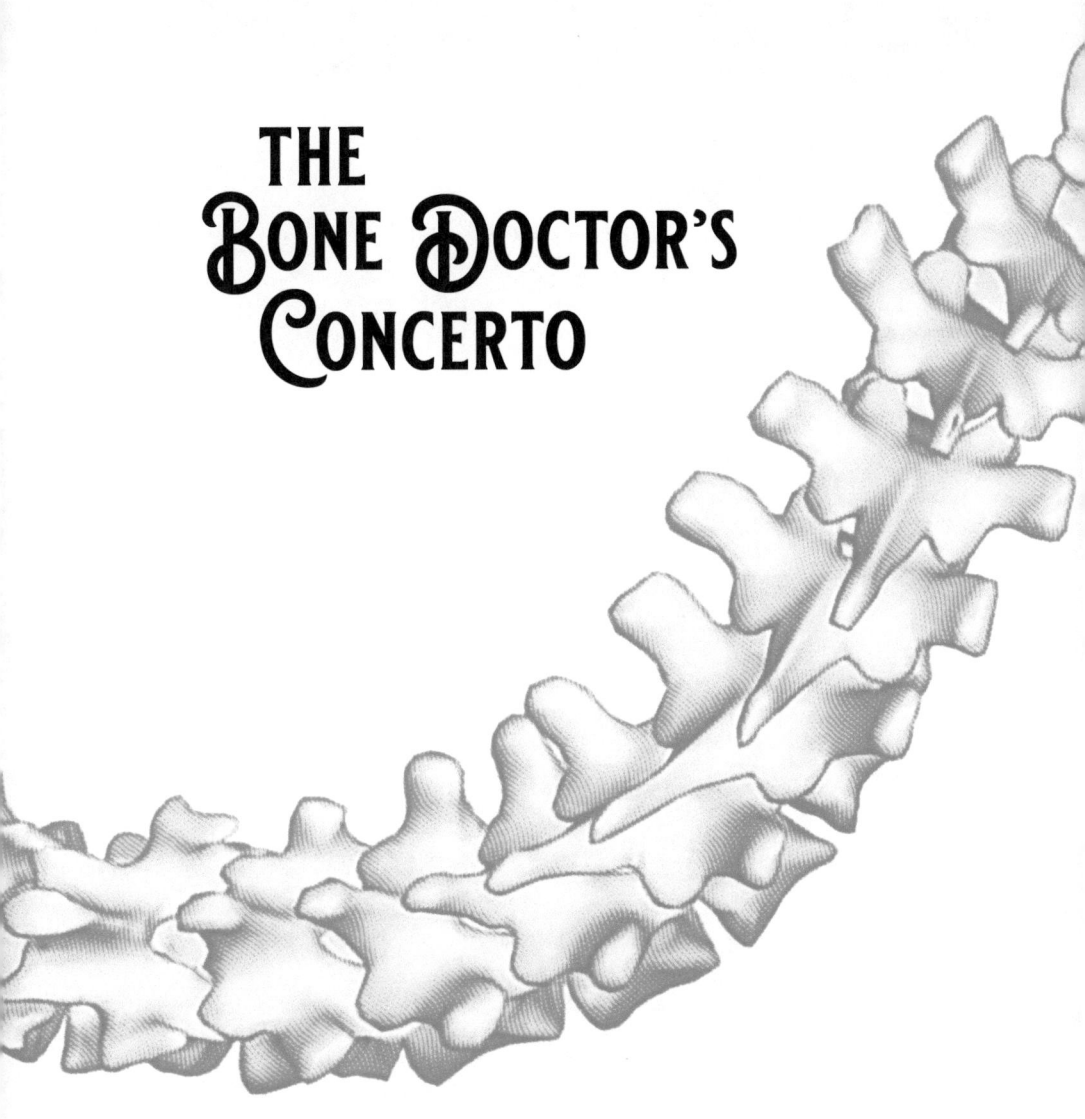

THE BONE DOCTOR'S CONCERTO

INTRODUCTION

I'm from Memphis, Tennessee. Specifically, I'm from Orange Mound, one of the first planned communities developed for freed slaves after the Civil War. The question of how I got from there to where I am now is hard to answer. This book highlights that journey.

Born into a rigidly segregated world, I benefited from a nurturing environment, education, God-given talents, a supportive family and community, multiracial connections, and just plain luck. The racism and negativity that challenged me growing up continues to challenge our country today. Each morning as I shave, the face in the mirror resembles the repeated subject that nightly news segments tell me I should fear: "rapist," "murderer," "doper." But less frequently do I see a face like mine under the headlines of "doctor," "brilliant scientist," or "surgeon."

I am not deluded that all possibilities are created equal. They were not in 1961 when I enrolled in the University of Tennessee College of Medicine (UTCOM), and they sure are not now. When I began medical school, the country was in turmoil with sit-ins, Freedom Riders, marches, protests—all in response to the rigid segregation in our country, especially in the South. The political, social, and cultural environments were so toxic that an African American male like me could never be completely at ease, even under the most benign conditions. As Dick Gregory would say, (and I paraphrase), "Any (n—) who isn't paranoid, is crazy."

As I write this, there is a persisting political force in this country, an undercurrent that may sweep away many of the positive features of our national landscape for people who look like me. We continue to contend with voter suppression, police brutality, and racial profiling. Our society has a long way to go toward communicating, relating, and accepting different attitudes and values. That's a fact and it must be faced head-on. As rhythm-and-blues artist Sharon Jones once said, "You have to look at life the way it is."[1]

The most important gifts I received from my mother were an understanding of the value of education and hard work. Both of my parents believed that education is something that can never be taken away, regardless of sociopolitical disenfranchisement. It was a pathway to success for my entire family. I would like to be remembered as someone who took maximum advantage of his education and talents and set out to make a difference. I believe it is important to always challenge yourself with high expectations. During my professional life as a pediatric orthopaedic surgeon, I surreptitiously also challenged my patients to be their best. Since 2008, unbeknownst to hospital administrators, every patient in my practice knew that if they brought in their report card with straight As, I'd give them $5.00 per A.

I am deeply honored that parents entrusted me with their children, traveling from near and far for treatment. Forty years of treating some of the most complicated spinal deformities, including over 27,000 surgical interventions, has been an honor and pleasure for which I'm eternally grateful. It doesn't get any better than that.

Basic human dignity follows the golden rule—treat people the way you would want them to treat you. To say I was occasionally demanding is an understatement; to say I was caring and determined is reality. My innate principles in my personal and professional life follow the MIID complex—motivation, industry, integrity, and desire. The ultimate desire for humans is to enjoy life and be happy. I have been blessed to have wonderful experiences with genuine opportunities and lasting friendships. I continue to strive to make achievement not a goal, but a lifestyle.

Music has played a significant role in my life. A good pianist learns to play all the keys—black and white—together. I challenge readers to recognize that just as all piano keys are needed to create a beautiful harmonic sound, all people—Black and white—are needed to make the world a better place. It is my hope that this book will reach young people who may be faced with what seem like insurmountable and exhausting barriers and show them how success can be achieved with purposeful hard work and support. This book has many chapters. My life's final chapter, however, has yet to be lived.

IN THE BEGINNING

I was born in Memphis, Tennessee on August 28, 1939, to Robert and Irma Crawford. Since my birth was at home (a usual practice at that time), an obstetrician from the John Gaston Hospital, a teaching hospital for the University of Tennessee College of Medicine (UTCOM), was sent by the health department to examine me. My family lived in Orange Mound, the first and one of the largest, predominantly Black, planned communities in the United States, second only to Harlem. Orange Mound was developed in 1890 on land purchased from a former slave owner for the purpose of building a self-sufficient community for freed slaves and their descendants, combined with the opportunity for home ownership. It may have been the first such planned development of its kind in the country. Tracts of land were available for purchase either outright or by indenture. Orange Mound was a community of single-family homes only. There were no apartment complexes or subsidized government housing developments within its boundaries during my early years. Everyone knew each other, and it was idyllic. To me, growing up in Orange Mound was as good as it gets.

Orange Mound was a self-contained community. We had everything we needed: grocery stores, service stations, pharmacies, funeral homes, churches, all run by Black individuals. There was an insurance agency owned by Fred Davis. Charles Lloyd Jr., one of the premier jazz tenor saxophone players in the country, lived there and it was his father, Charles Lloyd Sr., who owned the pharmacy near our home.

I don't recall leaving Orange Mound for the wider world of Memphis until I was about 5, and only then, perhaps, because my mother wanted to shop for Easter outfits or visit relatives who lived out of town. Those were the only times I interacted with the white residents of Memphis. My mother purchased our clothes on layaway in the bargain basement at Goldsmith's Department Store on Main Street, downtown. One of the interactions I remember was with Miss Dottie, who was a white salesclerk in the shoe department. She made a big deal about us coming there, so I was fortunate that I did not experience discrimination in the store. When I went to other communities in Memphis, I got on the bus and sat in the back, naively thinking it was a nice place to sit because there weren't a lot of people clamoring for my seat!

Even when we went out of town, Orange Mound and the people in it provided support because the community was so closely knit. Everybody's dad "owed one" to someone else's dad and it was reciprocal. If a group—Boy Scouts, Girl Scouts, fraternity, sorority, or similar club—was having an event in another town and travel was required, automatically there was a safety net and "friends" along Highway 51 or in other towns or cities. This was a pragmatic arrangement. At that time, African Americans were not allowed to stay in motels or hotels in the South. The *Green Book* was used to identify safe places for African Americans to stay when traveling throughout the region, but this connectivity network of acquaintances was also effective. The reciprocal arrangement provided security and spared African Americans going to the front desk of a hotel and having someone tell them, "Boy, you can't stay here." Or worse, be greeted with physical harm.

My paternal grandfather, Elijah Crawford, was born around 1879. He worked at the Memphis Country Club as a chef. As I grew older, I began to notice that many of the "colored" staff at the club were fairer in complexion than most African Americans living in and around Memphis at that time. In fact, all of the people in the front of the club—coat checkers, receptionists, waiters—were lighter skinned in complexion than the bus boys and other personnel.

Later, my grandfather purchased a parcel of land and opened a restaurant in the Orange Mound community. His family was from farther south and among the first group of African Americans to migrate north to Tennessee post slavery. Unfortunately, I remember very little about my Grandfather Crawford except that he played games with me from time to time as some grandfathers like to do.

Both of my Crawford grandparents were mixed-race and very fair-skinned. Grandfather Crawford's wife, my grandmother, Cordelia Beatrice Crawford, was of Irish and Cherokee descent according to family lore. She was born around 1885 in Tennessee. Now, I remember her very well. I thought of her as the white lady who came to visit us! Her parents nicknamed her "Lady" and that's all we ever called her. After Grandfather Crawford passed away, Lady had several boyfriends. She died at the age of 96, probably still living with a boyfriend!

Elijah and Lady's son, my dad Robert, was a laid-back guy and an entrepreneur. I don't remember him being at home much because he and my mother divorced when I was very young. What I do remember as a teenager are his visits and the fun things we did when he was trying to make up for not being around day to day. My dad was a Pullman porter and worked both regional and national routes in the 1940s. Pullman porter positions offered men the opportunity for travel and exposure to the wider world. The porters were all "people people"—extroverted and congenial, customer service–oriented types. As a porter, my dad was a member of the Brotherhood of Sleeping Car Porters. Formed in 1925 by A. Philip Randolph, it was the first labor union comprised of African Americans. As part of Dad's estate, I inherited his Pullman porter cap. I still have it, with the word "Porter" clearly displayed.

During World War II, the government placed a moratorium on the usual railroad commerce in order to allow the military to transport soldiers from the East Coast to the West Coast. When I asked my father why he wasn't in the military, he said that his service to the country was transporting soldiers.

Dad was a very proud man. He was a talented golfer and played in the Gulf States United Golf Association (GSUGA), the Black equivalent of the Professional Golfers' Association (PGA). He was also a tennis player and instrumental in starting my own life-long pursuit of the game; I played until I tore my Achilles tendon on May 30, 2013.

When Dad was not on the road as a Pullman porter, he worked at the Saddle and Spur Club in Memphis; he ran the bar and restaurant there. When I was accepted into Meharry Medical School in 1960, several of the club's physician patrons volunteered to assist me in any way they could. One of my dad's regular customers was a urologist who said that he would be pleased to let me use his freshman anatomy textbooks and microscope. This was very fortunate as microscopes were expensive, but helpful in learning pathology and microbiology.

Then I changed direction and enrolled in University of Tennessee College of Medicine (UTCOM) in 1961, now referred to as University of Tennessee Heath Science Center. When my father told the urologist that I was going to UTCOM, the man asked for the immediate return of his books and microscope. While Meharry Medical School was one of a few medical schools open to Black students, I was the first Black medical student at the University of Tennessee, and he didn't want to be associated with anyone who was integrating his alma mater. That was the end of that relationship. There was no visible anger on my father's part but this lack of support due to my race for my decision to pursue medicine at UTCOM was one of many I would encounter.

My dad's personality was friendly and smooth as silk. That said, he wasn't always around or supportive of my mother in raising and caring for me and my siblings, Robert and Gwen. As a teenager, though, following my mother's remarriage and start of a new family, I wanted to be around my dad as much as possible.

My father lived 84 years, and we remained very close throughout his lifetime. I kept in touch with him as I graduated medical school, married, went into the Vietnam War, moved to Boston, California, Detroit, and after I settled in Cincinnati. We spoke on the phone nearly every Sunday night. He was well read and considered it his responsibility to challenge his college honors-graduate son every chance he could. We vigorously discussed every single thing that there was to argue about. Dad was well informed and had either read the newspapers, spoken with someone influential, or was knowledgeable on the subject. So we'd get into long discussions about social issues, politics, sports, you name it. Robert Crawford Sr. was an authority on everything! But at the end of the call, he'd say, "Alvin, thanks for calling. I'll talk to you next week, OK?" I realize now that the topic of our last argument—the last time I spoke with him—was whether O. J. Simpson was innocent or guilty. We didn't agree on a verdict, so our conversation remains incomplete.

After my parents' divorce, my father remarried, and my sister Rosemary was born of that union. She was a brilliant student in high school and one of the first African American students to attend Rhodes College in Memphis. Rosemary subsequently graduated from Georgetown University Law School and now practices law in Pittsburgh, Pennsylvania; she was also a Federal Chapter 7 Bankruptcy Trustee. Rosemary ran for judge on two occasions, unsuccessfully, but she's informed me that it's not over yet and she'll try again.

In his later years, Dad lived alone. His doctor had become a friend of mine and he would call me from time to time to tell me what was going on. At some point, Dad had chronic indigestion. I talked to his doctor and he told me, "Everything's OK, but we're going to take him into the hospital for a work-up and a GI study." While they didn't find anything, Dad continued to have problems. Not long after that, he became dysarthric—losing control of his muscles for speech—and wasn't articulating very well. Dad went into a coma and died. Subsequently, they found out that he'd had a central stroke.

My mother, Irma Lee Meyers, was from St. Louis, Missouri. Her biological father, Grandpa John Glover, was an active member of a Memphis African American singing group, the Southern Male Chorus. The chorus sang around town and when I was a child, my mother took my brother, sister, and me to some of the concerts. My mother had a large extended family with numerous cousins who were the same age as me and my siblings. We always had friends because all of the cousins played together. We'd often physically challenge each other but were still cousins at the end of the day.

My mother's adoptive parents (in actuality, they were her maternal aunt and uncle) were William and Elizabeth Rogers.

Along with her older brother, Dan "Uncle Dan" Glover (not the movie star), my mother was brought to Memphis to live with them when she was around 8 to 10 years old. Her mother, Rita Jenrette had died due to childbirth (of puerperal sepsis), and sadly, the baby died as well.

My mother's marriage to my dad, Robert Crawford, produced three children: my older sister Gwen (born in 1934), my older brother Robert (born in 1936), and me. My siblings and I called her "Mother dear" or "Mud dear," which was the best pronunciation we could manage as young children. She was the consummate single parent who stopped at nothing to raise her children to be successful. My mother remarried when I was in high school. My stepfather, Clarence Oystern, worked for Standard Oil, which improved the economics of our household tremendously. From that marriage, I have two younger siblings, Clarice and Michael, both of whom are now living in Memphis.

My mother was a self-motivated, committed woman who raised three of her five children as a single mother, with all five of them attending college. She was the ultimate believer in hard work, the value of education, and the political process. Mother had staged and attended voting rallies when Black people were first allowed to vote, and drove a school bus to pick up and deliver the sick and fragile to the voting booths. She was an aggressive community organizer and extremely proud of her children. She was also a kind soul and every now and then took in a cousin or two who needed a place to stay.

But she had no difficulty in meting out punishment, if only to show us, in her words, "how much I love you." I remember spankings when she tearfully told us that it hurt her more than it hurt us.

My mother was the source of my interest in academics. Education was important to her, and she passed that focus on to me. She taught me that education was a permanent condition—once you know how to read, no one can take that away from you.

My mother was a practical nurse, having trained at Memphis City Hospital in a nursing program created through a federal initiative. She got a job at the Army depot during World War II, driving an Army truck. She often commented that for lunch, African Americans had to order food from the commissary kitchen because they could not sit inside at a table, yet the German POWs were allowed a seat; she always felt something was wrong with that picture.

Her nursing background, coupled with my mother's extended family's approach to infectious diseases, created an interestingly effective system for treatment. With mumps, measles, whooping cough, or chicken pox, the tactic was this: when one child in the family contracted it, all the kids would go to that house for a sleepover. Then every kid in the family was exposed to it at the same time, whatever it was. That was the way the kids in the community got through all of the infectious childhood diseases in fairly short order. The process of creating herd immunity has some scientific reasoning behind it. I've subsequently talked with infectious disease experts about this scenario and they said that the approach can work, although the advent of new vaccinations makes herd immunity unnecessary.

My Uncle Will owned a barber shop. When I was around 10 years old, I went in on Saturdays and cleaned up the shop, sweeping the floor and running errands. That was my first work experience.

As my siblings and I became teenagers, my mother came up with a clever game that proved educational. She would have us read the obituaries in the newspaper and then pick one to quiz us on, asking us to recall the birthdate, job, community activities, and other life events; in retrospect it helped us develop memory and reading comprehension in a fun way.

My mother's Grandfather Miller lived in Mississippi; her family had lived there before moving to St. Louis. I remember my great-grandfather's funeral—I was very young, 8 or 9 years old—and the whole family went down to Mississippi. It's interesting, the memories that I have of that experience. I remember that there were lots of white people standing outside the church during the service, looking through the windows. Many of them gave testaments about growing up with my great-grandfather—he had been a freed slave and was given a large piece of property post slavery. According to the stories in my mother's family, that acreage became the town of Miller, Mississippi. I remember the white people there particularly because they didn't look like me. Other than that, I don't remember much about the experience except that (to me) my great-grandfather was a very old man.

In 1954, I contracted nonparalytic polio, which was treated by the new wonder drug at the time, tetracycline. I remember that the doctor made a house call, and the health department came and did several blood tests. I'd had fevers for several days. One of our neighbors, a little old lady, bathed me, shrouded me in bay leaves, then made me sit by a warm fire. By her reckoning, bay leaves and a warm fire were the cure for just about anything. Fortunately, I never developed any paralysis or spasms. To this day, I don't know what cured me—the tetracycline or the bay leaves by the fire!

The poliomyelitis epidemic continued until around 1958. Orange Mound had one of only two public swimming pools in the city of Memphis where African Americans could swim. Kids from all over the mid-South came to Orange Mound to swim. But during the polio epidemic, the municipal public health authorities limited the number of people who could go into the pool. My mother said that we couldn't go at all because she did not want to risk my contracting it again.

Children are interesting, creative, and resilient though. Not being able to swim didn't sit well with my brother Robert and me. You can't tell active, enterprising 11- and 9-year-old boys that they can't go swimming in the summer! Before the epidemic, my brother and I went swimming almost every day, so we had to think of a plan around our mother's prohibition. In the summer, Robert and I were assigned chores to be completed during the day, when my mother was working. We would complete the housework and yard tasks, then hit the pool and get home before 4:30 p.m., because our mother came home on the 4:30 p.m. bus. Sometimes, in order to get all of the chores completed, Robert and I recruited our friends to help. Our plan worked well. We got those chores squared away every day, religiously. Then we went to the pool. Somehow our mother found out that we were swimming and we got spanked! How did she know? Eventually, one of us realized that our skin was ashy because of the chlorine. A minor hiccup. Undeterred, Robert and I concocted a new plan. We would shower afterward to get all of the ash off and slather ourselves in Vaseline. But Mom still figured it out! How? Well, mothers aren't blind. She could see that our eyes were red as beets. So then, again, the spankings came. It was the end of swimming for that summer.

My sister, Gwen, is the oldest of my siblings. She was a very bright girl and allowed to skip second grade. She was even the first female to be president of the student council at Orange Mound's Melrose High School. Gwen is a musician and a trained vocalist with a doctorate in music from Los Angeles State College. Her sons, Donald and Kevin Wyatt, are critically acclaimed musicians on bass and keyboard.

Growing up, I recall that with everything my brother Robert and I did, the question my mother always asked was: "Why can't you be more like Gwen?" We had to live with that because Gwen was perfect—smart, industrious, always told the truth—and wouldn't hesitate to rat us out if we were doing something that our mother had told us not to do. Robert and I didn't think very much of that!

Gwen read everything that she could get her hands on. When she became interested in music, she started taking private lessons in both piano and voice. Being the baby brother, I was stuck with the job of accompanying her to music lessons. I would joke that I had to go listen to her "scream at the piano." Usually, I ended up falling asleep. When her lesson was over, Gwen woke me up and we'd go home.

She did well in high school, too, and earned a scholarship in music to Rust College, a historically African American school with a Methodist affiliation, located in Holly Springs, Mississippi, southeast of Memphis. The Rust College Chorus, well-known in the African American community, toured "up North" each year, with an itinerary that followed the Mississippi River. Gwen is a lyrical soprano soloist and during one of those tours, she sang at an event in Grand Forks, North Dakota. Her performance must have been a success because she was subsequently offered a full scholarship to the University of North Dakota. That was the good news. The bad news was that it gets extremely cold in North Dakota. These were the days before we used the term "wind chill factor." Grand Forks was and is very cold! And it stayed cold for months. As Gwen described it, summer lasted only a week or two. Being from Memphis, she wasn't used to being very cold. But she stayed at the University, did well there, and graduated.

At the University of North Dakota, most of the faculty, staff, and students had never seen anyone who looked like Gwen. There was one other nonwhite person at the university, a young woman from the Philippines named Modesta. It was the fifties and school officials made them roommates because they had "a lot in common"—in this case, being brown in complexion. As a result, Gwen and Modesta became friends for life. They laughed about this "things in common" rationale. Modesta spoke Tagalog and Gwen spoke Memphis-inflected English and a smidgen of Ebonics. But the faculty and student body felt that they almost looked alike so they must have a lot in common (likely thinking "because they sure don't have anything in common with us!").

During the time I was in Southeast Asia during the Vietnam War, I spent some time in Manila with Gwen's former roommate and her family. She and her husband, a superintendent of one of the local unions, were well-connected. They let me use their car and driver, and I went all over the Philippines when I was on active duty at the naval air station at Sangley Point. I visited Olongapo at Cubi Point, Clark Air Force Base at Angeles City, Igorot Villages, and the rice field at Manawa.

After her graduation around 1955, Gwen took a teaching job at Philander Smith College in Little Rock, Arkansas. Later, when Nat King Cole was looking to form a group of background singers, the Merry Young Souls, Gwen auditioned and got the job. As part of the Merry Young Souls, Gwen was on several of Nat King Cole's recordings. Our mother was good with Gwen being a college teacher but was reluctant to let her go on the road with Mr. Cole, even though he was one of the top-grossing entertainers in the country at that time.

Nat King Cole was the first Black man to host a nationally televised variety program—called *The Nat King Cole Show*. The program was discontinued because Cole could not secure sponsors, as companies felt that Southern white people would stop using their products if they sponsored a Black television program. Despite this, it was said that Cole's record sales literally built the Capitol Records Building in Los Angeles.

While on tour with the Merry Young Souls, Gwen met and married Donald Wyatt, who was also part of the group. Eventually, the Merry Young Souls broke up. After Nat King Cole died in 1965, Gwen went back to school and earned her PhD from California State College at Los Angeles. Since then, she's performed at least three times at Carnegie Hall and was previously the music minister of Holman United Methodist Church in West Los Angeles. Her husband, Don, went on to join a musical group called the Creative Source, which did well in the seventies.

My wife Jeannie and I met Nat King Cole in 1964 at a show in Nashville. We had a great conversation with him and discussed several topics, including how I'd pursued music before becoming a doctor. I noticed that Cole always had a cigarette in his hand when he sang. No one knew then what it was doing to his vocal cords. He was a very pleasant man and wished me luck in the future. I, of course, wished him the same. Mr. Cole subsequently died of cancer in 1965, which was thought to be directly related to smoking. Nat King Cole remains one of the more memorable human beings that I've ever met.

My brother Robert takes credit (and deservedly so) for having taught me everything that I know in life. It was (and still is) an unbelievable relationship—he is my big brother, and I idolize him. Since he was older, he had to do all of the grunt work. Whatever "it" was, if it worked out well, he taught me what to do and how to do it. If it did not work out well, then he could tell our mother, saying that he knew I was wrong, and if I got in trouble it was because I was headstrong and did it in spite of his instructions. But I loved him anyway and knew that he would take care of me. Occasionally I would have to take one for Robert. Actually, I took quite a few for Robert.

We used to play mind games; I think we got that from our dad. Everything was a mind game. We lived on a street called Marechalneil, which was between Spottswood and Carnes Avenues; the intersection being the entry point to the Orange Mound community. These were the rules to our game: as cars went by, we'd have to know the make of the car, as well as its type, whether it was a cabriolet or sedan, and Robert always won.

Robert was a good athlete and a National Honor Society student. Orange Mound had the largest public park for African Americans in Memphis with facilities that included a swimming pool, playground, baseball diamond, and clay tennis and grass paddle tennis courts. Robert played football and was very good—he played quarterback—but he couldn't join the team because our mother was concerned that he might get hurt. So, Robert didn't go out for football until he was in the tenth grade. But once he did, he made the team and led it to two consecutive state championships. He was a highly touted athlete and received a scholarship to attend Tennessee State, which at that time was second to Florida A&M University in terms of getting African American athletes into the NFL. One year, the Tennessee State yearbook was dedicated to Robert because he was the MVP for the annual Orange Blossom Classic, a collegiate football event for historically Black colleges and universities that was comparable to the Orange Bowl. That year, the event matched up Tennessee State with Florida A&M University. Robert wasn't offered an NFL tryout because at that time the American professional leagues would not hire a Black player to one of the "thinking" positions like quarterback, even though the Canadian league was considering it. Robert might have been offered a tryout for defensive back because of his good hands. Candidly, Robert, as a quarterback, wasn't used to hitting or being hit, so it was not an issue. Today, many of the premier college and professional quarterbacks are Black.

Following college, my brother enlisted in the Army for two years. After his discharge, he returned to Memphis to teach and coach, first at Lester High School then to our alma mater, Melrose High School. During his tenure at Melrose, Robert coached both football and baseball and took the first African American high school baseball team to the state playoffs.

After graduating high school, I followed Robert to Tennessee State. I began my college career as a music major on a music scholarship. At the time I went to Tennessee State, football players could get a scholarship for their girlfriends. My mother asked the coach about a scholarship for Robert's little brother. Since Robert didn't have a steady girlfriend at that time, I got a football scholarship to college—and never played any football in my life.

Every athlete has a nickname: Robert's was "Bubba Crawford," so as his younger brother, I was "Li'l Bubba." Big Bubba was an athlete but since I was a music major, that had no social value whatsoever. At the end of my freshman year, I achieved the highest grade point average, received the Outstanding Freshman scholarship, and was recognized at convocation. With my mother's insistence, the university president, Dr. Walter Stovall Davis, took note and said, "Li'l Bubba has a brain. We need to do something about that." What he did was convert my music academic scholarship to a full football scholarship (with significant benefits in meals and lodging), and assign me to tutor three of his close friends' sons.

My family and hometown would have an incredible impact on my formative years and my educational path. Most of my success in life, I can trace back to the hard work I put into my education and the loving support I received from my family and friends in Orange Mound.

AS GOOD AS IT GETS

Melrose High School in Orange Mound was one of the best academic high schools in Tennessee. Our teachers were supportive and nurturing and gave their utmost to the students.

Erma Clanton, a former teacher in the Melrose school system, recalled the sense of pride parents and students had; the culture was very family-oriented. Everybody knew everybody. We all lived in the same community, went to the same churches, and played on the same playground.

In the sixth grade, I took the Stanford-Binet test and did well. There is no way that I could have known that the score would change my life forever; the impact was immediate. No longer could I take the fun courses. From that point on, my course selections were overruled by caring, nurturing teachers who wanted me to make something of myself. I was strongly encouraged to take science courses beginning in the seventh grade.

At Melrose, our cultural exposure included the fine arts and music. At the beginning of the seventh grade, students were sent to Mrs. Mae Ola Mebane, the choral music teacher, to audition for the choir. She sat at the piano, provided sheet music to a popular song, asked you to sing, and then would tell you if you should join the choir or if you should pursue instrumental music. I don't remember what the song was in my audition but before I finished the song, Mrs. Mebane stopped playing and told me that I couldn't carry a tune. That was the beginning and end of my choral career—and I never had to sing another note in high school.

I was told to report immediately to Mr. Richard "Tuff" Greene, the instrumental music teacher and band director.

I really took to instrumental music, from seventh grade through high school, and on to college. At first, I played trumpet but due to an overbite embouchure, I switched over to the treble-cleft baritone horn because it had a larger mouthpiece and the same fingering as the trumpet. I then switched over from brass to woodwinds and began to study the clarinet. By the tenth grade, having played both brass and reed instruments, I had decided that music was going to be my life.

I thrived at Melrose High School, graduating as president of my senior class and student band director. Music education was valued at Melrose. Being in the band was as important as being on the football team—and that was saying something considering the school had a state championship–winning football team! Every year, the band competed in a tristate (Tennessee, Arkansas, and Mississippi) band festival for Black students that was held in Stuttgart, Arkansas. The winners of the competitions had the chance to audition for the music faculty at Arkansas Agricultural, Mechanical, and Normal College in Pine Bluff, later merged to create the University of Arkansas Pine Bluff, the oldest historically Black college or university (HBCU) in Arkansas.

Hotels and motels that accommodated African Americans were rare to nonexistent, so band members stayed with local families during competitions. The Melrose High School Band won the senior band festival all four of my high school years. Unlike our competition, our band's repertoire included both Tchaikovsky and Rachmaninoff, and the blues. That was because of Tuff Greene.

Tuff Greene was appropriately named. He was the ultimate disciplinarian. When the marching band played during halftime for football games, we took eight steps for every five yards, just like the college bands. At that time, during the fifties, most marching bands marched to their formation, stopped, and then played. We were one of the first African American high school bands that played our instruments while we marched.

Mr. Greene was a stickler for perfection. If anyone made a mistake or misstep during a performance, all band members had to stay after the game and practice the entire halftime program over and over until it was perfect. The school kept the stadium lights on just for us. If you had a girlfriend or boyfriend in the band, you knew if someone had messed up during the program, because they might be a little late picking you up!

We performed high-stepping formations and played blues, rock and roll, and soul music. Once the African American college marching bands from Tennessee State University, Florida A&M, Morgan State, and others started playing and marching to popular music, John Philip Sousa marches were less likely to be performed. It wasn't long before the large state universities, including the Big Ten schools like Ohio State, Michigan, and Northwestern started doing the same thing, playing more popular music instead of traditional marching fanfare. Of course, they're given credit for the innovation, not my high school marching band. The records of history can be deceptive. As the proverb goes, "lion-hunting history would be different if the lions wrote it."

In high school, I tested out in the tenth grade and qualified for a Ford Foundation grant to attend Morehouse College in Atlanta. Several considerations, however, made the opportunity unattractive. First, it would be costly for me to leave home and live in Georgia, and second, by taking the grant, I would become a science and mathematics major in college. At that time, I wasn't sure that I wanted to be a science major. It would have also been a financial stretch for my family to send me to Morehouse, all the way in Atlanta, with two other kids, Gwen and Robert, in college at the same time. So, I turned down the grant and stayed at Melrose until graduation.

That decision turned out to be very fortunate for me when it came to my love life. During high school, I met my wife, Alva "Jeannie" Jamison, at a Jack and Jill Christmas party in Memphis. A friend of hers had invited me to the party. After the party, this friend got word to me that Jeannie wanted to meet me again. I called on her one day and said obnoxiously, "I understand that you want to meet me. Here I am!" I was her prom date for junior and senior years, both at my school and her school (Hamilton High School). We both went to college at Tennessee State and I was her debutante escort as well. At college, we didn't date each other, though we reconnected when we went home for breaks or for the summer. When we got married in 1963, people at Tennessee State were surprised—they didn't know that we'd ever dated!

During my high school and college years, I played saxophone in several bands, including a house band sponsored by WDIA radio, and a touring band with Sonny Williams and Tuff Green. I was even in a group that auditioned for *The Ed Sullivan Show*. While I was still in high school, one of my gigs took me to Texarkana, Arkansas, a town located on the border between Arkansas and Texas. The date was decided three or four months in advance, and we would be paid a percentage of the gate. We were playing so well it was decided that we wouldn't take a salary. By the time our actual concert date came up, however, the local Texarkana basketball team was number one in the state and on the night we were playing the concert, the town basketball team and the town had gone off to the state play-offs. Almost no one came to our concert and we hardly made any money. So, off we went to Little Rock because that was the big town in the area. We thought we could get some gigs there to pay for the gasoline that we'd need for the trip back to Memphis.

Looking back, I think that the community of Orange Mound was reluctant to accept integration for a variety of reasons. The caring, nurturing African American teachers were retiring and the students were not doing well academically with the new teachers that were hired in their stead. The word on the street was that the young, white, ideologically liberal female teachers being sent in to replace the retired teachers were, despite their good intentions, deathly afraid of the Black kids, especially the boys, and had difficulty relating to them. The boys were constantly being disciplined, reported, and/or expelled for alleged infractions. It was a turbulent time.

The reluctance to integrate was also a matter of pride. Our school had done a lot with very little and had achieved great success despite the roadblocks of segregation. When I was in the eleventh grade, Melrose High School students aced the standardized Spanish test given to students across the entire Memphis school system. The city school administrators accused our faculty and students of cheating because, in their minds, there was no way that Black students could have done so well considering our textbooks were third generation, recycled, and damaged. We took the test over, and, again, we did very well. After this, there was no follow-up or apology from the school board other than a notation that every Melrose student passed the test.

Erma Clanton recalled the process of integration in Orange Mound overall:

> When integration came, the students were scared; they didn't want to come into the restaurants downtown. I told them, "We've got to do it." So, I tried to get a group of students and a teacher to come with me and go to a restaurant that had been all-white for years. It was just a restaurant where you could eat corn bread, chicken, greens. And they [other patrons] looked at us as if...well, I won't go into that. But it was quite an experience for the students to eat in a restaurant with people of another color.

My experience with Orange Mound schools and the teachers I encountered there was truly as good as it gets. They taught me lifelong lessons that would support me in college and medical school, but also as I embarked on my own medical career. Tuff Greene, my band director, understood the importance of giving proper credit. I took that wisdom with me and decades later applied it to my employees.

MUSIC AT TENNESSEE STATE

After high school, I attended Tennessee State in Nashville for three years. In my freshman year, I began as music major. There weren't any privacy concerns back then. On a display case outside of the administration building, the professors posted test and final grade scores for all students. You could see everyone's grades; that practice would never happen now. Thankfully, during those years I made all As.

I played clarinet in the university concert band. On the side, I played the alto saxophone at the Subway Lounge in Nashville, now called Music Alley, and at several other clubs around there. I also played at Printer's Alley. Now, that was a big deal. It was during the rock 'n' roll period before the advent of fusion jazz. In those days, I woke up every morning to the song, "Wake Up, Little Susie," by the Everly Brothers. Later on, the music winds shifted and the tunes on the radio included "Stop in the Name of Love" by the Supremes. I was playing at The Hole; the New Era Restaurant, a student hang-out; and Brown's Cafe. It was a big deal if you played at Brown's. Brute Hayes, who'd been a big-time football player, opened up the bar and grill and all the kids went there including me. I spent a lot of unproductive, non-academic time on Printer's Alley but still managed to graduate with the highest GPA in our class. People are still trying to figure that out, including me.

Jazz or bebop was coming on the scene. One night I was playing at a place near the university and my brother Robert came by. We had a beer and talked after the set. I told him that I wanted to pursue a career as a studio musician.

With a late-night program like *The Tonight Show Starring Johnny Carson*, or now with Jimmy Fallon, they have a house band comprised of studio musicians. These musicians were (and are today) well trained and very talented. And they make a lot of money. It was a five-day-a-week show, involving playing for an hour or hour and a half, and you played all kinds of music. It was really exciting. Working this schedule, you could have a day job or weekend gig because you weren't on the road traveling.

In the fifties and sixties, hardly any of the guys in studio bands looked like me. I took it as a challenge, thinking "I'm from Tennessee State and we've got one helluva band!" But I also wanted a stable personal situation. Eventually, I wanted a family, and I didn't want to be on the road. I thought that being a studio musician would allow me to play challenging music, have a family, and teach—all things that I love. I figured that I could also play in a trio or small group in a bar on the weekend.

When I mentioned to Robert that I wanted to be a studio musician, he said, "A lot of the band directors are retiring so you shouldn't have any trouble at home getting a job as a band director." Hearing that was disconcerting because I wanted to be a studio musician, never a high school band director. So Robert asked me, "Well, what do you want to do?"

I thought about it. I knew the Tennessee State music department was like a conservatory. "I don't know how well I'd do in terms of the competition for getting into a studio band." If I wasn't able to be a studio musician, I told him then I wanted something challenging.

Robert said, "Why not medicine?"

I'd never thought about. Here I was at Tennessee State, and I made the decision to move from something that I loved, music, to study science. I was presented with the Freshman Award at Tennessee State for highest accumulative average in music. The next year, I received the Sophomore Award for the highest accumulative average in science. I took to sciences like a duck takes to water. They just came naturally.

So, at the end of my freshman year, I officially changed my major from music to physics and decided to pursue medical school.

It was difficult to make the switch. The department of music wasn't interested in giving up one of their top students. I stayed in school for the summer because I had to take organic chemistry, biochemistry, and the other courses that I needed as prerequisites for medical school. I was determined not to add time to my undergraduate education despite the major change. I had picked physics because it wasn't a structured major, which allowed me to take all of the prerequisite science courses required to prepare for the Medical College Admission Test (MCAT), without the electives required for a conventional major curriculum.

Jeannie remembers this period of transition. Her parents were concerned when we dated, because a life as a musician was not something they wanted for their daughter's spouse. Jeannie was pretty strong-minded and it became clear we were a done deal, musician or not. My brother Robert was a big football star and I became the "Crawford kid who makes good grades." The grading in my courses, especially in the math courses, was based on a curve. But the curve was only used if no one in the class achieved passing grades, which I did. That didn't make me very popular if most students did poorly on the exam.

It was 1960 and medical schools were just beginning to realize that doctors were typically from purely science backgrounds. Medical school applicants usually focused on the sciences and knew little about the arts, social sciences, or music. The testing service had modified the MCAT to attract more well-rounded candidates. It just so happened that when I went into the exam—and all of the exams were different—lo and behold, there was a fine arts exam. I was like a fox in a hen house! I did well on the MCAT and once the scores were out, I applied to Meharry Medical College in Nashville. At that time, there were two options open to me for medical school—historically Black Meharry Medical College or Howard University College of Medicine. The University of Tennessee College of Medicine wasn't even on the radar screen at that time. For African Americans, it just wasn't an option.

In the fall of 1960, I started at Meharry. I did well there and loved every minute of it. The biological science courses were very different from what I'd done before. After every exam the test scores were posted at the end of the hall for everyone to see, the same as they were at Tennessee State. At the start of medical school, students are usually told in their first anatomy class, "look to your right, look to your left. One of these people won't be there when you graduate." They are also reminded that both the number one in the class and the number fifty-four will be called "doctor."

My roommate at Meharry was the brother-in-law of a good friend of mine. He'd been a high school biology teacher who wanted to be a doctor. This was 1960 and there were a lot of veterans in graduate and professional schools, more mature people who were attending school on the GI Bill after serving in Korea. Some of them were married and had savings and financial support from family. We learned from each other. You could teach them details from anatomy and biochemistry classes, and they would teach you about life. It was a good trade-off. My experiences at Tennessee State and Meharry Medical School played a significant part in my educational pursuits and set me up for my next step at yet another school.

THE QUALIFIED APPLICANT

The process of integration was beginning to bubble up across the country. States in the South were being sued for failure to comply with federal integration policies. Although the 1954 Brown v. Board of Education of Topeka decision affected high schools, there hadn't been any definitive court rulings for colleges and universities. And there was substantial resistance to admitting African Americans to the major Southern universities. For example, the University of Tennessee said that it was ready to comply should there be a "qualified applicant," but argued "to date, no qualified applicants" had applied.

At that time, my mother was working as a practical nurse at the E.H. Crump Hospital for Coloreds in Memphis. Now my mother was very proud of all her children, so on any occasion—anywhere and at any time—she was more than ready and willing to tell you all about "my son, the doctor-to-be." On one of these occasions, Dr. William Speight, who was an ENT specialist and chief of staff at E.H. Crump, stopped her in the hall and asked, "Isn't your son in medical school?" My mother said, "Yes." In addition to his medical practice and hospital administrative responsibilities, Dr. Speight was president of the local NAACP. He continued, "You know that we're trying to get the University of Tennessee to allow Negroes into the university. They say that they can't find anybody qualified. We need a test case. Would it be OK if the NAACP were to use Alvin's medical college aptitude test scores?"

My mother asked if this would cause negative publicity and Dr. Speight assured her that it would not. So, my mother gave him permission. Later, she asked me what I thought, and I told her that I wasn't interested in changing to UTCOM as I was having a good time at Meharry, but didn't mind being used as a test case. I didn't think it would affect me one way or another.

The NAACP submitted my scores to the University of Tennessee. I was not the only test case they had and the scores for several other students were also sent. Privacy issues then weren't as much of a concern as they are now. The university responded publicly, indicating that, yes, they were making every effort to comply with integration. They said the College of Medicine had found a "qualified applicant," but that the individual had elected to attend another medical school. As far as they were concerned, the matter was closed. There was no indication that the qualified applicant was interested in transferring and so all was well. I was not contacted personally by the university and was not even sure that they were referring to me in their response.

My mother began to think about this situation, wondering if the applicant who was fully qualified to be admitted was me. "Let's take a look," she said. To do this, we had to validate all of the documentation with UT. In return, we received a letter from the university indicating that I was qualified to be admitted to the College of Medicine with a caveat that I was currently enrolled in medical school and had no desire to transfer.

Meharry was a private medical school and quite expensive. It was also in Nashville. The University of Tennessee had less expensive tuition and was based in Memphis, meaning I could live at home while attending school. My family considered this, along with the fact that my parents at the time still had two children, Clarice and Michael, in college. Gwen had graduated and Robert was graduating soon but my mother had mortgaged the house to pay for my medical school tuition and our family had other financial obligations.

Dean Rolfe (Daniel T. Rolfe, MD) had very real concerns about my desire to transfer. He told me I would have to withdraw passing from Meharry before I could go to the University of Tennessee. He argued and indicated that if I went to UT and flunked out, our community would lose one Black doctor. But if

I went there and did well, there was the potential of Meharry losing many Black doctors in the future to other medical schools, which could possibly lose the school financial support from the Southern Regional Council (SRC). This revenue was critical to Meharry's existence. Dean Rolfe didn't say it directly, but I got the message. He felt that this scenario could have a domino effect, that not only could our community lose many Black doctors but also Black medical schools, like Meharry and Howard University College of Medicine in Washington DC, would lose out on revenue they depended on.

This was a challenging decision for a 21-year-old to consider and I didn't quite know how to handle it. I had a conversation with Augustus "Gus" White about the possibility. He had worked as a lifeguard in the public swimming pool near my family's home in Orange Mound and he knew both Gwen and Robert. At the time, Gus was in medical school at Stanford University, so I thought he would be a good person to talk to about my decision. Funny enough, we would both go on to become orthopaedic surgeons. As an undergraduate at Brown[2], he had been the first African American to join a previously all-white fraternity and understood the reality of having only four or five African Americans in any class. We spent a lot of time talking about issues of race, culture, and civil rights. He recognized how challenging the situation was. He told me,

> Alvin this is a tremendous opportunity for you to make a significant contribution at some risk and cost to yourself. Who knows how good or how bad it's going to be. You are certainly in a wonderful position.

Both Gus and I shared a bit of Memphis culture. We saw how people navigated situations about race. We knew the same people, listened to the same music, danced similarly, were influenced by similar people, like Benjamin Hooks, who would later serve as the executive director of the NAACP in 1977, or Blair T. Hunt, the principal at Booker T. Washington High School in Memphis. We saw the way people managed or dealt with race. We understood the collective behavior of the Black school teachers, principals, and band directors we had in school who informed us as younger people and gave us a "kit" for survival. It was helpful to have someone to speak to about my decision and weigh the factor of my possible transfer. Gus understood, as I did, that we needed to be twice as good to be accepted, and what kind of path our decisions could pave for other potential Black medical students.

Eventually, I made my decision to transfer to UTCOM. "Let's go for it." I loved challenges and I knew that this would be a big one. I'd never considered going to medical school anyway, so in my head, if I flunked out—which I didn't think would happen—then I could always be a musician! I was a more than a little naive then.

Before I could enter UTCOM, I went for an interview with the vice president and provost of the school. He told me that the University of Tennessee didn't consider Meharry Medical College to be an accredited medical school and would not accept any transfer credits. However, he told me that I had the qualifications so if I was willing to start over from scratch, I could enroll. He noted that he was doubtful that I would succeed. That was my first "welcome" to the University of Tennessee College of Medicine.

Next, I went for an interview with the dean, who informed me that this was the worst day he'd experienced in his tenure as dean at the school. He said that if his father knew he was interviewing a candidate who looked like me, his father would roll over in his grave. And I thought, "Well, this is going to be interesting."

It was disappointing that UT didn't accept Meharry's grades because they said it was not an accredited school. Black people, but especially educators, looked up to Meharry. Erma Clanton recalled, "Someone else might have thought, 'Well, I'll just go back to Meharry, I'm not going to start over again.' That's what I admired about Alvin, he decided, 'OK. You're not going to accept the credits; I'll just have to bite the bullet.'"

I withdrew from Meharry Medical College and none of my credits transferred. It was as if I had never been to medical school in my life. I started at UT in March, spring quarter and finished thirteen quarters later. At the end of the first quarter, I had done well in most of the anatomy, physiology and micro-anatomy courses but was not appointed to the dean's list. The reason? The administration argued it wouldn't be fair to the other students to give me that accolade because I had already taken certain science classes at Meharry and had been exposed to some of the material. Quite the double standard.

Needless to say, I had developed a bit of arrogance, "hard-headedness" as one of my best friends said. I never considered failing or flunking out of anything. My mother had always told us, never assume the role of a victim, "They can beat you, they can kill you, but they can never take your education away from you." I didn't question my self-worth. I knew what I knew.

UNIVERSITY OF TENNESSEE COLLEGE OF MEDICINE

*A*t the time I attended UTCOM, the university was on a quarter system rather than a semester system. Medical students needed twelve quarters to graduate, and one course was one quarter. During the Second World War, the US government implemented the V-12 Navy College Training Program. This program was designed to create expedited courses and programs to increase the number of doctors that could join the armed forces and aid the war effort. The program ended in 1946, but the system of quarters and graduation requirements remained similar at UTCOM until the sixties.

Typically, medical students would take six quarters in succession with the School of Basic Medical Sciences. In these classes, medical students sat side-by-side with PhD and master's students. The faculty and staff seemed focused on working on their next grant. Race did not appear to be as significant of an issue with them, and the exams in these courses were largely objective, meaning there was less possibility of my success in the course being dictated by the instructor's personal feelings. This was followed by an off period, referred to as "6X," which included studying for state board exams. After passing state boards, students progressed to the School of Basic Clinical Sciences for six more quarters, then graduated. Students who didn't pass a class during a quarter had the chance to plead their case or repeat the course. This took some of the pressure off of students because they could simply take the course again the next quarter. Students didn't have to go a whole year or semester before realizing they were behind and would need to retake a course. The financial loss for retaking a quarter was also far less than for repeating a year.

When I began medical school at UT, I lived at home in Memphis. Eventually I moved into a hospital apartment at the aforementioned E.H. Crump Hospital, a training hospital associated with the university, because it was easier to be physically located in the medical center. The hospital was named for E.H. Crump, a man informally referred to by everyone in our community as "Boss Crump." Crump was a rich, powerful man in Memphis. Though he was unfortunately an enthusiastic, bigoted segregationist, he was good to "his folks." Clint Cleves, a Black man who worked for Boss Crump as a chauffeur-butler-manservant, lived on Cellar Street in Orange Mound. It was no coincidence that the first paved street with sidewalks in Orange Mound was Cellar Street. Mr. Crump made it his business to have that done for Clint Cleves. Cleves also owned a restaurant, The Four-Way Grill. Because my grandfather, Elijah Crawford, also owned a restaurant, I knew a lot of the restaurant people in the area. Mr. Crump made sure that Clint Cleves' restaurant was always well provisioned, regardless of the food source.

The E.H. Crump Hospital was built for the "colored folks." When I got to medical school, it became one of the University of Tennessee medical units. There were two jobs available to medical students: physical exam historian or x-ray tech. An x-ray tech didn't need much clinical exposure, only anatomy. After students competed the Physical Diagnosis course (usually taken late second year or early third year), they were qualified for the historian position. Now, in the twenty-first-century, Physical Diagnosis is taught in simulation labs using professional patients, but in 1962, medical students practiced on each other.

I was an x-ray tech for the first six quarters, on duty every fifth night at the E.H. Crump Hospital. Once I entered my third year of medical school and passed my board exams, I did histories, physicals, night calls, catheters and IVs, blood draws, and other routine checks. Of course, this was at a time when elective surgery patients were admitted to the hospital overnight for all procedures, whereas now, many procedures are often outpatient, same-day admissions.

At E.H. Crump Hospital, I met Douglas Wilson. I was already working at the hospital and had moved up in my position, so was tasked with finding someone to take my previous position. I found out that Wilson had applied and had been told there weren't any openings. He desperately needed the job as he lived far away from school and had to take the 5 a.m. bus every day. I was able to get him a position and my experience at E.H. Crump was all the better for it; we eventually became roommates at the hospital. Some of my fellow students were overtly bigoted and racist, but fortunately some were accepting and made it clear that accepting Black students in an integrated medical school had been a long time coming. Doug was one of those individuals.

I have an appreciation for the quality of treatment patients now receive at E.H. Crump. At the time I was in medical school, we didn't have phlebotomists like we do now. It was the medical students who performed the lab tests on service patients after 5 p.m. We did the hemoglobin, urinalysis, and the venipunctures. The only Black people on medical staff at the hospital were the lab techs who worked the night shift. When I was off-duty, I'd go downstairs where they worked, and we'd listen to records and talk. I hadn't been doing well on my labs but because they showed me how to do them properly, eventually I was performing better on the tests in class. A white classmate told one of the residents that I was taking my lab tests over to E.H. Crump and accused me of having the lab techs do them for me. He claimed that was why my results were so good. Of course, the resident never asked me about it and instead took the issue to the staff attendings. Those conversations caused a difference in one of my clinical grades in internal medicine and were very unsettling. This level of systematic prejudice that forced me to be on guard and defend my actions was not a one-time occurrence but rather an issue I have had to navigate throughout all of my education and career.

As a first-year medical student, I had to wrestle with prejudice from my gross anatomy tablemates, especially once they realized that they had to share the anatomy table with me. Few students wanted to work with me and during proctored exams, I noticed nobody was working with me on the cadaver. However, once it became clear that I was doing very well on the pop quizzes, interactions with my tablemates became more pleasant.

Because I lived in the resident quarters at E.H. Crump, in close physical proximity to the hospital, and because I did so many histories and physicals, I got to know the doctors who practiced there and they knew me. They'd say, "Look, I've got a case, would you like to come and help with it?" or "I have an emergency downstairs. Have you ever seen [such-and-such]?" I made sure they knew that I was available after I got my studies done and began to scrub in the surgical cases with the on-call attending surgeon. These were unbelievable opportunities. They gave me an on-the-job, hands-on surgical training experience much earlier than I typically would have had it in the usual medical school curriculum. They also exposed me to a variety of disease conditions and interactions with patients, clerical staff, nursing personnel, and attending physicians.

I also came to know the operating room (OR) nurse and she ran everything. She'd say to the attending staff, "You know, there's a medical student here, Student Crawford. He'd love to help." The doctor would think a moment then say, "Yes, I've heard about him. Give him a call and see if he's available." Decades later, as I developed my own spine clinic, the same practice of building relationships and connections helped me to develop and provide the highest quality of care to my patients.

After I took my first six quarters of basic sciences, I joined the US Navy Ensign Medical Program, also called "Ensign, 1915 Program." It was designed to provide an opportunity for qualified students to be affiliated with the naval reserve as commissioned officers while still in medical school. The program allowed me to receive a Navy ensign's pay if I went on active duty during school breaks. Once I reached my final year of medical school, I earned an ensign's pay throughout the school year as well. The program is now called the Health Professions Scholarship Program.

I was assigned to the Bethesda Naval Hospital in 1962 for an externship program. I ended up being at the hospital during the Cuban Missile Crisis. Elective surgeries were halted at that time, and the military took all the stored blood available and put it on the hospital ships so it could be readily available to injured troops. Trauma surgery, however, was still open. I was interested in getting as much patient care exposure as I could since I was trying to figure out if I wanted to be a surgeon. I scrubbed and participated in as many trauma cases as I could and that was good exposure for me.

In my first six quarters at UT, the exams had been objective. A new day dawned though, with my seventh quarter. This began the clinical medicine phase of my medical school experience. It was interactive and very subjective. It meant dealing with the personal attitudes of my educators and fellow students. There were people in the university medical community who didn't want anyone to think that they were friendly with me. During that time, I lost two study partners to some of the medical fraternities that I couldn't join, as well as dormitories where I wasn't allowed to live because of the color of my skin.

The clinical phase years of medical education were the most difficult sociopolitically. Students go on rounds and the professor asks constant questions. I learned the hard way that if I gave the right answer too often, professors stop calling on me, arguing it was "disenfranchising" the other people in the group. "Why don't we give someone else a chance to answer the question?" I often got that response.

During my clinical rounds, it was made categorically clear that I was not to examine white patients, except for trauma cases in the emergency room. Even then, I could examine a male patient but never ever touch a white female patient. It was common knowledge throughout the university hospital system that "he" (they were talking about me) was not to touch a white female and only touch a white male if there was no one else present who could do the job. During clinical rotations, I could only rotate at the John Gaston Hospital (the major teaching hospital) and the VA Hospital, which accepted Black patients. I was not allowed to work at Baptist Memorial Hospital; Methodist University Hospital, then called Methodist Hospital; or St. Joseph Hospital.

The first time a medical student performs surgery, the attending surgeon makes an assessment as to how well they proceed through several segments. At the time I was in medical school in the early sixties, typically the student would start with stitching up the surgery site at the end of the operation. If they did a good job, the surgeon would allow them to actively participate in other segments of a surgery.

In the current medical school environment, this set up is not always possible because of concerns about potential litigation and insurance demands. Medical students and residents are rarely given this type of authority. Today, medical students go through surgical didactic and then rotate through the surgical clerkships, such as OB-GYN (I was able to assist in the delivery of my daughter, Carole Kimberly Crawford, on September 13, 1963), general surgery, and neurosurgery. Surgical skills are best developed by repetition. ("The more tennis balls you hit, the more balls go over the net!") This is where I had an advantage with my medical school education. I literally lived in a hospital and did an unbelievable amount of surgical assisting. The work I had done at E.H. Crump to scrub in surgeries and learn from the attendings there paid off as I had more surgical exposure than any of my peers. I gradually was allowed to assume more responsibility under close observation by the attending surgeon. By the time I became involved in actual surgical procedures in medical school, I had already done over half of them several times and was familiar with handling tissue, suturing, and evaluating perioperative clinical situations. I learned quickly that I couldn't wait for people to give me opportunities, but instead needed to actively seek out involvement and continue to learn.

THE INVISIBLE MAN

There are still a lot of unknowns about the physiology of humans. What are endorphins? What conditions induce euphoria? Can being treated by a health professional that looks like you actually change your health outcome? Science cannot answer everything. In my medical practice, I have had experiences with several older Black men who'd say, "Son, I'm so happy to see you here. You'll be able to do so much good for our people."

I'll never forget one older Black man I treated when I was a medical student. He had congestive heart failure and diabetes. He hadn't been sleeping well because with his condition lying down put pressure on the lungs. His feet and ankles were so swollen he came to the clinic in slippers because his shoes no longer fit. I examined him and wrote out a prescription for diuretics. He squeezed my hand and said, "God bless you."

He returned two weeks later for a follow-up exam. As I examined him, I thought, "Humph. Ankles are as dry as a bone. Wearing his shoes, no swelling." I was feeling good about the progress of this patient.

I asked him, "How's everything going?"

He said, "I'm feeling so much better. I'm sleeping better at night."

"Good," I said to myself. I was almost giddy as I prepared to present my success to my medical attending staff.

His daughters were with him and said, "Doctor, he is really good. He's been telling everybody at the barbershop about you;

he's got all the family and the church members praying for you and you know prayer changes things."

Next, I asked "Now how is the medication going? Those are pretty big pills and I know that sometimes you can have trouble taking them."

At this, the daughters' expressions changed and they said, "Doctor, we have to tell you the truth. We didn't get the prescription filled."

He hadn't taken the diuretics at all. The swelling in the fellow's ankles and his congestive heart failure had cleared up seemingly on their own. Science might try to determine a medical reason for this, but I believe his recovery was because he was so proud that there was a young Black doctor on his case, something he thought he would never see in his lifetime. The impact of that cannot be discredited or minimized. He had prayed for me, and he had prayed hard to get better. And apparently, he did.

For me, this was an epiphany! The idea that prayer or positive thinking can have significant effects on health is not necessarily new and over the years, numerous studies have been carried out. There have also been a number of studies on the effect that having a medical professional of a similar gender or race has on patients of color. In a 2019 study in the *Journal of Race and Ethnic Health Disparities* it was found that a race/ethnicity concordance significantly increases the likelihood patients of color will seek and be more compliant with medical care—preventative or new health issues.[3] The man I treated was so happy to be treated by a Black doctor. In my career I encountered numerous situations like this. These occurrences made clear the level of trust that needs to exist between a doctor and patient. During my clinical work in medical school, I was the only Black man wearing a white coat and for many of my Black patients, the first Black doctor they had encountered. Several articles have inferred that prayer and good faith changes outcomes similar to medication."

I saw first-hand the significant benefit my race had on Black patients, but I also experienced first-hand the systemic prejudice because of my race in all areas of my social life and medical education. In medical school, I participated in team volleyball—the only sport available at the medical college. I would have played in my first year at UTCOM, but nobody was willing to play against an integrated team. Our team had to play all of our games in the University of Tennessee gym or at one of the local high schools because none of the other gyms would allow our integrated team to play, and Jim Crow laws prohibited integration. We ended up playing at a Jewish community center and we won the championship in my senior year.

There was a little hamburger joint that medical students at UT would go to when they had to study late into the night. One night, Doug was getting ready to go there and I asked if he could get me a burger, as I wasn't allowed to sit in the restaurant. He went in and was waiting for the order when a homeless man walked in. Despite his unkempt appearance, he was allowed to sit at the counter because he was white. If I wanted to get a burger myself, I had to go to the kitchen door and tell them what I wanted. They would take my order and money but would not let me in to sit with everyone else. Wilson recalled recognizing the difficulties I had in medical school due to prejudices against my race,

> I looked at that and thought, "This is absolutely terrible!" Here's my buddy Al, who is a quality person, a medical student. And here is this guy, just off of the street, and he's allowed to come here and my buddy is not. That taught me a major lesson as to what was going on and why something had to be done to overcome that inequality. It was awful.
>
> I struggled, my mother and I. My dad died when I was 15 and we had very little money. And we both worked and that's how we lived. I really had to struggle hard in order to be able to get into medical school, to get the money, but the whole point was, I had privileges which the African American student did not have and they had to work ever harder to have success ... it just hurt you to the core to realize just how persecuted these people were.

One time, Wilson and I were traveling to Nashville. We had to stop and get gas. I was terrified the whole time and even when we got back in the car. I kept telling him, "We just have to get the gas and get out of here." He didn't understand at first. He didn't have the same concern I did about being harmed, by the police or anyone else. It was a danger for me, a Black man, to be sitting in the front seat in a white man's car, especially in the South. The threat of being pulled over was looming over us the whole trip.

I think that for some of my classmates, my presence made them uncomfortable. Many were concerned that association with me would brand them as a "n----- lover." Many just didn't know how to relate to me and being 1961, plenty didn't see my life or the lives of other Black people as having any value. The dynamic was tricky. It was unsafe for Doug to associate with me, given the ramifications under Jim Crow. He took a risk being my friend, and thank goodness he did.

The reality of racism in the health care industry starts in medical school, beginning with the connections student are able to make with classmates and colleagues. There were so many socipolitical issues to face. At the beginning of medical school, there is less of a social component because I did my work and went home. The first six quarters are basic science courses and students don't participate in hands-on patient care. Most of our time is spent in laboratories and working on cadavers. In those first six quarters I did well with my work and had two study partners. But, as mentioned earlier, once I began my clinical phase of medical school, I became a liability. Suddenly, my friends disappeared. As we moved into our third year, many of my classmates wanted to join the fraternities and they didn't want to be considered a "n----- lover" because they were friends with me.

One of the students (an Asian fellow) I trained with had family in New Orleans and he would give me a lift to Mound Bayou, Mississippi. I was externing with Meharry Surgical and OB-GYN student residents there at the time. In our third year he stopped working or studying with me, however, because he wanted to be in a certain fraternity. While this wasn't uncommon, it still floored me that these things were happening. This was a time of rigid segregation and there weren't any faculty support groups encouraging inclusion as there are now. But I understood the sociopolitical capital that my classmates would lose if they associated with me—even if they wanted to—and I didn't let it distract me from my mission to earn my medical degree.

While I was the first African American to attend the University of Tennessee College of Medicine, more would follow. Samuel Walker was the second African American student to attend UTCOM. He was admitted about two years after I was. I'd known him in high school. He eventually left medicine, and is now an attorney practicing in Detroit, Michigan. I caught up with him again in 2013 in Indianapolis. It was the first time I'd seen him since the day I loaned him some textbooks in 1962!

Earline Houston was the third African American student to be admitted to UTCOM and the first African American woman to attend. Earline graduated in 1967. She, too, had grown up in Memphis and her family lived in Orange Mound. She graduated from Manassas High School, attended our church, Mt. Pisgah Christian Methodist Episcopal, and was very bright. Earline later became a psychiatrist in Philadelphia and did well in her field. Tragically, she died of cancer in 1986 at the age of forty-one.

I graduated from medical school on May 30, 1964. The ceremony was held in Ellis Auditorium, and it included students from the medical, dentistry, and pharmacy schools. In addition to diplomas, UT bestowed the Charles C. Verstandig Award, which was awarded to a member of the graduating class who "surmounts the greatest difficulty in obtaining a medical education."[4] I thought that I would at least be a candidate considering the difficulties I encountered in getting into and graduating from medical school, but I wasn't even in the running. As Ralph Ellison wrote in his seminal book, *The Invisible Man*, "I am invisible; understand, simply because people refuse to see me."[5] The fact that my classmates and educators didn't recognize the hardships I experienced—financial, personal, and sociopolitical— due to their prejudices against the color of my skin, was isolating. I was neither seen nor heard. It was as if I did not exist.

In a subsequent article in *Look* magazine, I was quoted as saying, "If I flunk out, there will be how many people flunking out?" I knew that I was going to be a success. The challenges and racism I faced only made me try harder to rise to the top. While I might not have understood it at the time, these hardships made me a better doctor. Being a doctor requires more than just intelligence and surgical know-how—compassion and empathy for patients is key to providing high-quality medical care.

On March 11, 1963, during my third year of medical school, I married Jeannie. Two weeks before I graduated there was a program for the wives of the medical students. We had been married over a year at that point and no one had informed her of the event.

After that mishap, the other wives invited her to take part in a little program they were going to have during the graduation. She recalled,

> I went to one of the homes of the students for a rehearsal and they were reading the parts. First of all, they wanted to know if I could read! They said, "Jean, would you read this?" Of course, I read it. But, they decided not to give me the part.
>
> Then when the actual affair took place at a local restaurant—it was a banquet—one lady was brave enough to befriend me. She said, "Let's go to the powder room." And I said, "Yes, I should go, too." In the restroom, there were about twenty women waiting in line. There were women behind me and in front of me. When it was my turn to go into the stall, I went in. When I came out, the restroom was empty. Everybody had disappeared. I remember thinking, I can't believe this! What happened? I was all by myself.

Years later, Jeannie and I were having dinner with Dr. Keith Gabriel and his wife at the Peabody Hotel in Memphis during the Pediatric Orthopaedic Society of North America (POSNA) annual meeting. The Peabody was considered a strict and socially aware kind of hotel. Jeannie remarked, "You know, this is the first occasion when I've been allowed to walk in the front door of this hotel." Keith responded "You're from here. How can you not have been to this hotel?" Keith and his wife were in disbelief. They were white and not from the South, so the possibility that we might not have been allowed in a hotel in our hometown because of our race had not crossed their minds. We left Memphis in 1964 and at that time there were plenty of places, the Peabody included, that didn't allow African Americans. We had never been to see Elvis Presley's house either for the same reasons, but that's another story.

Keith Gabriel has to be the most compassionate, empathetic postgraduate fellow I ever trained. He was always sensitive to the child patient's condition as well as the families' comfort or lack thereof during their treatment. The entire staff well remembers his standout presentations of children with unrelenting congenital/neurologic conditions bringing tears to their eyes, and I'll never forget the comments they made to me regarding his performance in the outpatient clinics. While I consider all of my fellows to have been special, his performance stood out.

Between 1964 and 1987, I had no contact with UTCOM. Why? Because I was naive and young when I left school and had some feelings about the school I probably should not have had. In addition, many of my experiences at the school with my colleagues and instructors had left a sour taste in my mouth. So the school and I lost contact.

But in 1984, while serving in the Navy, I met Bob Summit, a navy medical admiral who served as the dean of UTCOM from 1981 to 1997. In 1987, I was given the Outstanding Alumnus Award and went to the university to speak. I must have done a good job because after that, I was invited to give the graduation address for the medical school in 1988. Since then, I've returned as a visiting professor and developed some relationships with the younger faculty there. The College of Medicine celebrated its hundred-year anniversary in 2011 and invited me back for that milestone. They even wanted a picture taken of me as the first African American graduate. While I was there, I spoke to the Black Students Association (BSA) at the UT Health Sciences Center about my journey and experience. David M. Stern, who served as the executive dean of the Medical School and vice chancellor of Health Affairs at UT Health Science Center from 2011 to 2019, also served as the dean of the University of Cincinnati College of Medicine from 2005 to 2010. He is a good friend and a musician (he plays the clarinet). Together, we performed a Mozart divertimento for the

Daniel Drake Award ceremony at the University of Cincinnati in 2006. The Daniel Drake Award is named after the founder of the Medical College of Ohio, which subsequently became the University of Cincinnati Academic Health Center. This is the institution's highest academic honor.

IN THE NAVY NOW

As I've mentioned, my first experience with the Navy was at Bethesda Naval Hospital in the fall of 1962, during my 6X of medical school and during the Cuban Missile Crisis. Following graduation from medical school in 1964, I was assigned as an intern to the Naval Hospital Boston in Chelsea, Massachusetts. Later, one of my proctors told me that I was sent to Boston because "they" (naively) thought I would have less trouble as a Black doctor in Boston than in other locations. And here I thought that I was sent there because it was a top-rated hospital!

We lived in Boston in a third-floor apartment (in Allston) near Boston University. There wasn't an elevator! Jeannie's and my first child, Carol, had been born in 1963. In Boston, Jeannie was pregnant again, and caring for our young toddler, Carol. She recalled the day our second child, Alvin Jr., was born,

> One morning I woke up and said, "Alvin, I think my water's broken; I'm going to have the baby."
>
> He said, "No, you're not. It's too early for that, those are Braxton Hicks contractions. Just put your legs up like this ..."
>
> I said, "OK," thinking otherwise.
>
> He was doing an internship at Boston-Chelsea in OB-GYN. While he took a shower, I called the wife of one of the other residents who lived in another

building, and said, "When the guys leave, get over here quick because I'm having the baby this morning!"

"Did you tell Alvin?" she asked.

I told her, "That's a waste of time. Just get over here!"

She dashed over as soon as Alvin left. The police came (there was no EMS) and had to bring me down in a chair because I couldn't walk down three flights of stairs. I had the baby before I could get into the delivery room. They called Alvin at the hospital and said, "You have a Braxton Hicks baby here!" I named the baby after him. Later, I told Alvin, "I don't think this (OB-GYN) is a field that you need to be in. I think you need another field." Like orthopaedics.

Who chose the third-floor apartment? He did.

Medical interns worked every third night with only one night off. I felt like a zombie. I remember when Jeannie and I went to the World's Fair in New York City in 1964, I had to work seven consecutive nights in order to get one week off.

As I was finishing up my Boston internship the last day of June in 1965, my orders were to proceed directly to Alameda, California, where I had been assigned to the USS *Markab AR-23*, a repair ship. Actually, it was more like a floating factory patrolling the South China Sea. I spent six weeks training in Alameda and at the Naval Hospital in Oakland. There, I participated in grand rounds and connected with the orthopaedists there, asking where they trained and where they completed their residencies. I was then shipped out to the Western Pacific on a WESTPAC tour.

The route started in Pearl Harbor (Hawaii). It was there that the ship was outfitted for the Southeast Asia tour. From there, we went to Sangley Point (Manila), to Subic Bay in the Philippines, then Taiwan, and then Kowloon, Hong Kong. Next, we steamed out to Dixie Station off the coast of Vietnam. Once there, we provided supplies for and made repairs to destroyers and cruisers.

I was a general medical officer (GMO). When in port, one of my responsibilities was to be the industrial hygiene officer (IHO). I made rounds to local brothels, jails, drunk tanks, and hospitals to see if there were injured seamen. The IHO was also tasked with the review of the "Weekly Information Digest" (WID) which included updates on the best treatments for bacterial infections, skin conditions, and sexually transmitted diseases. We were also responsible for inspection reports of the local night clubs and houses of ill repute. We conducted a medical and administrative inspection while the shore patrol officer surveyed the neighborhoods.

During my rotation in Olongapo, Subic Bay, Philippines, I encountered a brothel that had a trademark or brand—the girls gave their customers a hickey on the lower part of their neck. The sailors displayed these as a badge of honor. I wasn't worried until I saw this brand on some of the officers, including the chaplain. I immediately realized that I needed to provide some serious counseling, as well as condoms and prophylactic antibiotics, for all of my shipmates.

It was unusual to have doctors on the ships in the Navy. The staff of the local military hospitals appreciated it when ships with doctors arrived in port, because the medical staff could take over as the on-call doctor, and replace one of the local doctors in urgent care and emergency rooms. That was only fair. After all, when you brought a ship in, there was the possibility of inundating the local ER rooms with drunken soldiers! But this way, I got to know some of the orthopaedic surgeons practicing in the region. My best experience was attending clinics and assisting with elective and nonthreatening injuries sustained in Vietnam while docked in Yokosuka, Japan. We'd talk, and sometimes I'd come over and assist with surgical cases. I was with the WESTPAC tour for thirteen months, during which I met Admiral Chester Nimitz, a highly decorated hero from the Second World War.

I had two pivotal experiences during my time with WESTPAC. The first took place when we were "coming into colors" at Pearl Harbor. When returning to port, there is a lot to do, including cranking up the lifeboats and arranging the decks. The lifeboats are unsecured when the ship is out at sea in case it hits an iceberg, or is hit by a torpedo or typhoon. When the ship returns to port, those boats are cranked up and secured. The boatswain's mates carry out that task by using crank handles. On this occasion, one of the crank handles flew out of a sailor's hand and ricocheted, hitting another sailor in the head. This sailor was standing up front on deck at attention for review. I was on the top deck in the pilot's nest when this happened. The sailor was knocked unconscious, and we couldn't resuscitate him; the young man had a severe cerebral concussion. He was taken off the ship and sent to Tripler Army Medical Center in Honolulu, where he later died. That was probably the worst thing that I saw during my time on the USS *Markab*.

The second pivotal experience occurred because I did something very stupid. The USS *Markab AR-23* was experiencing typhoon conditions as we traveled from Pearl Harbor to Manila. I was up in a stateroom where the officers' quarters were located. In typhoon conditions, those on the ship are supposed to stay put and sit with a life preserver on in their stateroom. But I spaced out; my life preserver and all of my gear were down in the sick bay (the medical department). I said to myself, *if the ship goes down, I won't have any of my stuff*. So, I tried to go back down to a lower deck to sick bay—in the middle of a typhoon.

When there's an emergency condition, the quarters and compartments of the ship are locked so that if the water comes in, it is sectioned off. I wasn't thinking about that at the time though. I started heading downstairs but couldn't make it so I decided to go *outside*. That was the worst thing I could have done! The wind was blowing me up and down and soon I was only focused on staying alive. The wind blew me against the side rail—the rail that was pulled up when ships are coming into port. I thought about that afterward. Finally, I got down to sick bay where my equipment was and it was locked. Of course. I pounded and pounded on that door but it was clear I was stuck. There was no way I could get back through the ship because all of the compartments were locked. And I sure as hell wasn't going back outside. I could've been tossed overboard, and they would have never found me, considering the sharks in the water. I wasn't wearing a dog tag so even if they'd found my body, they wouldn't have known who I was. All this for a life jacket. Go figure. This experience put things into perspective, and I recognized there were important things that I wanted to do in this world. I also learned to *always* have my life jacket close by while at sea.

The USS *Markab* is a big ship. It's not a "tin-can," which is Navy lingo for the destroyer class ship. It's second in size to a cruiser or carrier, and the carrier deck is large enough to play baseball on. Outside of Okinawa, returning from Southeast Asia, we had an engine failure, of all things. This was ironic because the *Markab* was a repair ship, not one that typically needed repairs itself. In an embarrassing turn of events, we had to be towed into Okinawa by small Army tugboats. I didn't even know that the Army had tugboats!

Wherever the *Markab* docked, other ships would up come alongside to be repaired. The staff also did a lot of regional tours, touring during the day, remaining on the ship at night. During our time in Panganiban Falls in the Philippines, I had the opportunity to visit with Dr. Lichauco, the world's leading ichthyologist. He had, at that time, the largest collection of fresh and saltwater fish in the world. I spent a day with him and his wife, going through the various categories and species, and learning about the genetic experiments that he was doing. In 1965, not much was known about molecular genetics or about the heredity and familial characteristics of fish species and coral. I have always been interested in learning from well-researched doctors and scholars and this was an opportunity to learn about a topic I wasn't as familiar with by one of the best in the field. I am a strong believer in getting whatever education you can when its available.

Community action and engagement are part of the work that the military does when in other countries. We went into the communities to paint, do repairs, or build a school. As a medical officer, I gave health lectures and organized blood drives. At the end of my thirteen-month tour of WESTPAC, I left the ship in Okinawa and flew back to Travis Air Force Base in Solano County, California. My time on the USS *Markab* had run out. My replacement picked up the ship in Okinawa and I flew to my family in Southern California.

The navy was the best experience of my early adult life. I was academically sound, pursuing excellence and adventure, and contributing to the medical field as much as possible. Outside of the military, however, and out of uniform, no one of importance paid much attention to me, whether the attention was positive or negative, and it was mostly negative. I was fortunate to be in Elmo "Bud" Zumwalt's Navy, and boy did it make a difference. The standards for excellence were set and it became a matter of providing equal opportunity and achieving successes. For once in my life striving to be the best with hard work and dedication paid off, was rewarded, and I was loving it.

BOSTON TO SAN DIEGO

My thirteen months in the Southeast Asia theatre ran from September 1965 to June 1966. After my time was up on the first of July I returned home to California, where I was reassigned to Long Beach Naval Station. Now I had the status of General Medical Officer (GMO), which put me in a good position to find on-the-job training. I was training as a primary care physician in the orthopaedic clinic at the Long Beach Naval Hospital, which was located on a hospital ship (I believe it was the USS *Hope*). We saw patients and performed surgery, all on the hospital ship. I also attended rounds at the Los Angeles Orthopaedic Hospital. Fortunately for me, a couple of colleagues I worked with in Yokosuka, Japan—Ira Woodstein and Bob Gledhill—had previously been on staff for a residency position at the hospital. I interviewed with Dr. J. Vernon Luck, the medical director and CEO at the hospital, and was accepted for a residency.

At about the same time, I attended a meeting of the Society of Military Orthopaedic Surgeons (SOMOS) in San Diego and met Larry Bingham, chief of orthopaedics at Naval Hospital Boston in Chelsea, Massachusetts, where I had done an internship after my graduation from medical school. He told me that one of the residents selected for 1966 had turned down the position and he had a vacancy.

"People are still talking about you and your performance as an intern at Chelsea," he said. "Would you like to come back?"

It was a difficult decision, to choose between a residency in Los Angeles or one in Boston. If I stayed in Los Angeles and did my residency at the fabulous Los Angeles Orthopaedic Hospital, after three years I would be done and could start my practice, enjoy Southern California with my family, play tennis year-round, and live the good life. A return to Boston meant that I was obligating myself to the Navy for at least two more years upon completing my residency. But I decided that the prestigious "Boston" label would be equally as good, and since I didn't plan to go into private practice anytime soon, I should take advantage of it. I returned to Boston and started my residency in orthopaedic surgery at Naval Hospital Boston in 1966.

The return to Boston was difficult. At that time, the city was at the center of one of the most contentious school integration situations in the country. The downtown and South Boston areas were hot beds of bigotry and brutal racism. In some ways, it was worse in Boston than it was in Mississippi. A popular mayoral candidate there, Louise Day Hicks, who opposed the desegregation of the city's public schools, ran her campaign on a slogan: "You Know Where I Stand." The atmosphere in Boston was tense. Hicks lost the election by only 12,000 votes. But I returned to the city anyway.

I started at Naval Hospital Boston in Chelsea, and from there connected to Massachusetts General, Boston City, New England Baptist, and Boston Children's Hospital. Naval orthopaedic surgery residents were required to do a year at an outside facility for their pediatric training. Captain John "Jack" Howard MC, USN, my chief at Naval Hospital Boston, wanted to get me out of the military and into the Harvard system. Dr. Art Pappas—the chief of orthopaedics at Boston Children's Hospital and a professor of orthopaedics at Harvard Medical School—was reviewing fellowship applications. I had previously rotated through the system during my residency and was already known by the Harvard staff, so at Jack's request, I prepared a proposal that he presented to Dr. Pappas and it was accepted.

Jack Howard and his family "adopted" my family throughout our time in Boston, and we remained friends until he died at the age of 91. He was an amazing human being, a fine surgeon, and a wonderful educator. He taught clinical community orthopaedic surgery and was an incredible resource for human anatomy. He could direct any surgical procedure. Jack often reminded me, "Alvin, I can't make you smarter, but I can teach you how to stay out of trouble."

I learned later that there had been an interesting meeting between Jack and Art Pappas. Jack presented my credentials. After Art Pappas reviewed them, he said, "Have him here at 7:30 a.m." Then, Jack said, "Dr. Pappas I need to tell you something. I don't know what your politics are or anything but this kid is a Negro." And Art said, without missing a beat, "Well, do you think he can be here at 7:30?" Art Pappas was a good chief, which made my fellowship year very enjoyable and educational. Art had been a football player during his college years at Harvard and at some point, was the team physician for the Boston Red Sox and the Boston Bruins. Sometimes we got tickets to the hockey games when Bobby Orr (Hall of Fame hockey player for the Bruins) was playing. Art was also a part-owner of the Boston Red Sox.

Art was a tough no-nonsense kind of guy whose strength was legendary. A "Pappas unit" was a term that the fellows coined, meaning if someone had enough strength to lift and carry two children that were wearing plaster body casts, they could lift a "Pappas unit." Art left during my fellowship year at Boston Children's Hospital when he was selected to start up the orthopaedic program at the University of Massachusetts at Worcester. John Hall, who was previously at the Hospital for Sick Children in Toronto, came in to take over.

I won the Outstanding Resident Award from the Boston Orthopaedic Club while at Boston Children's. During that time, I was a "free body," that is, I was a resident being funded by the Navy. This was a good deal for Harvard Medical School and Boston Children's because they didn't have to pay me anything although I was paying with two years of my life for every year of training! I did not waste this training. Along with my fellowship with Art Pappas and then John Hall at Boston Children's, I did another fellowship at Massachusetts General Hospital with Otto Aufranc, the leading hip joint reconstruction surgeon in the world. I was also granted a leave of absence to teach freshman anatomy at Harvard Medical School, which I enjoyed.

I met John Anthony "Tony" Herring in 1968 while at Boston Children's Hospital. He was a junior resident and I was a senior resident. Our first real encounter was when Tony had reached the stage of what was called "the ward senior resident." The tradition was that the ward senior made decisions and the "super senior," who was the managing resident, would intervene if there was a problem. I was his super senior.

Tony recalled, "We would make rounds, and everything I recommended to do he would countermand" and say, "No, we don't do [that]. We're going to do [this]." I was really frustrated and so finally, one day as we were going from one ward to another past the cast room, I grabbed him by the arm and said, "Come here a minute." I closed the cast room door and said, "Look, dammit! I'm the ward senior; I'm supposed to make some of these decisions! And if you don't quit bugging me and countermanding everything I want to do, I'm going to knock the hell out of you!" He's only about four inches taller than I am! And I didn't really know how I was going to carry that out! But he sort of stepped back and said, "OK. Let's try that and see how it works."

Subsequently, we realized that we both played tennis, so we decided to get together for a game. We didn't have much time, so we tried to play on a court at Harvard, which was an indoor court. It was very hard to get these courts, and even then, only hour slots were allowed. So, when we finally got a court time, it was 9 p.m. on a Sunday night. This was in the middle of winter and there was snow on the ground. We started the game and I had the first serve. Tony claimed he saw the ball go out into the alley and said, "That was out." I replied, "No. That was on the line." And he shot back, "No, the ball was out. Play two." And then I said, "No. The ball was in play." To which he repeated, "No, it wasn't in the alley, it was out." So now we were standing at the net together, a few feet apart, arguing, "The ball was in!" or "The ball was out!" After about forty-five minutes of this, we realized that we'd used up all of our time on the court without actually playing. Not only that, but we had come in one car and had to drive home together! We argued about this all the way home.

Quite recently, I told Tony something he had not realized. I told him that when I was at Children's, I was not appreciated there because I was from another program outside of Harvard, and some students viewed me as coming in and taking work away from the Harvard residents. I think people resented me there for that, and my race. But when Tony pulled me aside and challenged how we worked as ward senior and super senior, I realized that he was just treating me like anybody else. He wasn't playing patty-cake to be nice and didn't care about my race. He just wanted a fair situation. I figured that we could probably be friends based on that and fifty plus years later, we still are!

The Harvard Orthopaedic Department had access to a home in the Vineyard Haven community of Martha's Vineyard where residents and their families could stay. I worked as the attending urgent care physician at Oak Bluffs Hospital on the island while completing my fellowship in 1969. Oak Bluffs was a predominantly African American community on the island and the location of the only hospital. During one of my shifts, from late in the evening to overnight, there were lots of phone calls coming in from news networks—NBC, CBS, and ABC—wanting to know if Senator Kennedy's body had been brought in. It didn't mean anything to me at the time. I answered each one of them, "No, it had not." Everybody at the hospital got sort of giddy that night, wondering, "What is going on?" When I got home, I remember telling my father-in-law about it, thinking it might be a sick joke, then going to bed.

The next day, it came out that a young woman named Mary Jo Kopechne had attended a party with Edward "Ted" Kennedy and they left together. For whatever reason, his car had gone into the river. They found her body in the car and they were looking for him, because they assumed both he and Kopechne had been in the car, and either he would have survived or his body would have been found. But no body had been found and no one had heard from Senator Kennedy. It was later found out that Ms. Kopechne's body had been taken to the morgue and handled as if she were a nonperson. She was never brought to the hospital for medical assessment.

This was the same week that Neil Armstrong walked on the moon in 1969. I remember staying up and watching it, hearing "one step for mankind" on our little black and white TV. Funny enough, years later, I would serve as a director of Ohio National Financial Services Insurance, where he was a fellow board member.

While I was staying on the Vineyard, Jeannie and I had her parents and sister and our two kids staying with us. These two disparate events will always remind of my time and experience at Oak Bluffs Hospital.

Timing is everything. I finished my fellowships in Boston in 1971. A few years before, President Nixon had formed a commission to develop a plan for an all-volunteer armed forces. In 1972, Congress moved towards implementation of the plan, and the draft expired in 1973, creating, in effect, the Modern Volunteer Army (MVA). I had put my soul on the line, committing to the "two-for-one year" obligated service for all training outside of government facilities, which meant that I had eight years to pay back to the Navy. With the implementation of the MVA, these contracts were null and void so in the end, I didn't have any payback at all. I had done two fellowships, and didn't owe anything. Go figure!

The underlying reason that I made the decision to incur such an obligation with the Navy was because, at the beginning of my medical career, I'd planned to go into academic medicine. I reasoned that once I left the military after completing my obligated length of service, I'd be 43 years old and still young enough to transition to an academic career. The change in military pay system allowed me to have a stable assignment and develop a quality pediatric division.

I was one of the first pediatric orthopaedic sub-specialty-trained surgeons in the military. I was placed on a five-year variable incentive plan (VIP) and sent to God's country, the San Diego Naval Hospital. The VIP was designed by the service to encourage retention by duty station elongation stability and income enhancement. I implemented the pediatric orthopaedic and scoliosis service at San Diego, for which I was awarded a Navy Commendation Medal.

I was like a kid in a candy store in San Diego! Naval Base San Diego was and still is the largest naval base in the United States west of the Mississippi. Any child that had a pediatric orthopaedic condition requiring treatment, whose parent was stationed west of the Mississippi, was referred to me. It was the most optimal control group for clinical research. Regardless of the diagnostic condition, the children were well fed and nutritionally stable as opposed to the indigent, nutritionally challenged patient population in most medical school training programs. Nutritionally stable children aren't always found in teaching hospitals. I was also able to make the eleventh Naval District tennis team, and played the clarinet with a Dixieland band called the Yankee Air Pilots, so named because of the naval pilots who played in the band. We were the best band for many nonprofit groups in the region—we played for free in exchange for food and booze!

In addition to the unbelievably good working conditions, the social life in San Diego was great. The admiral in charge of San Diego Naval Hospital was Herbert Stoecklein, one of the nicest men I have ever met. He loved to entertain and had a near photographic memory. Admiral Stoecklein took the time to brush up on the family history of every member of his staff and delighted in being able to call his staff's wives and children by their first names, to know where the children attended school, and activities that the family enjoyed. He also played tennis, especially doubles tennis. Admiral Stoecklein was always interested in knowing whether I was in clinic or in surgery or if I was free to play tennis. One of the dentists on staff, Russ Tontz, was Stoecklein's hitting partner and traveled with him all over the United States.

The Vietnam War was winding down and the Navy, like all of the military branches, was downsizing. They began to regionalize the service using the Berry Plan. The Berry Plan allowed a physician to complete his or her postgraduate training and not be drafted. The rationale was that servicemen could be better used if they had advanced training. Tony Herring, my colleague/tennis nemesis from Boston Children's, was on the Berry Plan and was allowed to finish his medical training. The regional approach to assignments was messy, the East Coast military made assignments to the South or East, but not to the West Coast. Somehow, through the Bureau of Medicine and Surgery, I was able to get Tony assigned to San Diego. We had gotten over our tennis tiff, somewhat, by that point.

It was 1972 when Tony showed up at the San Diego Naval Base. His hair was down to his shoulders when he went to the induction center to get his ID card. The personnel there told him, "There's no way we can take your ID picture in uniform. You've got to get rid of that hair."

So, Tony went to the barber shop on base to get his hair cut. And they told him, "We can't cut your hair unless you're in uniform or have a military ID card." Completely frustrated, Tony said, "OK, I have my uniform, but I can't wear my uniform (and get my picture taken) because my hair is down my shoulders." And the barber and credentialing service personnel both agreed he had a problem, though they didn't do anything about it. Tony couldn't get his hair cut because he couldn't wear his uniform to get his ID card. And he couldn't get his ID card because he couldn't get his hair cut! In fact, Tony couldn't even get on base as an officer. We laugh about this today; it's a classic Catch-22 situation. He did eventually get his hair cut and received his ID.

During this time, I became interested in writing and publishing articles on my work. The population that I served was the military, meaning it was relatively transient, so it was difficult to maintain adequate follow-up. The aforementioned Alfred I. duPont Institute in Delaware had the best pediatric orthopaedic database in the United States, proving a virtual patient population in records. It was similar to the Shriner's Hospitals network in that they also maintained all of their own records. I made a request of the US Surgeon General to do an additional research fellowship in Delaware.

The waiting list for the fellowship was two years. I appealed to Admiral Stoecklein and thankfully the request was granted. Creatively, if I took a five-month sabbatical plus thirty days of leave I could complete a six-month fellowship. I went to the Alfred I. duPont Institute as a research associate. The admiral allowed me to do the fellowship without adding another year to my obligated service. I thank God for helping me to play tennis.

The duPont Institute documented everything. I had wanted to go somewhere for a research fellowship where I could get the work done quickly and efficiently. What I needed was access to research, librarians, and coordinators, all of which duPont had. The doctor in charge of the institute, Dean MacEwen, gave me several projects, including one on neurofibromatosis. He was the president-elect of the Scoliosis Research Society. We used to have research meetings on Sunday mornings. I wasn't particularly interested in neurofibromatosis—I wanted to study something more interesting. I went in one Sunday morning after he'd returned from a conference in South Africa and he asked, "How are you doing? How are your projects going?"

I told him, "I've got all of the basics from Wilmington General hospital nursery."

"What about your project?" He was referring to the assignment on neurofibromatosis.

I decided to pivot. He said, "But the project I gave you?"

"The clubfeet are doing well..."

"I mean your project. Your project. I gave you the project of neurofibromatosis."

I said, "You've got to be kidding me. Nobody wants to do..."

He told me for the next half hour why it was important for me to do neurofibromatosis. The conversation was ugly. But I left with the firm understanding that if I wanted to be a pediatric orthopaedist, neurofibromatosis was something to which I needed to give a lot of my attention.

I had to start at the duPont Institute on or around the first of July in 1971. Jeannie was a teacher and couldn't come with me right away because she had to get her things together after the school year ended. There were at least three weeks before Jeannie and the kids arrived. During those three weeks, I lived in the duPont estate mansion. Before I arrived in Delaware, I had asked the duPont Institute about finding an apartment. MacEwen said, "Why don't you stay in the mansion?" And I thought, *What the heck is he talking about?*

The duPont mansion is set back in the woods on the site of the Institute. The duPont family had gone on vacation, I think to Italy or Florida. They didn't need the mansion, so I lived there for three weeks with no one else there except the security personnel and Tom. Tom was Irish and a butler and valet by training. His father, grandfather, and others in his family had all been butlers as well. Tom said to me, "Dr. Crawford, if you're going to live *here*, you need a butler and a manservant." He told me that he would lay out my clothes at the foot of the bed, wash them as needed, instructed me as to what to do if I wanted breakfast in my room, or if I wanted to come down for breakfast. Living alone in the mansion without family gave me time alone to contemplate life: my marriage, its future, and my career path of commercial versus academic practice. I utilized a Zen principal in changing the vector of my life arrow. I had picked up a Hibachi pot in Japan; at the time, I loved meat, and we cooked outdoors quite a bit. For this transition in behavior, I "stopped eating the meat of animals that carried their young" (this was the seventies and I lived in Southern California) as a part of the process of restraint, withdrawal of, and redirecting my arrow. I have continued that dietary restraint since.

The mansion had a bowling alley, a movie room with first-run movies, exercise area (at that time, a true rarity), fencing room, and dance studio. It seemed like it was a Rockefeller level of luxury! The three weeks I stayed there were unbelievable.

And the tennis ball Tony Herring and I argued about? Yes, that issue has been conclusively resolved in my mind. The ball was out.

First day of first grade.

Senior Class Officers

Alvin Crawford,
PRESIDENT

High school graduation.

First year of college.

"Mr. Brains" after completing his undergraduate degree.

Nearing his graduation from medical school.

Alvin and his siblings; (from left to right) Rosemary, Robert, Michael, Clarice, Gwen, Alvin, and Aubrey.

Alvin and his future wife Alva Jean "Jeannie" together at senior prom.

Alvin and Jeannie on their wedding day with Crawford's parents.

Three generations of Crawford men: Alvin, Alvin Jr., and Robert from top to bottom.

Crawford pictured on a surgical trip to Ahmedabad, India.

Crawford with a Marine division at Camp Pendleton, California.

Crawford pictured on a surgical trip to Germany.

Crawford pictured on a surgical trip to Shanghai, China.

Crawford pictured on a surgical trip to Seoul, South Korea.

Dr. Crawford's first staff at Cincinnati Children's Hospital.

The first diverse surgical department at Cincinnati Children's Hospital Medical Center.

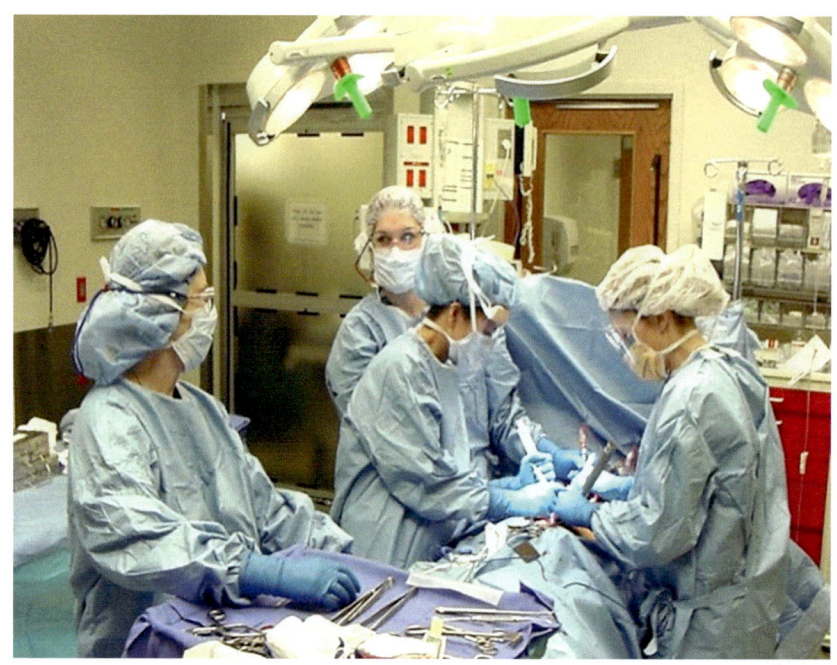

The "testosterone-free" spinal surgical team.

Caribbean Orthopedic and the JR Gladden Orthopaedic Society meeting in Barbados; one of the largest meetings of orthopaedic surgeons of color.

(From left) Roy Emerson, Marty Relsin, Cliff Drysdale, Mel Anderson, Alvin Crawford, Fred Stolle, Neal Fraser, John Newcomb, and Owen Davidson at a tennis camp hosted by Newcomb in Texas.

Crawford with American tennis player Arthur Ashe.

Crawford pictured with Dean MacEwen and John Hall.

Crawford and John Howard, the orthopaedics director of the Boston Naval Hospital.

EUROPE ON FIVE DOLLARS A DAY

Near the end of my pediatric orthopaedic fellowship at Harvard's Boston Children's Hospital in the spring of 1971, before I left for San Diego, I decided I wanted exposure to the European approach to orthopaedic surgery in the skeletally immature. Art Pappas helped set up a traveling fellowship for me at institutions in France, England, Belgium, and Germany. It was a tremendous learning experience. In medicine, as in life, it is important to push one's boundaries and explore new opportunities. I have worked to pursue many international opportunities in my career and employ a global perspective to advancements in orthopaedics.

My first professional visit on this trip was at L'Hôpital Cochin in Paris. I worked under the direction of Dr. Merle D'Aubinge, who was particularly known for joint reconstruction. I followed this with a visit to the Hospital for Sick Children at Great Ormond Street (now called the Great Ormond Street Hospital for Children) in London, which was considered one of the best pediatric orthopaedic centers in the world. Mr. George Lloyd Roberts was the chief of the hospital (in the UK, surgeons are addressed as "Mister"). While in London, I met two other fellow Americans, George Simons from Northwestern University and Paul DeRosa from the University of Indiana, both of whom were residential fellows at Great Ormond Street. I also had the chance to meet Arthur Ashe, who was competing at Wimbledon. That was an exciting experience for me! Years later, Ashe, who is also a member of my fraternity, Kappa Alpha Psi, visited Cincinnati during a Cincinnati Association of Tennis Professionals tournament. In 1986, Ashe was awarded the Laurel Wreath Award, which I would go on to earn in 2013. The Laurel Wreath is the highest honor presented to a member of Kappa Alpha Psi fraternity, for extra-meritorious achievements in service to the fraternity or in human endeavors, national or international. Of over 105,000 members only seventy-one were awarded since its inception in 1911; I am eternally indebted to Donald Washington (deceased) who worked tirelessly getting this honor validated without letting one failure deter him.

In Belgium, I visited the Thalidomide Center, working under the direction of Dr. Ernst Marquardt. The Thalidomide Center was the treatment facility for international patients who had sustained intra-uterine complications as a result of the mother taking the drug thalidomide for nausea during pregnancy. The drug had caused several congenital limb anomalies. Dr. Marquardt was especially known for developing prosthetic limbs, and wealthy patients from around the world were referred to him. I spent three weeks at each country and learned a lot about European approaches to orthopaedic surgery. I would go on to travel to many countries in my career, sharing my own knowledge and learning about other developments in various aspects of orthopaedic surgery.

Jeannie and I took advantage of my time in Europe, and after my daily tutorials we took some time off to travel. Thankfully, back home, Jeannie's aunt watched the kids for us while we were gone. We visited Europe using the guidelines of the then-bestseller, *Europe on Five Dollars a Day* by Arthur Frommer. Not surprisingly, Jeannie and I had quite different views on the merits of this system. I rented a Volkswagen and we drove around Europe, staying in local hotels and bed and breakfasts. In France, our lodgings included a bed so old it had a large dip in the middle—any attempt to start the night on one side was futile as we both always ended up at the center. Jeannie's memories of the trip are a bit different than mine. She recalled,

> Horrible.
>
> I wanted to go to Europe. And when we had to go on $5 a day, I said, I will not ever go on any trip with a limited amount of money like this again. Period. That

really let me know Alvin's attitude towards M-O-N-E-Y. That was a hard trip! It was 1971.

From then on, whenever Alvin said, let's go on a trip, I would say, "No. I don't think so." If I go anywhere, I'm going to have some real cash in my pocket or somewhere on the side. The next time I went to Europe, it was on a tour. I'm not saying it was perfect, but it was different than Europe on $5 a day!

One of the places we visited was Munich, Germany. At the time, they were building the stadium for the 1972 Olympics, which we visited, as well as the Olympic Village. Unfortunately those Olympics would go on to be the site of the Munich massacre, where five Israeli athletes and six Israeli coaches were killed on September 5, 1972 by the terrorist group Black September. Jeannie and I also visited the Dachau Concentration Camp Memorial Site, and Auschwitz-Birkenau in Poland.

I made the decision to pursue orthopaedics in my senior year of medical school and that decision was reinforced while I was in the Navy during the Vietnam War. In medical school, students have to make the decision to pursue what was called "cut to cure" or "medicate to cure" disciplines. Those who didn't like blood or surgery could pursue "medicate to cure" paths such as radiology, pathology, anesthesia, or becoming an internist. Being a surgeon though was a "cut to cure" position. In the third year of medical school, students start to home in on the specialty they want to pursue. At that time, some of the "bright" kids in medical school wanted to be neurosurgeons, so at first, I thought that I wanted to be a neurosurgeon, too. But I soon learned that with surgery, I didn't want to just save lives, but also wanted to tangibly, visibly, make people better. Hardly any of the major medical institutions accepted Black students into neurosurgical programs, and coupled with that, I recognized neurology wasn't a path for me. Neurological procedures, while possibly lifesaving, can leave patients in very different states. I wanted to perform procedures with more visible results. I specifically liked working with kids—kids just want to get better so they can play with their friends again. Adults are much more complicated. Children don't care what the doctor looks like or who they are. I wanted to help them be well enough to pursue their best lives. If I could do that for them, then I was the greatest person they ever met. It didn't matter what their father or mother said or thought about me, if the child said, "Doctor Crawford's OK," then I was.

Surgery intrigued me and I rose to the challenge. But I was also very aware of the differences in orthopaedic surgery and other types—such as neurosurgery or invasive surgery of the internal organs. I practiced pediatric limb-tumor surgery for twenty years and saw, time and time again, that tumor surgery does save lives. But tumor surgeries of the bone are different from those involving the internal organs. In limb surgery, the focus is on saving the limb. A diagnosis is made from a biopsy, the surgeon cuts the tumor out, and then appropriate chemotherapy is used to remove residual tumor or surgical spillage. If a repeat biopsy shows a significant part of the tumor was killed, the patient qualifies for limb salvage surgery. The child is fitted with a prosthesis and continues to do most of the activities they were used to doing. Doctors can often predict the success of chemotherapy by using microscopy to determine the percentage of tumor successfully controlled in a presurgical biopsy. As much as I liked surgery, however, I didn't have the heart to perform extensive abdominoperineal resections, which were part of my oncology training. With the diverse portfolio I gathered during my fellowship in Europe, I returned to the United States fully equipped to begin a career as the director of a pediatric orthopaedic service, at a time when there were no Black pediatric orthopaedic chiefs of service.

Orthopaedic surgery can improve patients' quality of life in multiple ways. A patient with knee pain from osteoarthritis can have a knee replacement procedure and be ready to get back on the tennis court. I wanted to see my patient able to resume active lives and purse the activities they had enjoyed before treatment. I enjoyed witnessing the visible improvement from treatment or surgery. Upon returning to Boston, I entered a total joint arthroplasty fellowship under Otto Aufranc, the premier hip arthroplasty surgeon in the United States at the time. He asked me if I would join his practice in Boston after completion of my military service. I considered his offer, but I knew my goal was to be a director of a pediatric orthopaedic center. I had done all this training and knew I didn't want to end up performing one specific surgery, such as hip or knee replacement, for the rest of my career. I wanted diversity in the care I could provide. So, instead, I continued my training at Boston Children's Hospital for the next few months, working with pediatric orthopaedics. I loved it.

I then moved to San Diego and was having a great time in the navy, focusing my work on pediatric orthopaedics. But I realized that this state of affairs could change if the succeeding hospital CEO did not buy into the concept of specialized pediatric services. At the San Diego Naval Hospital, the orthopaedic service was binary, meaning one side of the clinic was active duty, the other dependents and retirees. If a new CEO determined that service should only be provided to active fleet and their adult dependents, then pediatric orthopaedic patients could be referred to a nonmilitary affiliated children's hospital. I had known I wanted to specialize in pediatric orthopaedics since medical school and my experience in Europe had taught me about the different approaches and developments in orthopaedic treatment and surgery. At San Diego, I didn't want to lose that place due to a change in hospital structure. I ultimately set up the first full-service pediatric orthopaedic service in the military. I subsequently received a commendation medal for my efforts and would continue to center my career on increasing access to pediatric orthopaedic care.

HENRY FORD HOSPITAL AND BEYOND

In 1975, my military service obligation was coming to an end, and I began to look for civilian orthopaedic positions. Unfortunately, I soon discovered there were not many available to me. I'd done well in residency and won the Boston Orthopaedic Club's Outstanding Resident Award, as well as a Carl Berg Traveling Fellowship with the Orthopaedic Research and Education Foundation, but I quickly learned that not many positions were open or accepting of Black applicants. Only two positions came to my attention: one was at Stanford Children's Hospital and the other was at the Henry Ford Hospital (now flagship facility for the Henry Ford Health System) in Detroit, Michigan. The Stanford position paid less than my military pay, so that was off the table. But the Henry Ford Hospital presented a unique opportunity.

The hospital was initially financed by automotive pioneer Henry Ford and opened its doors to patients on October 1, 1915. At the time I was applying, Henry Ford II (Henry Ford's grandson) was continuing the family's philanthropic commitment to the hospital and was dedicated to its success. In 1973, the Ford Foundation, though not associated with the hospital, provided a sizeable grant as part of a ten-year expansion program in research, education, and medical treatment. I applied to a position as a senior associate orthopaedic surgeon and joined the hospital in 1975.

I had a great experience at Henry Ford. Prior to this, I had never been in a place with such innovative, well-maintained resources. The hospital had considerable funds available for research, and projects with clinical implications needed only to show a profit within seven years. I'd never seen anything like it. This was around this time of the Livernois–Fenkell riot in July 1975 that erupted after a white owner of a bar shot and killed a Black youth. There was significant prejudice against Detroit, and the hospital was not immune. It was clear to me, arriving in the city shortly thereafter, that if Henry Ford Hospital with its stellar resources, were in any other city than Detroit, it would have been recognized as one of the preeminent medical facilities in the world.

The University of Michigan (UM) allowed its junior medical students to do clinical rotations at Henry Ford Hospital. Initially, the majority of students who took advantage of this opportunity were Black. The resources Henry Ford had available for testing were amazing. Medical students could order a test in the morning and have the results back that afternoon to support or refute a diagnosis. This quick turnaround just wasn't an option at UM. The Henry Ford clinical experience focused on more common disorders and was less esoteric. University of Michigan medical students who did their clinical rotations at Henry Ford were consistently doing well on their boards, and soon the competition for getting a clinical rotation spot at Henry Ford skyrocketed! For medical students, quality clinical experience was essential to obtaining competitive board scores, which in turn determined if the student matched in their specialty of choice.

Henry Ford Hospital used the same model as the Mayo Clinic, Johns Hopkins Hospital, and the Cleveland Clinic. These hospitals employed a closed staff of physicians who worked exclusively in and for the hospital; everything was streamlined and kept internal. A patient could come in the morning for an evaluation, consult with a doctor, have x-rays taken at the lab, and leave with a document at the end of the day to take to their primary care doctor back home.

Henry Ford Hospital was a pioneer in many ways. For example, during my years at Ford, one of the administrative fellows, Vinod K. Sahney, wrote a proposal for a satellite hospital unit. This was not a common approach to hospital healthcare at the time. The process was structured much like the auto assembly line for which Henry Ford made his name: patients could obtain different treatments and services at locations around the city at satellite medial facilities—each part or piece comprising the whole of their treatment. This gave patients more options for locations they could be treated at and increased the services that could be provided. Maybe a patient just needed a tune-up such as a cardiac stress test or hernia repair, or maybe they needed a more invasive surgery such as arthroplasty/arthrotomy (knee replacement surgery) or colonoscopy—most of procedures could be performed at the satellite hospital, not just the main downtown campus. Today, almost every major medical center in the United States has this structure.

I had met Robert N. Hensinger in 1973, when I was at the duPont Institute and he was attending staff. While I was in Detroit, Robert was at the University of Michigan, Ann Arbor. During that time we connected often. During my Carl Berg Fellowship, when I traveled around the United States and visited a number of hospitals and orthopaedic departments, Robert had been the only doctor to invite me to dinner at his home. Robert also knew Dennis Lyne, a Johns Hopkins-trained orthopaedist, who had initially helped recruit me to Ford. Dennis was a good friend of mine from my Navy days at Boston Naval Hospital.

One thing Henry Ford didn't have, though, was a designated children's hospital. It had a pediatric pavilion within the in-patient treatment building. But I wanted to be an orthopaedic director of a free-standing hospital that was exclusively for children. The only children's hospital in Detroit was the Wayne State-affiliated Detroit Children's Hospital. This was 1977 and I was acutely aware that there wasn't a pediatric hospital in a major teaching center that had a Black orthopaedic director. I would later become the first, but unfortunately, after me there have not been any directors of pediatric orthopaedic surgery in a major children's hospital in the United States that look like me.

When I considered leaving Henry Ford Hospital, there were several opportunities open to me including one at the University of Virginia Medical School. I went through the interview process and got a call back from the head of the department. He said, "We can't wait to get you here. We think you'll be a fine addition to our staff. And you and Dr. [So-and-So] will make a great combination."

"What do you mean by that?" I asked him.

He said, "Our young acting director is excited that you may be taking the job and can't wait to work with you. I've decided that it would be good for you to bring him along. The two of you will work very well together as codirectors of the division."

I said, "I don't think so." I had worked tooth and nail in medical school and in my residency and fellowships, fighting for my spot each time. I was not going to accept a shared directorship, so we ended our negotiations.

At about the same time, Ed Miller, director of orthopaedics at the University of Cincinnati College of Medicine, initiated a search for a division director of orthopaedics at Cincinnati Children's Hospital. Ed wanted to establish an in-house academic service run by University of Cincinnati staff. At that time, the Freiberg orthopaedic group was providing most of the orthopaedic services at Cincinnati Children's. Aaron Perlman, who was with Freiberg, was the director, and Bernie Bacevich, Mike Rosen, David Greenfield, Richard Weimann, Jim Willis, and Dick Jolson were on the clinical staff. Ed Miller took a chance, hiring me to be an in-house orthopaedic director. I also understood the pressure this put on me as the first Black doctor hired in the position and one of few Black surgical division directors in the nation. Failure could have any number of ramifications.

Cincinnati had passed a tax levy in 1975 that provided funds for both treating underprivileged children and training doctors. Passage of the levy transformed the entire concept of medical training for the treatment of children. Before the tax levy, the Cincinnati Children's Hospital was an Episcopalian institution for mostly private patients. Poor children were treated at Cincinnati General Hospital (now University Hospital). Funding from the tax levy allowed for the development of a university division of pediatric services that would operate from, and be physically located in, the Cincinnati Children's Hospital. Someone was needed to oversee the orthopaedic department, which is where I came in, as full-time university faculty.

Ed Miller and I talked about how I could shape the position and what the specifics would look like. For the most part, we agreed. Aaron Perlman, however, said, "No, I think he should just come down and do research to get started. Sooner or later, I'll retire and then he [Crawford] can take over." That wasn't what I wanted. I wanted to provide clinical services and direct the training program, not just research. We negotiated that point for a long time, but it just wasn't working out. At one point during this process, Aaron even flew up to Detroit and got a room at a motel near the airport. He really wanted to talk with me. And we did talk—for most of that day. Finally, Aaron said, "You know, I've looked at your resume. And I think you would be good for Children's. If you decide to come, I promise that I will retire within the year and you'll take over completely. I'll put that in writing."

I told him, "Yes, I can come only if you'll agree to continue to be active on the attending staff as *I'm* directing the division. That will be fine with me."

Still, no deal. I would come as director but a university employee. This issue had not been completely resolved. The Freiberg group had been recruiting a pediatric orthopaedist to take Aaron's place. I got the opinion that the University's intent of establishing a pediatric orthopaedic division with an in-house director had not been discussed with the attending orthopaedist on staff at Children's. There were a number of communication issues between the University, the Freiberg group, and Children's.

One of my last visits to Cincinnati before officially joining was on May 28, 1977, the night of the Beverly Hills Supper Club fire in Southgate, Kentucky, just across the Ohio River from downtown Cincinnati. I remember that night so well. I went over to the ER to visit with some of the residents and attending physicians on duty. John Beavers, one of the residents, told me what was going on with the fire. All the doctors on duty were asked to come over to the hospital but John had actually been on the scene in Kentucky to help out.

In a fire, there are usually people who've been burned, are bleeding, or are traumatized. There are always broken bones. But John said that he was waiting outside of the supper club and as they brought the victims out, they were dead but looked as if they were asleep. There was no evidence of trauma. They had died from the smoke and toxic fumes, which didn't leave a visible mark. The scene was chaotic. People were screaming, looking for their relatives. Some would run back into the building and fifteen or twenty minutes later, they, too, were brought out as victims overcome by smoke inhalation and toxic fumes from the fire. John recalled it was eerie not to see evidence of trauma in people who were obviously affected and had died from it.

In the end, this recruiting visit to Cincinnati didn't work out either. The only thing we agreed on was that we needed further discussion. Of course, the story does have a happy ending as eventually the issues were worked out and I took the position as director of the pediatric orthopaedic division at Cincinnati Children's Hospital. But this wasn't until December 7, 1977, when the issue was finally resolved. By that point, I had been in conversation with Ed Miller, Aaron Perlman, and others at Cincinnati since July! It had been a long, arduous process, but I also knew my worth and stood my ground in the negotiation process. My family remained in Detroit, and I moved to Cincinnati and took an apartment in Morgan's Hall, the married students' dormitory, from December 1977 to July or August 1978. When school was out, Jeannie and the children finally joined me in the Queen City.

PEDIATRIC ORTHOPAEDICS AT CHILDREN'S HOSPITAL

When I started at Cincinnati Children's as the director of the pediatric orthopaedic division, at first there was no one there (as in, based at the hospital) full-time. There were very few surgeons seeing uninsured patients. The orthopaedics practice was run as a satellite facility through the Freiberg group and others who maintained offices off-site. Virginia "Ginny" Niemeyer was assigned to my limb clinic as a part-time registered nurse in 1978, splitting her time between my department and the ENT (ear, nose, throat) hearing-impaired clinic. She recalled,

> When I met Dr. Crawford, I was apprehensive because the hospital hadn't really planned for him. I remember the uproar: "Where was he going to go? What was he going to do?" He didn't have any staff; they pulled a secretary out of another office to assist Dr. Crawford and they found an office for him in what was then called "The Pavilion Building."

At that juncture, Cincinnati Children's evolved into a general pediatric hospital that treated all children, paying and nonpaying. Except for the newborn nursery, pediatric patients who previously were treated at Cincinnati General were automatically transferred to Cincinnati Children's. Funds from the levy previously earmarked for indigent care were then available to support treatment for all.

The timing was good for me. The funding from the tax levy benefitted Children's tremendously. Before its passage, paying customers could go to Christ or Good Samaritan Hospital for pediatric care. Every hospital in the region (Mercy, Bethesda, St. Luke's, and St. Elizabeth's) maintained a pediatric unit, but because the levy passed consistently, Cincinnati Children's became the primary recipient of the funding, which allowed it to build facilities and a reputation that was so excellent that parents didn't want to take their child anywhere else for treatment. It soon became too expensive for other hospitals in the region to take care of very sick children, so except for ambulatory conditions like pediatric hernias or specialties such as ENT, most other hospitals eventually decided not to anesthetize patients below a certain age and instead refer their pediatric patients directly to Cincinnati Children's. This gave Children's a large array of patients along with the tremendous responsibility to provide excellent care to all.

The delivery of medical services was changing, too. In 1977, patients who were not able to pay or had limited funds for medical treatment were mostly treated by resident physicians, who were under supervision. These residents generally did a good job, but there wasn't always consistent and comprehensive staff supervision. Once funds became available from Medicaid and the tax levy for the treatment of financially disadvantaged patients, then the hospital was able to support attending staff physicians for all patients. This provided more accountability within the process as staff physicians were compensated by the insurance carriers and Medicaid for the services provided.

At the beginning of my time at Cincinnati, there was one orthopaedic nurse who worked with me. There was no office because there had never been an in-house chief who actually worked out of the hospital. In the past, physicians "attended" the hospital but had private offices located elsewhere in the city. I had to pay for my personal office out of my salary from the university. The renovations needed to make the space usable were going to cost $10,000. For this, I applied for credentials from the Children's Hospital Board of Directors. The board president at that time was Lonnie M. Wright. Lonnie had an interesting perspective on my position. "I don't know exactly what you're going to do here," he told me in one of our meetings, "but it may not be as easy as you think. You'll have to find a physical place to hold your clinics. We'll see if we can get clinic space down in the Holmes Hospital."

At that time, Holmes Hospital treated well-to-do, insured patients who wanted to consult with a university doctor. Few patients voluntarily chose to be treated at Cincinnati General Hospital unless they were financially destitute, and/or at risk for survival from a serious, life-threating injury. At that time, patients who were insured or had the financial resources chose other hospitals in the city, especially Holmes. To give a sense of the atmosphere at Holmes, there was a staircase in the foyer with a chandelier hanging from the ceiling. The Procter, Taft, and Holmes families were among those who initially funded and professionally managed the hospital, which opened its doors in May 1929.

It was Lonnie's opinion that I couldn't attract insured patients to the Children's clinic environment and should instead set up shop at Holmes. The shift for Cincinnati Children's to become the University of Cincinnati's pediatric hospital had not been in effect very long and the reputation of Children's still had a way to go. Insured patients were used to being treated in a private office, not clinics at large hospitals. He didn't think I could get both the financially disadvantaged patients and the moneyed patients to seek treatment at the same clinic. Lonnie told me, "You can't see private patients in childrens' clinics. You can't see patients in the clinic. No, no, no."

I said, "You know, I just left a place where I managed a clinic *and* a clinic office. While I was there, I treated patients from Michigan Social Services and I also had a patient whose father made cars imprinted with their last name. So I think we can get them to come." I was determined to make high quality pediatric orthopaedic service the goal of my practice, and not focus on getting only certain patients to the clinic.

When I first arrived, they had multiservice examining rooms for all patients in the clinic. In the waiting room at the clinic, all the families sat together like a big festival. A voice would come over the PA system saying, "Mary Jane, please take your child to room [so-and-so]." I immediately didn't like the lack of respect—no "Mr. or Mrs. [_____]" at all. I wanted to change this and create a more welcoming, respectful environment but the initial response was, "well, it's just a clinic." This was a recurring issue I ran into—

coming up against preconceived notions about how and what a medical clinic should be and the kind of patients I should treat. Challenging preconceived notions was something I knew about all too well.

Before the outpatient department was built, the old orthopaedic clinic was just a small section of the total outpatient department, in the back on the right-hand side of the building. It was next to both the hematology clinic, where many patients were receiving blood transfusions and chemotherapy, and the fracture room, with the patient rooms around the corner. All the disciplines were jammed together, one right after the other. They were held on different days: general orthopaedic, foot clinic, spine clinic, and so on.

Every Friday, there was a scoliosis clinic. Afterward, we met in an inside room where the orthopaedic residents discussed the patients that they'd seen that morning. They were responsible for viewing the x-rays that day if I wasn't there.

Pediatric orthopaedics is an orthopaedic subspecialty. Growth plates separate a pediatric case from that of an adult. An injury to the growth plate can cause angular deformities (i.e., a crooked bone) or impede normal growth as the child develops; the bones won't grow as they should. In addition, there are genetic disorders and syndromes unique to children that are out of the purview of the adult orthopaedist. Today, most doctors would, by default, send their pediatric patients to Cincinnati Children's. But it wasn't that way in I arrived in 1977. A patient was considered a customer. There were plenty of situations where parents with resources preferred their child (the patient), be treated in a private office rather than at Cincinnati Children's clinics. There were a number of physicians who would not send their kids to me for treatment.

It was important to me to pursue excellence in my skills and be patient-oriented. I had quite the job on my hands—combatting the stigma against my race and how I chose to set up my clinic. My rationale was that a clinic is not "just" a clinic and that we would have to do something different to treat all patients with dignity and respect. I had different criteria for each diagnosis. We initiated changes, improved the appearance of the clinic environment, and instituted separate clinics so that it wasn't just a big bastion of patients waiting to be seen. Today, parents bringing their children to Cincinnati Children's Hospital will go to one of the clinic halls. There's equal treatment and no one's name is outed on the PA system. Patients have an appointment, are told when they will be seen, and are assigned a room number. It was important to me then, and it is important to me now, that patients are treated with the utmost respect. My staff and I changed the whole fabric of the Cincinnati Children's Hospital outpatient clinic system by presenting an environment where all patients—insured, uninsured, paying, and nonpaying—are treated with dignity and high quality care. In a fundamental way, orthopaedics was very active in leading the change of the entire hospital outpatient clinic system.

Each morning, my residents and I would meet early, have a "prayer" session, in other words, review the trauma patients and emergencies admitted overnight, and then go through *Tachdjian's Pediatric Orthopaedics*. I would assign chapters and had developed a syllabus with 1,200 slides.

In 1973, when I was stationed in San Diego along with Tony Herring at Balboa Naval Hospital, I invited Merhan "Myke" Tachdjian, MD to be a visiting professor at both the San Diego Children's Hospital and the Balboa Naval Hospital. Dr. Tachdjian was the reigning authority on pediatric orthopaedic surgery. He had trained at Boston Children's Hospital and was the director of orthopaedics at the Children's Memorial Hospital in Chicago. He had just written *Tachdjian's Pediatric Orthopaedics*, which became the definitive textbook on pediatric orthopaedic surgery. The current version was edited by doctors at the Texas Scottish Rite Hospital for Children, including my friend John Herring.

Another quick aside about Dr. Myke Tachdjian. Myke had also developed the first definitive pediatric orthopaedic review course, which took place in Chicago. There was no other course like it in the country that was fully dedicated to pediatric orthopaedic surgery. Pediatric care was just then (early to mid-seventies) becoming an issue for our orthopaedic specialty boards. The pediatric orthopaedic review course was an amazing endeavor with over 400 attendees who trudged through lectures from 7 a.m. until 10 p.m. Every attendee was focused on writing down the pearls of wisdom that would get them through their board exams. The course location would later alternate between Chicago and San Francisco. Myke was a tremendous mentor and strengthened my knowledge base by giving me lecture assignments in his international courses. The course was named the International Pediatric Orthopaedic Symposium (IPOS) and it's still going on today. His impact on the pediatric orthopaedic field is immeasurable.

Efficiency was key to my practice, and I wanted on-call residents to be located in the hospital, ready to go when needed, and with quick access to patients. Michael O'Brien was one of my first residents at Cincinnati Children's. He recalled:

> One thing I remember is that he showed up and wanted to know who was on call that night. Somehow, he learned that we stayed overnight at home when on call, not at the hospital. He said, "Not anymore." So, I, unfortunately, was the first one to take in-house call at Children's Hospital. The next morning when he came in, I was in his office. I believe I was taking a shower. He was wondering why I was in his office, and I said that I had slept in his office because I had nowhere else to sleep. That night he found us a call room—a real "nice" room without windows as I recall.

The specialists usually see referred patients rather than direct walk-ins, except in the case of emergency admissions. Most surgeons get their patients from "patient care" referrals. This makes up most of a surgeon's practice. Surgeons might also get referrals from medical school colleagues, neighbors who work at insurance companies, or friends who belong to the same country club. But this assumes the surgeon has been a part of a certain culture that created these connections, which I wasn't. Instead, my practice started out, quite literally, from trauma. I received cases from the emergency room, for example, when a kid fell out of a tree or was in a road accident. By doing a good job with their treatment, the child's parents might recommend me to their friends in need of an orthopaedic surgeon. And that comment begets a referral and begets another referral. That's how it works and how I built up my repertoire. Patients return or recommend if they receive quality, respectful care. It's not an insurance thing, it's not a country club, social setting thing, and it's not a religious thing. For a parent, it's satisfaction with the care of their child. I built up my patient pool by putting people first and relying on good work, not monied connections. Kids are especially loyal—if their doctor helps them run outside and play again, the doctor is their hero, regardless of their parents' socioeconomic or political positions, or how they were referred to begin with.

But it was still more difficult to attract the well-to-do and private patients; that took a while. Most of my first patients had state aid. It is important to keep perspective—things don't change just because you, the new guy, came to town. People are treated well before you arrive and will be treated when you leave. And building a pool of patients based on good work, while rewarding, does take time.

The aesthetics of a clinic cannot be underestimated. They were not attractive settings. The renovated orthopaedic clinic was adjacent to the garage loading docks. One of my recruits rightly questioned whether anyone would want to bring their child to see me in that environment. Combine this with a myriad of sociopolitical attitudes in Cincinnati in the seventies and it was clearly the uphill battle I faced in trying to develop a premier department.

Angela "Angie" Strader became a nurse in my spine clinic, but before that, she was my patient. She recalled,

> What I remember is the atmosphere. First off, the orthopaedic department was located in the basement of the hospital. You followed a maze through the hospital and there was yellow tape on the floor—we called it the Yellow Brick Road. You followed this into a dungeon area. The department was, literally, in the bowels of the hospital next to the loading

dock. It was old looking, it was not pretty. I remember walking into the waiting room and being completely freaked out.

The waiting room was filled with children of all ages wearing the most horrendous-looking casts. Some of them were wearing a "halo" which is a metal ring around their heads (screwed into their skulls) and sitting in chairs with weights on them. And here I am—a perfectly normal healthy kid who has a spine deformity, scoliosis, but besides that, I am fine. I walk in and it (the clinic) looked like a torture chamber.

I was here without a defined supportive budget, since it was not a university-supported facility, so my staffing decisions were based on work output and remuneration. I finally recruited another pediatric orthopaedic surgeon in 1983, Dennis Roy, though at that point I was billing enough for three people. Whether it was the economic (academic medicine versus private) or sociopolitical environment that impacted this, I'll never know. Billing has nothing to do with income, especially if you're billing a welfare system. Collecting is important.

Hard work has its benefits and its drawbacks. In my first six years at Cincinnati Children's, I personally treated the majority of self-insured (nonpaying) fractures that required intervention. In the early nineties, I was called into the CEO's office and informed that there had been an ongoing investigation of fraud in my practice by the State of Ohio concerning billing charges to the state's Crippled Children's Fund. The investigators had monitored my daily activities, including those from the outpatient clinics and surgery. During the investigation of my division—an investigation that I had not been informed of—*The Cincinnati Enquirer* published my payments from the State of Ohio, and the contribution of the division (me) to the hospital's bottom line was second in revenue generation to pediatric radiology (which had eight to ten radiologists, as opposed to pediatric orthopaedics being just me). This was before academic medical programs began requiring an attending surgeon to cover every case. During this time, any non-insured patient seen in the Emergency Room service, whether I saw them initially or not, could be billed in my name. And reimbursement rendered only when I saw them in follow-up clinic. It's interesting to note that the payment to the doctor was about 17 percent of every dollar billed at that time. Most volunteer attending surgeons did not submit a bill from the clinics because of the difficulty of getting reimbursement from the state. My billing to the state was alarming because there had not previously been as much billing with the same population group. Previously, most patients at Cincinnati Children's were private, and because I had agreed to accept self-pay and Crippled Children's Fund, the state was now receiving orthopaedic service bills.

My meeting with the CEO was a surreal experience. In that meeting, he was happy to inform me that I was found not guilty of any fraudulent activity, but continuing to work as I did without an associate was not good for my health. From that point on, my awareness of the institution to which I was committed was heightened. A line from Joseph Heller's novel *Catch-22* came to mind: "Just because you're paranoid doesn't mean they aren't after you."[6] I realized that I hadn't been paranoid enough. No one gave me a head's up about the state investigating me. I had been left hanging. I realized I needed to be on guard and more aware, making an extra effort to keep detailed accounts in case I was called into question again.

As I finish this book, Cincinnati Children's Hospital has been named number one in the United States in the Best Children's Hospitals rankings. Pediatric Orthopaedics ranked number three out of the top fifty medical centers. I rest my case.

THAT DR. CRAWFORD

N ot long after I interviewed and agreed to come to Cincinnati Children's, I gave a presentation at a local luncheon. There I met one of the more renowned pediatricians in Cincinnati. She was enthusiastic about my presentation and congratulated me on my new position, saying that she was looking forward to the day when I would be here, and telling me that she would refer all of her Black patients to me. I remember thinking, "Gee! Thank you very much!"

From that conversation, I recognized the subtext of her message—that Black patients were the only patients that she would ever refer to me. Interestingly, I would go on to treat some of her non-Black patients. In that case, the parents and the patient assumed it was because that particular pediatrician didn't know about my practice. I operated on the patient, who, fortunately, did very well after surgery. The next week, I told the pediatrician that I'd operated on one of her patients. She replied, "That's good! I'm so happy about the outcome." And then I told her the patient's name, knowing that in no way would she ever have referred that individual to me. She gave me an incredulous look—one that was familiar, having observed a lot of those looks over the years.

Now, that conversation was before HIPAA regulations, when medical staff might meet in the hallway and openly discuss patient care information. Fortunately, that can't be done anymore. While I was grappling with the difficulty of starting a clinic and attracting patients, I had to battle the prejudices of doctors like this pediatrician who believed I should only treat Black patients. I had to make sure my work was twice as good to combat this kind of intolerance. Eventually, this doctor came to terms with the fact that I treated many of her patients, Black and white. But the only patients whom she ever directly referred to me were Black.

There were other situations where doctors and other medical professionals would come in from around the country to observe some of the procedures that we were doing at Cincinnati Children's. Sometimes they came uninformed, their consultants having neglected to tell them that I was Black. I remember being at the operating room (OR) scrub sink with a visitor and he asked me if I was going into the OR with Dr. Crawford. I told him that I was. He assumed that I was a technician or orderly.

He said, "I came to see him do [such-and-such] procedure. Is he pretty good?"

I thought about it for a moment and said, "Yes, he's pretty good."

He went on to tell me, "They say he's an asshole."

To that, I said, "Well, maybe so, but maybe not," and we exchanged a few more remarks about the procedure. He was still unsure about going in. I asked him, "Are you really interested in this procedure?"

He said yes, so we talked a bit more. Because I knew so much about the upcoming procedure, he finally said, "Boy, you must work with him a lot."

We went into the OR together. He wasn't scrubbed or anything. This was at a time when you could invite a physician into the OR to scrub or observe the procedure with you. The process has changed now, and credentialing has become a more standardized involved process. The scrub nurse saw me coming in and she said, "Dr. Crawford, is this a visitor? Will he be scrubbing?" The poor guy almost lost it!

I had friends and colleagues around the country involved in residency training programs. My colleagues and I wrote a number of journal articles where the fact that I'm Black, of course, was not mentioned. My team and I have written lots of papers so it's not unusual that academic societies were familiar with some of our work. One year, I was attending an academic society meeting, sitting at a table with a doctor from one of the Los Angeles programs. He asked if I was Dr. Alvin Crawford.

I said, "Yes, as far as I know."

He asked if I'd done any writing. And I said that I had. Then he asked, "Are you *the* Alvin Crawford?" Again, I told him that I thought so.

He said, "I can't wait to get back and tell the guys!"

I said, "What're you talking about? Tell them what?"

"We didn't know you were Black! We hear about you in the journal clubs and the surgical groups all the time, and we never knew!"

I said, "I'm very much Black!"

Some of my colleagues would say that society has gotten past this—that they don't have to tell people my race when talking about my work. I certainly don't think anyone's race needs to be disclosed in an academic article, but I do think it is important for Black medical students or aspiring doctors to know my background. As the adage goes, "you can't become what you can't see."

In the late seventies to early eighties, I didn't need to be told that there weren't many doctors on staff who looked like me. I knew it. Occasionally, though, I was reminded more overtly. I was treating the daughter of one of the Black nurses at the hospital. The young lady had scoliosis. As I scheduled the surgery, the nurse asked, "Will Dr. Clements be helping you?" Not having been in Cincinnati very long, I didn't know a Dr. Clements. I asked her if he was on staff.

She replied, "Yes, Dr. Ambrose Clements is the only community African American surgeon on staff at Cincinnati Children's Hospital and he operates on all the Black patients." I made sure it wasn't long before Ambrose and I met in person, and I recounted the conversation to him. He was the nicest, most laid-back guy! He told me, "Yes, I'd be happy to scrub with you. I don't know much about what's back there in the spinal column … but I'm sure that it will be fine." Ambrose was a very good doctor, but he wasn't a spine surgeon. I was reminded that my presence meant that Black patients now had the option to go to a Black doctor and have access to expertise they'd not previously had. And as it turned out, Ambrose's and my children were already acquainted. For me, it was good to meet him, beginning what I assumed would be a lifelong friendship, but unfortunately, he died quite young.

Also, around this time, Cincinnati was one of several cities that took part in an interactive call-the-doctor-style television program that aired on Sunday mornings. The scenario worked like this: the producers selected a medical condition and invited in doctors with a background in that condition. The condition was presented on-air with a brief explanatory lecture by a medical professional. Viewers were allowed to call in and ask questions and the studio doctor and consultants would provide answers.

One time, a pediatric orthopaedic condition (scoliosis), a condition seen most frequently in adolescent white females, was chosen, and I was invited to participate on the show. I was asked to bring an assistant with me to help demonstrate the basic scoliosis school screening examination, which is customarily performed on young women in grade school. My assistant bent over, and I stood behind her to trace the alignment of her spine, showing how I check for a curvature. It didn't occur to me that there would be consequences for, what was to me, a routine process. I performed this examination so frequently it didn't dawn on me that on screen, the examination might trouble some viewers. Within an hour of the airing of this program, the station received calls questioning my sanity at having a young, white, woman bend over while I examined her back from behind (unfortunately for me, that was the camera angle.) My enemies questioned my sanity while my friends expressed dismay at my choice of specialty.

I hadn't given any thought that there would be sociopolitical consequences to such a mundane process. I recognized that I would need to do extra work to always be aware of how I was perceived, something my white colleagues didn't have to encounter. I took the situation as a learning experience and never ever again forgot who or where I was in my professional interactions.

I attended a luncheon in July of 2014. A report presented at the meeting identified the city of Cincinnati as the most segregated city of its size in America. Neighborhoods in Cincinnati are still unfortunately divided along racial lines. As Mark Twain was rumored to say, "If the world comes to an end, I want to be in Cincinnati. Everything comes there ten years later." Efforts towards racial reconciliation evident in other cities still have a long way to go in Cincinnati.

When I started at Cincinnati Children's, I had several young African American training staff coming to me as a mentor. They would talk with me about some of the situations they had to face, such as a patient in the ER saying, "I'm not going to let this Black doctor touch my child." This kind of sentiment was frequent, and I was one of few doctors who could understand what it was like to be told this. It was interesting how egalitarian the hospital could be in some situations and not in others. If a patient refused to be treated by a Black doctor, rather than stating, "if the patient refuses to be treated by the doctor on hand, then they refused to be treated," the hospital's position was, "we're here to treat your child and the child's disease is the issue." Another doctor would be assigned to the case. It was a slippery slope because many parents might argue, "I don't want this person treating my child" for any number of reasons.

On one occasion, I had a patient who was the grandchild of a major industrialist in Cincinnati. The patient had a tumor on his thumb. I had operated on several children with this condition at Henry Ford Hospital in Detroit and had good results. The father and his son, who was the patient, came to Cincinnati Children's. The son was about 9 or 10 years old. I told them that the thumb would have to be partially removed because of the cancerous tumor.

I told the father and son about the chemotherapy, and that we'd have to get the biopsy to determine the exact pathology. Tumors are rarer than people think, especially in children. A biopsy was obtained and then a tumor board convened with the pathology department (today, it would include an oncologist, radiologist, and geneticist). We queried the top five pediatric orthopaedic centers in the country and asked them how they were treating this type of tumor, what procedures they were using, and what the results were. Surgery is only a part of cancer treatment; there's chemotherapy, as well, which has to do with medications and the sensitivities of the tumor. The biopsy is just the beginning of a much longer process.

About a week later, the kid came in again, this time accompanied by his grandfather. The grandfather took one look at me and asked, "Are you Dr. Crawford?" I said, "Yes."

He said, "OK. I need my grandson's records and x-rays."

I asked, "Are you a physician?"

He said, "No, but I'm going to find one to take care of this."

I said, "OK. Not a problem."

I knew immediately what was going on. This man had megabucks and he was going to find a doctor who wasn't Black to take care of his grandson. He took the boy to a doctor at the Cleveland Clinic and asked, "Can we bring our grandson here for surgery?"

The Cleveland Clinic doctor said, "Yes, you can bring him here. But if my grandson had this problem, I'd take him to Dr. Alvin Crawford and he's in Detroit."

The grandfather said, "You're saying there's a Dr. Crawford in Detroit?"

The Cleveland doctor said, "Yes. Now, I don't know about your politics, but Crawford is Black."

The man said, "Alvin Crawford?"

And the Cleveland doctor said "Yes."

The grandfather responded by saying, "Crawford's in Cincinnati. We'll go back and see him." Apparently, this was enough to change his mind. I performed the surgery here at Cincinnati Children's and fortunately the child did well.

That was 1978. Now, the healthcare industry has changed and one of the reasons is insurance. Insurers mandate the particular care provider. The patient goes in for an appointment. They may not like the color of the doctor's or provider's skin or something else about them. But unless the patient feels strongly enough about it to pay the copay and/or the out-of-network expenses, the doctor they have is who will be treating them.

Over the years, I've gotten the comments from staff, residents, and fellows from time to time to the effect of, "I don't want to be on his rotation because he works everybody so hard, but if my child had [_____] condition, I'd want him to take care of it." That's more important to me than what anyone thinks of me personally. I can live with the disparaging comments or the lack of confidence in my abilities because of my race. People may have these opinions but at the end of the day, I will still provide my best treatment for my patients.

I've done it many times.

I encountered another circuitous referral involving a patient who was the daughter of two University of Cincinnati professors. The child had an advanced scoliosis deformity. Her parents took her to a university doctor in town who told them to take her to a specialist in St. Louis, Missouri. He had advised them that if she was his daughter, that's where he would take her. Following his advice, the family arranged for an appointment in St. Louis. The consulting doctor there asked the parents if they had heard of Dr. Crawford at Cincinnati Children's. "If she were my daughter," he told them, "I'd take her to see Alvin Crawford." The family returned to Cincinnati, and I treated their daughter. She was a joy of a patient, brilliant, and eventually wrote her high school senior paper on the subject of scoliosis. The correction of her spine was quite good, and, with appropriate permission, we used unidentifiable photos of her as part of the illustration in a pediatric textbook on scoliosis. Subsequently, the young woman graduated from medical school and became an ophthalmologist. I consider myself fortunate to have been part of her treatment.

In the early eighties, there was a senior attending pediatrician here whose son had a tumor on his neck. The bone scan technology was in its infancy then and just coming into use. We didn't even have MRIs. The child got a CT and a bone scan, which revealed that he had a tumor around the neuroforamenae, the small opening between lower cervical vertebrae where the nerves and blood vessels go through. Before I came to Cincinnati, critical pediatric orthopaedic surgical problems like this were sent to the Children's Hospital of Philadelphia, often referred to as CHOP. Many of the doctors here in Cincinnati were trained there and they knew people at CHOP who were "gods" in the world of pediatric surgery.

This child's father was a professor of pediatrics at Cincinnati Children's so he closely followed the treatment of his son. When I told the father, "We're going to have to operate on him," he talked to people around the medical center and they told him, "You want to take the child to CHOP." Then the father talked to my predecessor at Cincinnati Children's, Aaron Perlman.

Aaron told him, "Why would you take him anywhere? Crawford is a better surgeon than pretty much anyone in pediatric orthopaedics right now. Why don't you let Alvin do it?" After considerable discussion, the professor brought the boy to me. It was a complicated situation because the tumor was located in a difficult spot. Surgery could injure the blood vessel or the exiting spinal nerve causing loss of motor or sensory function above and below.

My team performed the surgery with intra-operative bone scanning, a first for our institution. The child did well, grew up, and became a pediatric subspecialist just like his father, and is now a professor at a major medical center. For the Greatest Living Cincinnatian ceremony in 2014, I wanted to share this story. I called the father, now retired, and told him that I was going to include this story in my remarks and wanted him to be aware of that. He became emotional and told me, "We think about that all the time."

NAVY RESERVE ACTIVITY

When I came to Cincinnati Children's in 1977, I continued my active Navy reserve duty, becoming what is popularly known as a "weekend warrior" because I was on duty during the weekend, providing physical exams. I had always wanted to be an admiral and decided that I was willing to stay in the military reserves as long as was necessary to achieve this goal. Unfortunately, this wasn't in the cards for me. From 1988 through 1990, the military began to integrate the active-duty forces with reserves. The rationale was that instead of being a "back-fill" partner, the reserves and National Guard would be online in conflicts. Becoming an admiral required attendance at National Defense Security seminars and contingency meetings, all of which would conflict with my duties and responsibilities as a department director with an active practice plan and financial target goals. There was no way that I could attend the required seventy-plus active-duty days per year and maintain my position at Cincinnati Children's.

So, I was a captain and later became a commanding officer of the Cincinnati Naval and Marine Corps Medical Reserve Unit on Gilbert Avenue. We took our physical fitness test running the track at Walnut Hills High School, a grueling task replete with its share of orthopaedic injuries. There were only two to three physicians for over three thousand individuals in the unit. As a result, I added another layer of doctor/patient interactions, not associated with my Cincinnati Children's practice. A large part of my job was performing the required annual physical exams.

On one occasion, a young white woman from the Appalachian region came in for her physical exam. In her conversation with the officer of the day, she categorically stated that she had never been examined by anyone like me (implying a Black male doctor) and never would be. The officer, who was also a line officer, told the young woman that her promotion package needed to be sent to the Navy Bureau that day in order for her to maintain her pay grade and her eligibility for promotion and retirement. A requirement of the package was a physical exam, and I was the only doctor available that day. The officer told her, "If you don't want him to exam you, I'll understand. But your promotion data won't be sent in, essentially ending your career. I suggest that you have a seat and give this some thought." It was interesting. What the woman may not have known was that every female is examined with a female medical corpsman present in the examining room. It wouldn't have been just the two of us. After sitting for an hour or so, she decided to move forward with her physical exam and have me examine her.

In addition to performing physical exams, while on active duty, I taught pediatric orthopaedics on behalf of the Surgical Advisory Committee (SAC), and supervised Naval fellows from the committee assigned in Cincinnati. And, of course, I was "called up" when international circumstances required it.

Jumping forward in time a bit, in 1987, an Iranian passenger plane mistaken for an F-16 fighter aircraft was shot down by the US military while flying over Iran's territorial waters in the Persian Gulf. This incident precipitated international discord and was of particular concern in Southwest Africa. I was dispatched to the western coast of Africa as part of a West African Training Cruise (WATC). I was assigned a PC-3A, which is an antisubmarine warfare airplane (ASW). We picked it up in Tampa, Florida, spent several planning days in Puerto Rico, then proceeded to the African continent.

Most of the countries in that region have favored-nation status with the United States. This allows their citizens admission to military academies, schools, or positions in government for their respective nations. We started out in Dakar, Senegal, and from there went to Lagos, Nigeria; Accra, Ghana; Malabo, Equatorial Guinea; and finally Libreville, Gabon. Gabon, a former French colony, is where Dr. Alfred Schweitzer became famous for treating people stricken with malaria. We went to São Tomé and Príncipe, which are islands off the coast of Nigeria, and then visited the New London (so named in colonial times) Medical School in Ibadan, Nigeria, one of that country's largest cities. It was there that the local staff asked me about Ben Felson, who was at the time the University of Cincinnati Medical Center chief of radiology and a tennis enthusiast. I knew him very well and we swapped "Felson" stories. The medical school faculty used his book in their classes and were impressed that I knew him in person. I also visited Dr. WEB DuBois's home in Ghana, where he moved in at age 93 and passed away two years later in 1963.

Our naval mission was sociopolitical. We would land in a country—twenty-six men, including a musical band, a group of construction battalion troops (CBs or Seabees), and three intelligence officers (also known as spies). In undertaking this cruise, the US Navy was using us "to show the flag" (and the force) of our country and we weren't alone. The Cubans put on boxing matches, the Chinese presented wrestling matches, and the Russians conducted war games and dancing. In West Africa, we provided medical education, such as critical care courses and treatment, as well as other community engagement efforts such as repairing schools and playgrounds, or helping to clean up neighborhoods. When we landed, the intelligence officers left the plane immediately at one end of the tarmac and we didn't see them again until we were ready to leave. We never knew what they did when the left the plane.

I learned many aspects of international relations during these missions and, in truth, we did more than just show the flag. I performed medical consultations and saw patients, and during one of these consultations, a local elder in Nigeria taught me a lesson in compassionate and empathetic medicine that I have never forgotten. At the city square in Lagos, I examined a teenage boy who had polio with severe contractures of the lower extremities. He couldn't walk and sat on the side of the road to beg. While I couldn't strengthen the muscles ruined by polio, I could release the contractures, brace him, rehabilitate him, and possibly change the course of his life. It had the potential to be a great story and seemed like a win-win situation—a positive image for the United States and a life-changing outcome for the young boy. I scheduled the boy for surgery to release the contractures and the Armed Forces Media was set to film everything. At 10 p.m. the night before, I had a conversation with one of the community elders, who took me aside and told me, "Son, maybe you shouldn't operate on that kid."

Misunderstanding him, I said, "No, I can do this."

"Let me explain," he said. "That kid is on the square every day, limping, crawling, and begging."

I said, "I know. That's where we first saw him."

The old man continued, saying, "This boy begs for alms and with that money, he supports an entire family, two generations of people. He has no other skills. If you fix him then he's walking almost normally. But he will need braces and physical therapy, which we don't have. Nobody gives you money for walking normally. And if you have no other skills or talent then you can't go to work for anybody. More important, the whole family loses their financial support."

I thought about that for a long time. There have been many moments in my life that truly have given me an education, and this was one of them. It was a humbling experience, to understand that I couldn't fix everything and, in this case, trying to "fix" him with osteotomies would not make his or his family's life better. One needs to think of the comprehensive consequences of surgical intervention in any situation. The local elder understood the dynamics of the patient's role, the environment, his financially supporting the family based on observers' caring response to his obvious deformity and disability—I hadn't realized that. Strong lesson learned.

ADVANCES IN SPINAL SURGERY

In expanding the orthopaedic department at Cincinnati Children's, we covered all the pediatric orthopaedic conditions. There was an existing fracture clinic, as well as cerebral palsy, myelomeningocele, and scoliosis clinics. Most of the patients visiting the orthopaedic clinic at Cincinnati Children's were service (welfare) patients. Private patients still typically visited offsite offices, not the hospital clinic. We were understaffed; I came to Cincinnati in 1977, and it wasn't until 1983 that I was able to hire another full-time, permanent orthopaedic surgeon, Dennis Roy. As the department developed and grew, I was able to bring on more staff, allowing us to set up specialty clinics and perform more sophisticated procedures. But most of the new hires were interested in treating everything except the spine. It was understandable—with every spine surgery, there is the potential the child could become paralyzed from direct or indirect injury to the spinal cord. Every surgery involved risk—the spinal cord could be injured from dissecting tissue, suffer from a lack of the blood supply, or perfusion in a crooked position. A patient might even become paralyzed after significant correction was performed, without the root cause ever being known.

The worst job I've ever had to do is come out of the operating room and tell a parent that there has been a problem and a chance their son or daughter had been paralyzed. That's so incredibly difficult. I make sure to share this experience with postgraduate fellows, especially those who are going into spine surgery, so they understand the severity and risk of the procedures they will be doing, and also the significance of making sure parents/patients are given enough information to make an informed choice about the procedure.

In the early eighties, neurological monitoring during surgery was fairly primitive and limited as to the problems that could be detected midsurgery. We used what was then called the "wake-up test." Back in 1976, I cowrote a paper in the journal *Anesthesia & Analgesia* on the use of hypnosis to ensure the accuracy of the wake-up test in scoliosis surgery. After the instrumentation, general anesthesia was lightened, and IV morphine administered. When the patient woke up, they were asked to move their lower extremities. If they could, that was good. If they could not, that was a serious concern. My team, which included audiologist Robert Keith, participated in a lot of innovations in the world of spinal surgery. Now, the process is extremely sophisticated. Surgeons can utilize multimodal spinal cord monitoring—transcranial evoked, somatosensory evoked, or neuro-evoked potential monitoring—instead of solely relying on the wake-up test. More recently, spinal cord mapping can provide surgeons with the precise location of an issue. There's a simultaneous read of the neurological system during the entire surgical procedure so any problem is instantly picked up. Surgeons can reverse, abort, or prevent a neurological problem from continuing. We don't have the problems now that we used to have, which is an enormous benefit to the patient and surgeon.

Spinal correction surgery is a relatively young specialty. The major advances in spine and spinal instrumentation have come about in my lifetime. Any surgery on the spine is a big operation and puts the patient through substantial metabolic and physiologic stresses. Before the sixties, anesthesia wasn't developed enough to transcend the length of a spine surgery safely and dependably. Surgeries in general were just beyond the "open drop ether" method. This required positioning the patient on their back. In most spine operations, however, the patient need to be lying face down. Progress in anesthesia, as well as positioning, managing blood loss, preventing infections, and neurophysiological assessment, has truly changed spinal surgeries.

Before advancements in portable assessment radiology (image intensification fluoroscopy), when inserting pins in patients, it was almost like putting them in blind because the patient was large and a portable x-ray couldn't provide the contrast—the shadows of the pin—to make sure the pins were being placed in the proper location. Fortunately, radiology improved so that we could do a better job of pinning.

At one time, the primary treatment for scoliosis was a Harrington rod, popularly known as a "jack in the back." It started as a straight ratcheted rod with attachable hooks at the top and bottom connecting to the vertebrae. Correction was carried out through lengthening the construct by ratchetting the hooks up onto the rod; it stretches longitudinally and straightens the spine. It wasn't until the early eighties that Yves Cotrel and Jean Dubousset (called "CD" from the initials of their last names) of Paris developed instruments that accommodated the fact that the human back is not straight but curved when viewed from the side. When the spine is curved from the front (coronal plane), it's called a "scoliosis." When seen from the side (sagittal plane) there is "kyphosis" in the upper back (hump back) and "lordosis" (sway back) in the lower back. Cotrel and Dubousset were the first to write about putting curves in the rod to accommodate the normal anatomy. A further development was the ability to attach the rods at multiple levels, and therefore stretch, as well as compress, on a single rod. The "jack in the back" only allowed the spine to be stretched to straighten the back out. The CD is a version of segmental spinal stabilization with universal correction and compression distraction forces on the same rod. Now, orthopaedic surgery has ventured into rigid fixation curved rods and screws with the ability to rotate, distract, and compress the spine independently, using the rod to obtain anatomic correction.

Bruce Honsaker joined the spine clinic as a registered nurse in 1980. He had been at Children's as an ER nurse, having previously been a medic in the Army. He worked in the clinic daily and helped apply connective plaster to create what was called a Risser type "jacket." This was no easy feat—especially if the patients were teenagers—to lift them, and a twenty-pound casting jacket that went from pelvis to neck, off the Risser casting table. Both brains and brawn were necessary. Bruce was somewhat of a reluctant recruit at first but soon settled in with our team as a casting nurse specialist.

Ginny Niemeyer, who I mentioned earlier, was a registered nurse with a master's in education. She joined our team in 1983 and her education background gave her keen insight into understanding and relating to children. She recalled,

> The spine presented a whole different way of thinking of orthopaedic nursing. The learning curve was changing. Over the years, I learned exactly what Dr. Crawford wanted when it came to spinal treatment, so that I could answer questions for the parents. I developed an outpatient protocol for his patients prior to surgery (including taking vitamins and iron) and made sure that they complied. Then I set up a program for them to visit the hospital prior to surgery. I took them around the hospital, coordinated the pre-op blood work, educated the patient and the family as to what was going to happen, and explained the post-op follow-up. Early on, Dr. Crawford started out with casting, then transitioned to using braces. Later, with instrumentation design and technology it was possible to bypass the cast and brace entirely and have the patient standing and walking within a day.

One of my patients in the mid-eighties, Eric Ruby, later returned to my practice when his son was my patient in 2017. He recalls,

> It's amazing how the treatment of scoliosis has changed over the years. Dr. Harrington's rods, which I had placed in me, were revolutionary when he invented them. Prior to that, the kids had to be in body casts for months and months. Alvin was a pioneer in spinal fusion with the modified Harrington rod innovations. That eliminated the casting but still

required some prolonged bracing. I know that after my surgery, I was in a brace for about four months to allow the fusion to heal which was part of the routine then. Also, postoperatively in the hospital, I remember the Stryker frames that Dr. Crawford routinely used, that was the most challenging part of the whole recovery because you're totally immobilized. You want that fusion to set up and all that work to bear fruit and fuse, it's imperative that you don't move. We were on that little waffle iron-rotating bed and that's one of the biggest memories that I have about that surgery.

Now, in 2017 my son went home postoperative day number two; he was never in a brace and never immobilized in bed; they want them up and walking immediately. But the actual fusion process, where they do the pedicle screws … it's just different. The spine is immobilized, that allows those fusions to take place without the need for all that bracing. That's a big advancement; it's great for the patients and that's the way medicine is. Onward and upward; everybody's always trying to improve on previous pioneers' work.

My experiences before I came to Cincinnati cemented my interest in the complexity of the spine. Two of the fellowships I have held affirmed my decision to focus on the spine—with John Hall, the Chief of Pediatric Orthopaedics in the Harvard medical system and with G. Dean MacEwen at the Alfred I. duPont Institute. They were some of the most innovative leaders in the field of pediatric orthopaedic surgery and became mentors to me. They each served as president of the Scoliosis Research Society.

I also understood that to continue to focus on the spine, I needed to keep exposing myself to premier spine centers and surgeons to learn about advancements and developments in spinal care. In the United States and Canada, I visited the UCLA Medical Center with Marshall Urist, who went on to develop bone morphogenic protein (BMP); the Rancho Los Amigos National Rehabilitation Center in Downey, California; Newington, Connecticut's Children's Hospital; the Hospital for Sick Children Toronto with Robert Salter; the Alfred I. duPont Institute, Wilmington, Delaware (where I had previously done a research fellowship in 1971) with Dean MacEwen; and the Campbell Clinic in Memphis, Tennessee with Fred Sage.

At Cincinnati Children's, the orthopaedic department maintained a totally academic approach. Protocols (currently called clinical pathways) were developed for almost every orthopaedic condition, all of which was documented in a database. The database began with punch cards and evolved into spreadsheets. Whatever series or process we did, we documented it, and made presentations to improve our visibility on the domestic and international scene. Those presentations raised us to a level where we were recognized on a regional and national scale, and as our papers and results became more comprehensive, we received international recognition as well.

Along with this academic approach, I also had some more interesting, perhaps less-academic methods of procedure. Lance Bolin, who worked as my lead physician's assistant in 2004, recalled:

> Actually, it scared me the first time I heard it. In the OR, once you get to the point where he's (Crawford) bending the rods for scoliosis surgery. When he bends the rods, he sings a song, "Spine-maker, spine-maker, make me a spine!" to the music of "Matchmaker, Matchmaker" from Fiddler on the Roof.
>
> And when he does bone grafts, he does a chant, putting in a bone graft. But it's secret. He does it as he's sprinkling the bone graft into the wound.

Jose Herrera-Soto, my fellow from 2002–2003 corroborated this tale:

> Basically, what you do is, when you are putting in a bone graft, you do almost like a tribal chant, calling

the gods of bone fusion so that the surgery will not fail and will heal. So now, my fellows do that too! (Which is creepy, but they do.) I remember when I was in Orlando one day and we didn't do it. One of the residents called me immediately, very upset. He said, "Dr. Herrera, we didn't do the bone chant!" So we had to do it over the phone! He made a new rule for the bone chant—maybe Dr. Crawford should know this rule: If you do it (the bone chant) within twenty-four hours, it's still valid. The patient did OK so I guess it works.

(Note: The actual wording of the chant is a closely held secret known only to the doctors and nurses present in the OR. The penalties for leaks of this information are severe.)

THE CINCINNATI INCISION

When I came to Cincinnati Children's, I had heard of Dr. Nicholas "Nick" Giannestras, a well-known foot surgeon with a practice in Cincinnati. I assumed foot surgeries primarily filled his time. Shortly after I settled in Cincinnati, though, I learned that he was also a spine surgeon, working out of a clinic at Good Samaritan Hospital, also in Cincinnati. The clinic included a service that dispatched vans to rural counties in the Appalachian areas of Ohio and Kentucky to perform scoliosis screening examinations. The mobile teams carried "Crippled Children Service" surgical consent forms and completed them for patients whose scoliosis screenings were positive, so they could be brought to the hospital for treatment. I soon realized that, as a member of the Scoliosis Research Society moving into this area, my status could impact his operation and his operation could limit my access to patients. Giannestras suggested that we meet in order to head off any potential conflicts. At that time, I was performing a fair amount of clubfoot surgeries, something that interested Giannestras. Conversely, he was performing a substantial number of scoliosis surgeries and I was interested in scoliosis patients.

We met in December 1977 at the Bankers Club overlooking Fountain Square in downtown Cincinnati along with Alfred "Fred" Kahn, MD, who had recently completed the Toronto Sick Children's Pediatric Orthopaedic fellowship. Fred was also interested in scoliosis. After a lengthy conversation, we made some decisions. Giannestras would give me a partnership in the Good

Samaritan Spine Center and, in return, I would give him a foot clinic at Cincinnati Children's. This could have been one of the worst political decisions of my career, though it thankfully worked out well. Hospital politics can be interesting and challenging.

The Freiberg group attended Cincinnati Children's clinics and had no interest in Nick Giannestras ever attending any clinics there. But Nick, Fred, and I consummated the deal in December over drinks and cigars. Almost immediately, I started work in the Giannestras Spine Center and Nick began preparing to attend the Cincinnati Children's foot clinic. He had contracted with Picker X-ray Electronics for a grant to use computed tomography to study clubfoot in young children.

In February 1978, while in New Orleans attending the American Academy of Orthopaedic Surgeons (AAOS) meeting, Nick developed a urinary retention that was initially thought to be a prostate problem. However, a biopsy revealed a renal malignancy. He returned to Cincinnati and died in the spring of 1978. Though our partnership was short lived, we developed an important surgical innovation.

Nick had initiated a transverse foot incision, a utilitarian incision that had a variety of applications. We collaborated on extending the anterior limbs of the incision and using it to treat clubfoot and other foot disorders. Nick and I gained a bit of worldwide acclaim for this procedure. It was soon a standard treatment protocol: clubfoot operations most likely involved the Cincinnati incision. While the incision is an aggressive approach, it generally received (and still does) good results. But it was also "surgeon sensitive," which means that its success was heavily dependent on the skill and experience of the surgeon.

Nick and I had both agreed to call the application the Cincinnati incision and I published it under my own name in the *Journal of Bone and Joint Surgery* in 1982.[7] Sadly, Nick Giannestras died before the article was submitted and I was unable to obtain permission from his famiy to use his name in the publication. The legacy and use of the incision, though, still continues.

There are other ways to treat clubfeet. Currently, it is treated most predominantly with a procedure developed by Ignacio Ponseti that was used routinely in the fifties. It involves percutaneous soft-tissue release and casting. Because it is dependent on parental compliance—meaning parents had to be heavily involved with weekly cast changes—it lost its popularity in the seventies to other methods—Vince Turco's oblique, Norris Carroll's dual incisions, and the Cincinnati incision. It didn't regain popularity until the advent of the internet age, which reintroduced other methods. And, in contrast to the Cincinnati incision, it's minimally invasive.

Cincinnati Children's orthopaedic division increased our vector of development and encouraged more of everything—more fellows, more research, and more publications. As I stated earlier, I was at Cincinnati Children's for six years as the only full-time pediatric orthopaedist before another was hired. Within four or five years after that, we were able to hire another and offered a job to Eric Wall. Five years later, Charles Mehlman arrived, followed by Twee Thi Do, Junichi Tamai, Diane Von Stein and Atiq Durrani. The team and prestige at Cincinnati continued to grow, as did our international reputation, in part because of the innovations, like the Cincinnati incision, developed in my department.

INTERNATIONAL PATIENTS

*A*s our international reputation as a premier pediatric orthopaedic department grew, so did our number of international patients. These patients gave our division much-needed public relations. The wealthy Organization of the Petroleum Exporting Countries (OPEC) nations could refer patients to medical institutions anywhere in the world or would bring in doctors from across the globe to their respective countries. It wasn't unusual for patients from the OPEC member countries to travel to the United States for medical treatment.

My first international patient, who was a native of Iraq, was referred to me by one of my orthopaedic residents at Henry Ford Hospital. The patient's father was a PhD candidate at Wayne State University and his mother was a head nurse at the Jordanian Army Medical Center hospital. Both parents were well-connected politically in Amman, Jordan. The child had bilateral clubfeet. He had started his treatment in Detroit with a cast, but it wasn't working so he ended up coming to Cincinnati, where we performed his surgery. The child responded well to treatment and went on to become a member of the Jordanian national soccer team. As a result of his parents' connections and the success of their son's surgery, I was invited to visit Jordan in 1981 to consult and operate on patients. Jeannie and I flew over on an El Al jet and landed at the Queen Alia International Airport, which was named in honor of the third wife of His Royal Highness King Hussein. The jet was a 747 and we were the only passengers seated in business class, an experience I will never forget.

Later, I had the opportunity to operate on another Jordanian child in Cincinnati. There was a lot of press in *The Cincinnati Enquirer* on that situation. The child was brought here with a tumor that had originally been thought to be scoliosis. I operated on her and the outcome was successful. The child's father was a major general in the Royal Jordanian Army, and he invited me to return to Jordan in 1981 not only to perform more surgery but to also have an audience with His Royal Highness King Hussein of Jordan.

To have an audience with the king was a life-changing experience! I even had to bow before him. People who were granted an audience were positioned below him. I was impressed by the king, particularly of his knowledge of what was going on within the borders of his country. I felt that I was a small fish in Jordan, but the king knew every single thing about me and what I was doing from the moment that I got there. It was a singular honor.

In Jordan, a king is a god on earth to the people in his kingdom. Several well-armed guards came to pick me up from my hotel. They brought me to a room that was dimly lit. The king wished me well and hoped there would be a continued connection between Cincinnati Children's and Jordan. Later on, one of my first fellows from Jordan, Dr. Farley Nasser, who came to Cincinnati as a postgraduate fellow and worked with me for about a year and a half, ended up returning to Jordan. Out of all of my fellows, he has probably achieved the most political success. He was appointed the minister of health for Jordan and now has two sons who are orthopaedic surgeons.

While in Jordan, I asked about the rest of King Hussein's name and was bluntly told that the rest of his name was His Royal Highness. When I met him, he was well-guarded. I was informed that there had been thirty-three attempts on his life. Usually in the kingdom a royal was in danger of being assassinated by a relative, most likely one who was in line for the throne, but that had changed when the Taliban and other terrorist groups gained power.

I was in Jordan for several weeks. The first week that I was there, our team had three full days of operating on club feet. I was considered to be a clubfoot specialist and so that is primarily what

I was doing. For a lot of the migratory Bedouin tribes, clubfeet were fairly common because there is a hereditary genetic transmission factor.

Bedouins are passionate, loyal people who never fail to show their gratitude for service. While I was in Jordan, I was informed that the father of one of my patients was planning a dinner for me following the surgery and had slain the family's best goat in my honor. This was a problem since I didn't (and still don't) eat meat. A Jordanian colleague from the medical center made an effort to postpone and subsequently cancel the dinner in order to avoid a disaster. If I were to attend the dinner and not eat the goat, it would have greatly offended the child's father and none of us wanted that.

The perioperative management of patients in Jordan was a new adventure for me as well. Following surgery, it is customary for family members to converge on the patient—to see, hold, and feed their child as soon as the operating room door opens. I had to deliberately delay the patient's exit from the operating room until he or she was stable enough and physically prepared for family members to touch them. The minute the doors open, the family is committed to taking the child from you. It can be a very challenging situation if the patient is weak or not yet stable.

After a week of surgery, I took a long weekend off. First, Jeannie and I visited Aqaba, Jordan, a seaside community across from Eilat in Israel. At that time, there was no relationship or trade agreement between Jordan and Israel. It was an unusual situation. I could look across the bay at the Israeli people on the Eilat side and they see could Aqaba, but there was no communication or connection.

From Aqaba, we took the road towards Damascus, Syria, observed the Golan Heights, and then returned to Jordan to visit the city, Petra. Petra was an unbelievable UNESCO World Heritage Site. The architecture was built in the fourth or fifth century BCE by the Nabataean culture and is one of the new wonders of the world. The architecture was beautifully unique. The structure was built from the top down and is carved out of a mountain.

Though I was mostly treating clubfoot in Jordan, the doctors at the King Hussein Medical Center eventually asked me if I treated other conditions. I told them that in the United States,

I mostly operated on cases related to scoliosis conditions. The doctors were surprised, having lined up all these cases of clubfeet because they thought that was all I did.

Beginning the next week, I operated on clubfeet and everything else! In the meantime, one of the crown princesses had broken her arm and it was in a cast. Her mother brought her to the medical center for me to examine it. We removed the cast and took x-rays. The mother said, "It's really severe, isn't it?"

I tried to reassure her. "No. A child of this age—and she's in good health, she'll remodel the fracture and do fine."

"Aren't you going to have to do extensive therapy?" the princess's mother insisted. "She won't be able to use it [the arm]. Won't she need physical therapy?"

I said, "No. Once we take her out of the cast, she'll do very well."

One of the two doctors present—Nabil Attollyah and Fouad Hassan were my primary hosts—took me aside and said, "Dr. Crawford, you're missing something here. This child is one of the crown princesses. The mother wants you to follow up with this child in your clinic in Cincinnati because then she'll have to bring the child to the United States, and that will give her the opportunity to go shopping in New York! That's where she's going with this conversation. You just haven't picked up on it." I never would have picked up on that! Fortunately for the princess's mother, we made an appointment for her in Cincinnati.

When we first visited Jordan in 1981, we could not go from Jordan to the Golan Heights or Eilat because flying between Israel and Islamic nations was tricky in the eighties. I returned to Tel Aviv to speak to the Israeli Orthopaedic Society years later. Because of my lecture schedule in Tel Aviv, I wasn't able to go with Jeannie to Jerusalem, the Wailing Wall, or other historic and cultural sites. Together, however, we were able visit Masada, the Dead Sea, and a few of the ancient sites mentioned in the Bible. Tel Aviv was a very comfortable, laid-back city, but I was always aware of an atmosphere of tension, developing as a result of the Palestinian-Israeli conflict.

Among the many people I met at the Israeli Orthopaedic Conference were Shlomo Weintrob and Dror Ovadia. Dror is a spine surgeon whom I had met forty years earlier at Henry Ford

Hospital when he came to visit his uncle in Detroit. Since that time, I've also met him at Scoliosis Research Society meetings, and in the summer of 2016, Dror came to Cincinnati as a visiting professor at Cincinnati Children's.

While I lectured at the conferences, Jeannie visited Jerusalem. She recalled,

> My guide was originally from Europe but had moved to Israel and her major in college was the history of this area. We visited many of the historical sites that you read about in the Bible. I got the chance to ask her questions about biblical events and told her "I want to go to see the place where Christ was buried, where the Last Supper was." She said, "No problem. But it's in the area where there is a lot of shooting going on." I don't remember exactly where that was. She told me, "I live there and I know where to go so that nothing will happen."
>
> So while Alvin was doing lectures and performing surgery, I visited Tel Aviv and Jerusalem. I went to the place where the Last Supper was believed to have been held, where Christ was first buried, all of these locations. It was just amazing to learn the stories and to see believers of all of these religions visiting there to study, together. I saw many Orthodox Jews, learned how they live. The women have to cover themselves and wore wigs. The men tie a leather strap (tefillin) around their arms, wrapped seven times to symbolize the loving relationship between the Jewish nation and God. Alvin asked me later, "Why did you go there, so close to danger?" I told him that I was with a person who knew the way through.
>
> Over the years, whenever Alvin went somewhere and I went along, I got to spend time with the local citizens, especially the women, who would tell me about their lives and culture and what their habits were. It wasn't like I was on a guided tour with a group. I really got to know people, on a one-on-one level, to

ask questions to learn how we are alike and how we are different. I knew them personally.

Upon returning to the States, I was contacted by the secretary-treasurer of the emir of one of the Gulf States. He brought his child to Cincinnati Children's for treatment. Now this was quite an undertaking. The patient and family arrived with an entourage that included nannies, bag handlers, housekeepers, and more. They took over the whole floor of a local hotel. I performed the surgery and while the child was recovering after the surgery, Jeannie and I went out to dinner with the parents. Post-op the child was in a big cast that went from his toes to his chest. His mother said, "It's so warm in my country, he'll be miserable over there in that cast. We'll have to take him somewhere cool." So, they rented a place in Laguna Beach, California so that the child could recuperate there.

And then the mother said, "I don't know if I want to go out there [Laguna Beach]." Their servants could care for the child while he recovered. She asked my wife, Jeannie if she'd like to go to Paris to shop for "a bit" (as in six weeks) while her son recovered! This suggestion was followed by silence on my part! After the surgery (which, fortunately, had a good result) there was an interesting conversation between me and the child's father concerning the number of my bank account.

"Bank account?" I said, thinking that he referred to my ordinary banking account.

"Your Swiss account," he said. He explained that he intended to deposit my fee directly into my Swiss account, which was what they did for other doctors. In his opinion, my salary wasn't enough, and the hospital wouldn't give me much of the money owed me for performing the procedure. (Boy, was I naive! He was so right!) He also felt that by depositing my fee into a Swiss bank, I wouldn't have to pay taxes. I was rolling with laughter. I had never considered I would ever have a Swiss bank account.

Sometime later, I learned of another interesting encounter between this patient's father and one of the administrators in hospital admissions concerning payment for the medical services performed at the hospital.

"Do you have insurance?" the administrator asked.

He said, "No."

She said, "Well, are you on welfare? Do you have a green card?"

Again, the answer was "no."

"You know that you have to pay for this," she told him.

He said, "Yes, I know." Then he picked up a leather valise and opened it. It was full of Cook's traveler's checks. Cook's is the European equivalent to American Express. The case was medium-sized, made of alligator skin and filled to the brim. The admissions clerk turned pale and immediately called security!

You can imagine how quickly the word got around. People made up all kinds of excuses to come visit our department. For weeks after this, the water cooler conversation was, "When is Crawford going to get another one of those patients?" Well, we did, many. One patient I treated had a parent who was an executive producer for a major television network, and rewarded our spine team with Olympic games tickets and seats to the US Open tennis tournament as well as mugs, bags, and the like. Another patient had a parent who was a writer (or showrunner as they're called) for a CSI-type television program called *Bones*. He was so pleased with the treatment of his child that he incorporated a "Dr. Crawford" character into one of the episodes. The character was a doctor in a neurofibromatosis clinic.

One of our international patients precipitated a case presentation that I had to make before the diversity advisory board of the American Academy of Orthopaedic Surgeons. The patient was a young female from a devout Muslim family who had severe scoliosis.

As part of her pre-op workup, we performed a pregnancy test. This step is routine and performed presurgery on every skeletally mature female because of potential unintended consequences of anesthesia on a fetus. This girl had a positive pregnancy test. For a young unmarried Muslim woman, a positive pregnancy test created a very difficult situation. In some locales, it could allow her father to punish her to extremes depending on the interpretation of his religious beliefs.

We had to deal with that. She was 17 or 18 and preparing to attend college here in the United States. Her father didn't want her to go to school here because her boyfriend attended the college. We repeated the test; it was positive again. We talked with the patient who said that she had been sexually active, although not for about three or four months. We took further x-rays and the film didn't show a fetus. Then we did an enzyme test. The young woman was definitely not pregnant. Eventually, we figured out that whatever condition she had in her blood caused the false positive on the pregnancy tests.

The dilemma that we went through was arduous. I spoke with the chief of staff and the ethics committee as to whether I could withhold this surgery. We understood the risk in informing her parents about why we were running additional tests and why we might have to delay the surgery. The family had traveled a considerable distance to Cincinnati with servants for the patient's mother and a nanny for the other children. They had gotten a block of hotel rooms. This visit was an investment for them. Thankfully, the conversations ultimately did not reach her parents. The discussions took place between me, the patient, and the aforementioned chief of staff and ethics committee. Once we were able to prove that she was not pregnant, we went ahead with the surgery. I might not have been so sensitive to or aware of the delicacy of the situation had I not been exposed to the culture in majority Muslim countries. This wasn't something that can be learned through textbooks—only through lived experiences and recognition of the complexity of every patient's background.

The young woman did well postsurgery. She went on to an American university and received her master's degree. She later called me and asked if I would operate on her older sister, who also had fairly severe scoliosis. The sister had been too afraid to have the surgery before but was now interested since her sister's outcome had gone so well.

MISSION SURGERY EXPERIENCES

Not all of my international surgery experiences were with wealthy patients who were able to come to Cincinnati. Medical missions made up an important part of my work. Spine procedures are complicated and lengthy, and are challenging under even the best conditions. But when a spine surgery is performed in some international venues, as I have done on medical mission trips, the medical team can be additionally challenged in a variety of ways. There are many factors that can inhibit efficiency in surgery, including language barriers, anesthesia and oxygen supply, control of blood pressure, and blood loss. Spine operations require very large incisions and there is always the possibility of the patient losing a lot of blood. A lack of methodology for blood replacement, or an anesthetic method for maintaining the blood pressure throughout the procedure (spine surgeries can range from two to seventeen hours), can have very serious consequences. Metabolic concerns, musculoskeletal problems, or neurological tissue damage due to lack of oxygen are all challenges in surgery that are exacerbated when outside of familiar surgical environments. The availability of anesthesia or blood products, such as a blood banking system, can be a significant worry in some international venues.

Such concerns were evident in work I did in Mexico in 1974. Tony Herring and I went down to the American British Cowdray (ABC) Hospital and Mexico City Shriner's Hospital to do a set of Luque procedures (sublaminar wiring of the spine to the rod, usually to a Harrington rod) with Dr. Eduardo Luque. Tony and I first encountered Dr. Luque back in San Diego. Tony recalled,

> One day, while Al and I were working together in San Diego, I happened to attend a lecture by Dr. Eduardo Luque from Mexico. I was impressed with his inventive and very unorthodox ideas about scoliosis surgery. He [Luque] was a very dynamic speaker, and looked a lot like Salvador Dali with his handlebar mustache. While many of his ideas sounded a little crazy, I was impressed that he was able to do scoliosis surgery with rods and did not have to place the patients into casts. He said that Mexico was too hot for body casts.
>
> At Al's suggestion, I had gotten a traveling fellowship from the Orthopaedic Research and Education Foundation. I was able to include a trip to Mexico in that fellowship and I invited Alvin to accompany me. We arrived, tennis rackets in hand, and were in for quite a show, both on the medical side and the social side.
>
> In the hospitals we were able to see some truly revolutionary surgery using rods and wires to correct scoliosis. Wires of this sort had never been used for this, and the insertion of them had some real risks. At the same time we could see how powerful the method was to correct the deformities, and how the patients were able to return to their lives without a cast or brace. At times we were able to help the anesthesiologist with problems that arose in surgery.
>
> On the social side we really got to know Dr. Luque. He took us to his country house which was situated on a small mountain. There he had his own handball court and beat us all regularly. He was a really flamboyant guy and much fun to be with. Naturally Al and I got in some hotly contested tennis matches while there. In the end, we were the first Americans to observe his work in Mexico. From that we formed

a group called "The Segmental Spinal Instrumentation Study Group" and spread his ideas throughout the scoliosis community. This work changed the way scoliosis was treated throughout the world. Because the rods could be contoured, the shape of the patient's spine was much closer to normal than with the older Harrington method.

As Tony said, the Luque procedure was developed because the heat in Mexico did not allow for children to be placed in casts and there weren't government resources to provide bracing. The sublaminar wiring provides independent fixation with no need for external support. Luque's original design allowed the child to grow, and repeat surgeries were performed to lengthen the segment of the spine bridged by the Luque construct. This was the first of the "growth modulation" surgeries for the spine. We did about seven cases in four to five days. We had a situation where several patients lost their circulating red blood cell volume. The blood was replenished but it was with extreme difficulty and put inordinate stress on the surgeons. As mentioned earlier, handling blood loss can be additionally challenging in international venues, where standards and resources are different.

There's an excitement in doing mission surgery but it is important to develop plans to take into consideration the challenges and possible complications that performing surgery away from standard US hospitals might present. To avoid some complications with anesthesia, my team would bring our own anesthesiologist on missions. Another useful surgery tactic that we implemented was the "huddle." The concept is similar to that used in football. A team "huddle" and "time out" were used to review every step of the procedure, point by point. This emphasized the importance of communication among team members. The communication infrastructure also included a preoperative huddle, which is arguably just as effective as conference calls here in the United States. The team lead would tell the operative team in the destination country what the clinical requirements are and would request photographs and x-rays in advance. From that, the team would develop a list of considerations and then meet to make a decision as to whether or not they wanted to take on the case. The team considers the risks and benefits for the patient and the team, and determines whether it's in the patient's best interest for them to perform the procedure. If the patient has resources, they might be able to come to Cincinnati Children's for the procedure. If that is not an option, then the team might apply to a philanthropic organization to provide the means for the child to come here. At the end of the day, surgeons prefer to do the intensely complex procedures with their own team in their own venue, in my case, at Cincinnati Children's. If that is not possible, the "huddle" provided a space for communication, and made sure all the factors and details were laid out before any decision was made.

In some countries I traveled to for medial missions, consistent electricity was a problem. On any given day, there may be any number of intermittent power outages. In an operation on something as critical as the spinal cord, loss of ceiling lights and electricity can be detrimental. They may be out for a short period of time before the generator might kick in, but the uncertainty of it makes the operation very risky. This is another reason why surgeons do their best surgery at home. The barriers to doing the best surgery often have little to do with the technical aspect of the surgery, and are heavily influenced by the environment. This is not to dissuade surgeons from medical missions, but for this reason, my team would turn down cases where there was a high risk of neurological injury or paraplegia. We could not in good conscience subject a child to those risks in a potentially precarious environment, especially when the concern was a clinical deformity.

There are also cultural considerations in medical missions. Countries have their own laws and in some of them, the doctor is ultimately responsible for the medical outcome. Bacteria have the advantage in surgery and even though medical teams wash their hands frequently, wear masks, and follow hygienic guidelines, there is always a chance the patient may get an infection. In fact, three percent of patients do. Depending on the surgery location, the penalties can be severe. For this reason, before a team takes on a case, they must be aware of the laws and idiosyncrasies of the country and every venue in which they might work. There is always a risk for an unexpected consequence, and patients and their families are clearly made aware of the goals, risks, and benefits of the procedure first.

Another unfortunate situation I have encountered, and one that medical teams need to be aware of, is the "disposable patient." On occasion, a patient who has no resources is scheduled for an intricate procedure. A medical team is brought to the host country but is unaware the surgery is really a means to provide surgical exposure and training for the local medical team, not necessarily for the good of the patient. When the patient leaves the hospital operating room, it may be the last time they are seen by any physician. The procedure may go well but due to lack of finances, the patient isn't followed up by the medical staff afterwards. A medical team needs to be cautious when operating internationally and do everything it can to ensure that the hosts provide appropriate postoperative care and maintenance on the patients once the team leaves the country.

When I went to Shanghai over the course of a few years to perform a number of surgeries, I would test the team there by following up months later asking for information and x-rays. This was my way to ensure the patient was being cared for postoperatively. I was aware there was an ugly side to being the "professor who comes in to help the poor children." I needed to ensure the child would be properly cared for and given medical attention after their surgery. Being aware of the situation ahead of time allows the team to make inquires to ensure the cases they take on are always first and foremost in the best interest of the patient.

The Cincinnati Children's Hospital pediatric orthopaedic division has launched several medical mission trips over the years. These trips involve travel to an isolated location and performing surgery, usually gratis, on underrepresented patients who wouldn't normally have access to the type of care that we provide at Cincinnati. There are a couple of models for mission surgeries. I've done mission surgeries where I was the attending surgeon and a former resident set up a busy schedule with hours of patient consultations in an outpatient setting, answering questions from parents or grandparents. I've done many of these kinds of trips all over the world. In this approach, however, I could not conduct complex or complicated surgeries because I did not have access to the necessary facilities or technology. The only instances where I have performed complicated surgeries internationally were in situations where a former resident or fellow is on staff and has a surgical team in place that is similar to the team that he or she experienced in Cincinnati. The international facility I worked in that comes to mind as one very similar to the facility in Cincinnati was in Pakistan.

The other model, which is efficient but expensive, is the model where we would take a team from Cincinnati Children's, including a primary or critical care person, an anesthesiologist and anesthesia team, peri-operative nurses, and possibly another attending surgeon. Probably the most sophisticated team that we assembled was when we went to Shanghai for three consecutive years, 2005 through 2007. These ventures were coordinated by Dr. Charles Mehlman. The trip was sponsored by a religious organization called Healing the Children. We took a nuclear staff from our operating room along with an anesthesiologist, scrub nurses, peri-operative nurses and two attendings, Mehlman, and myself. Because we brought our own team, we were able to do surgeries with major complexities. We supplemented these endeavors by enlisting the participation of colleagues who lived in the region (Singapore, Hong Kong). Because of our regional colleagues' willingness to join in, we were able to perform three complex spine cases simultaneously at Shanghai Children's Hospital.

Kathie Hays accompanied our orthopaedic team to Shanghai each year, where we worked on severely scoliotic children; we were the last resort for many of them. She recalled,

> Crawford is big on pictures. He has pictures of every patient he's ever worked on, every surgery. The families would come in with their child. He [Crawford] would take a look at them, look at their x-rays, and try to figure out how he could help them. We were there about ten days. It was one interesting case after another. They [our hosts] didn't have the same equipment that we have here. For one young lady, we had to put her in traction. Because we didn't have the items we needed, we make-shifted a traction device for her—he [Crawford] figured this out on his own. It was pretty neat.

Charles Mehlman recalled,

> The fellowship part started in July 1995. We did it with an A team that we took with us: our A team spine, OR nurses, spinal cord monitoring people, to make the surgery as safe as possible. If we did one thing for our Chinese colleagues, we'd like to think it was that we raised the level of their game by making the surgery safer with the monitoring.
>
> We go through and do the cases. Alvin shows all of his amazing-ness, his physical stamina, the ability to stand and work and do what he does. I'm not ashamed to say that I don't like standing that long now let alone someday when I get close to his age. I don't want to stand and work! (I want to see the results of his DNA test to see if there's some alien DNA in there. That's my prevailing theory!)
>
> So now, a couple of years have gone by and I'm back there with him doing our follow-up clinic in Shanghai. He's examining a child and taking some photographs and he's sitting there smiling, a big Cheshire cat smile as he was examining a child he operated on two years before. I said, "What?" And I'm thinking a rude guy comment is forthcoming and he says, "It should be illegal." I said, "What should be illegal?" He said, "It should be illegal to have this much fun doing good for fellow humans."

Our last visit to China was in 2007, prior to the Beijing Olympics. It had been three consecutive years—we'd had a good run and it was time to end that venture.

In 2013 I traveled to Gujarat, India to do work at the PNR Polio Hospital. I was also presidential guest speaker for the Indian Pediatric Orthopaedic Society. Two of the Indian fellows, who went on to become attending surgeons at Cincinnati Children's, had trained there. So, it was like going back home for them. One of the fellows Viral Jain recalled,

It's a little different there; Ahmedabad [city in Gujarat] is where I trained during my residency and spent a lot of years there. Crawford let me be the mentor of the team and he would stand on the side. People there know him and respect him a lot. It's a different culture; if you have a mentor who is really accomplished, then you have a lot of respect.

We did simulcast surgery which allowed surgeons from the community to observe procedures, live from the operating room. As I think about this now, I think about how improvements in technology have made video lectures and simulcast video of surgical procedures possible. In 2012, the Indian Orthopaedic Association invited me to give an eponymous lecture at their annual meeting in Jaipur. The trip gave me the opportunity to visit the Golden Triangle of India: Delhi, the location of the top medical school in the country; the resort community of Jaipur; and Agra, the location of the Taj Mahal. That was pretty exciting. Our team also visited Ahmedabad and experienced its annual kite flying contest.

While this visit was not entirely sponsored by the local organization, we were able to bring people from Cincinnati Children's Hospital Medical Center (CCHMC), including an anesthesiologist, peri-operative nurse, and, in this particular case, a team of neuro-monitoring technicians from Evoke Neuroscience, a Cincinnati corporation. They were kind enough to allow us to use their equipment, as well as perform the neuro-monitoring during the surgeries. In doing that, they also trained members of the local medical team in the techniques that were being used.

I performed mission surgery in Greece three years running thanks to Marios Lykissas, a former fellow of mine who was an attending and junior faculty at the University of Ioannina. There was an annual course in place at the university that focused on the foot, mainly because the director was an orthopaedic foot surgeon. Under Marios's guidance, we set up cases and made arrangements to perform complex spine surgery at the same time. We also visited Thessaloniki, the second largest city in Greece, and performed surgery there. The relationships that we formed in Greece, the multiple surgeries at multiple institutions along with the academic components (we collaborated on several papers as well), were invaluable on both sides. In 2015, I received the Doctor Honoris Causa Professor of Medicine title from the University of Ioannina, a singular honor.

After 2016, we temporarily suspended our cycle of mission surgeries because of some complicated legal and financial issues. It has since been restarted and a number of our postgraduate fellows now have the opportunity to participate. The mission surgery opportunities certainly enhance the quality of the Cincinnati postgraduate pediatric orthopaedic fellowship. The relationships and knowledge gained from these medical missions helped the development of the orthopaedic department at Cincinnati Children's and the larger pediatric orthopaedic global community. I also firmly believe that giving back should be a vital part of a surgeon's work, and by participating in these medical missions, my team was able to support patients and help local medical teams provide better care in the future.

GLOBAL RELATIONSHIPS

My international connections and travel were a means to continue to learn about spinal and pediatric orthopaedic care from a global perspective. This has always been an important part of my practice and led me to develop valuable relationships in orthopaedics and beyond. One of my early adventures (excluding my time in Southeast Asia with the military) was to Bali, with stops in Hawaii, Hong Kong, and Singapore. During my time at Henry Ford Hospital, I was asked to accompany a group of Ford auto dealers who had won the trip as a reward for reaching a national car sales goal called: "Winning Ways 77." I was the attending physician on this trip. There were several destinations to choose from and I chose Bali, because of all the choices, I didn't think I'd ever visit Bali. Off I went (with Jeannie, of course) in a chartered jet, with about fifty other couples, carrying my physician's bag filled with medications. What I remember most about this adventure is the contrast between Singapore and Bali. Bali was tropical and relaxed. Singapore was cosmopolitan, structured, and modern with automated toll booths and—this was 1977—a system of CCTV to monitor traffic.

In November 1977, I was a visiting professor at the Chinese University of Hong Kong, Department of Orthopaedics and Traumatology, a professorship endowed by Wu Jorge Yee, a Chinese billionaire. For approximately ten days, the visiting professor assumes directorship of the department and supervises surgeries and clinics. Dr. Jack Cheng was one of the orthopaedic professors we visited at the university. During my visit I was inducted into the Chinese American Orthopaedic Association. While in Hong Kong, Jeannie and I lived in Sha Tin Province, which has one of the largest McDonalds in the world. After days of eating spicy food, I uncharacteristically said, "I need a break today!" and on that day we went there.

One of the most exciting visiting professorships I ever had was the Gordon Batman Lecture series in Indianapolis, Indiana on May 14, 1992. We finished the lectures and teaching activities, and my host Dr. Terry Trammell, a spine surgeon said, "Al, I'd like to take you down to the pits..." He hadn't prepared me for what he meant, but told me it would be exciting. He meant the pits of the Indianapolis 500 racetrack. He went on to show me the most elaborate laboratory of electronic, computerized systems of monitoring physiologic changes of drivers' heart rate and blood pressure changes during the race. In addition, motor engine function and tire pressures were all simultaneously monitored while the races were going on. I had no idea how sophisticated the activity was. The pit crews competed in the speed of changing tires, refilling gas, oil changes, and more, and all this activity while the fans were watching the track. Little did I know. It had to be one of the most exciting afternoons of my career. Terry was the medical first responder for the Indy 500 series driving meets, and he saved the lower legs and feet of several world-famous drivers. He would go on to earn the Louis Schwitzer Award in 2021 for developing methods to optimize motor sports safety, and he wrote a book on the subject. As a matter of fact, he ended his career as the official medical expert of Indy car racing, traveling around the world with the matches.

I also had the chance to visit Japan in 1998. There I taught a course on video-assisted thoracoscopic surgery (VATS) using a pig for demonstration purposes. I unwittingly committed a faux pas during the presentation, however. As part of the course, I wanted to show the observing doctors several examples of actions that could get them into trouble during surgery, and potentially kill the patient. After illustrating a surgical technique, I cut the aorta and the spinal cord. Upon cutting the spinal cord, the pig jumped once then didn't move again. Then I cut the aorta. The chest cavity filled with blood and the pig bled out. When I'd finished and turned around to take off my gloves, I saw that my hosts were standing behind me with their hands clasped in a prayer position. They were reciting prayers for the pig. Later, one of my Japanese fellows told me that in some of the Japanese religious traditions, animals, especially larger animals like pigs, are revered. The attending doctors were praying for the pig's soul. It probably didn't occur to them that I was going to cut the aorta or the spinal cord, but I wish I had been warned or given a heads up to avoid that situation. In so many of my travels, I was introduced to ideas or practices that I would not have known otherwise, and that, I believe, has made me and my spine clinic a more understanding, culturally aware establishment.

Randall "Randy" Wolf, who was with me on my visit to Japan, recalled,

> I was lecturing at a major Japanese meeting on minimally invasive thoracic procedures and brought Alvin with me so that he could directly give the orthopaedic perspective on this to thoracic surgeons. The inventor of some other device offered to take us to the best sushi restaurant in Tokyo for lunch. I don't think Alvin ate sushi very much. He was a little apprehensive about the whole thing. If you've had sushi, you know that sushi comes with wasabi which is similar to horseradish. In Japan, it's very fresh. They shave the wasabi right there and put it on your plate. I could be wrong but I don't think Alvin was familiar with it. Because he took a big hunk of that wasabi and ate it. It seemed to me that he turned green…his eyes were watering…

In 2009, I was selected to be the senior Scoliosis Research Society (SRS) traveling fellow. The society selects the best and brightest from the new members biannually, and the North American group travels alternatively to Europe or Asia, with the international group coming to North America. The domestic (US) group included Jacob Buchowski, a spine surgeon out of Washington University in St. Louis, who had trained at Johns Hopkins; Frances Shen, a tumor spine surgeon trained at the University of Virginia; and Frank La Marca, MD from the University of Michigan. Dr. La Marca's participation was notable because he was a neurosurgeon and, at the time, there weren't many neurosurgeons who were members of the SRS and possibly, none who had participated as international traveling fellows.

The SRS set out to do an international tour offsite every other year. This particular year, 2009, the tour included visits to the major Asian spine centers: Hong Kong, Beijing, Tokyo, Dokkyo, Seoul, and Singapore. The agenda included presentations (by me and the junior fellows) in each location along with surgical exposure that could be observation and/or participation. In addition, we structured the program to allow us time to interact with local surgeons about procedures that they were doing.

About two days before we were to embark, international public health authorities declared that the H1N1 virus (popularly called swine flu) had become a worldwide threat. We were advised by the travel authorities to reconsider our international travel plans because of the potential of fatalities from this virus. By this point, we had invested a lot of sociopolitical capital in setting up this tour. It's not easy to set up a multivenue Asian itinerary. I consulted with the board of the SRS as to whether we should continue. In the United States, H1N1 wasn't considered a real problem but within the Asian community, it was. Some of these countries hadn't given severe acute respiratory syndrome (SARS) its proper attention a few years previously and thousands of people died. As a result, the public health authorities in this region were now more aggressive in the management and quarantine of people who might have been associated with H1N1. Nevertheless, after many discussions, we felt that the positives outweighed the negatives and our team elected to go.

I flew from Detroit to Tokyo then on to Hong Kong. At the end of my first day in Hong Kong, after we'd given our lectures and presentations, our team went out to dinner. During dinner, I got a call from the hotel where I was staying with a message that the minister of health for Hong Kong needed to speak to me and it was urgent. I remember thinking I didn't know that we'd gotten to that high of a level! When I returned to the hotel, the hotel clerk told me, "We have someone here to see you. But first you need to go to your room, get your bags and check out."

I said to him, "But I'm not ready to check out."

He told me, "No. You're ready to check out."

There was a delegation from the department of health waiting for me in the lobby. A man who acted as the spokesperson for the group asked me if I'd been sick. I told him that I hadn't.

He asked me if I'd had a cough and I told him, "No." Then, came more questions.

"Have you had a headache? Do you have a fever?"

I said, "No. What's going on?" The desk clerk pulled out an instrument which is used to check body temperature. It's commonly known as a fever gun. Just as I'd told him, I had no fever. Then they asked if I remembered being in Japan and I said that I did and that's where this scenario really began. In Japan, before we were permitted to leave the plane, the authorities went around to every passenger and tested them with a fever gun. Those passengers with no temperature could leave; those with a temperature were escorted off by health authorities and taken directly to a hospital. Apparently, there was a woman on my flight who got off the plane in Japan and was, subsequently, admitted to the hospital with a high temperature. Even though I didn't have a temperature, I was considered potentially contaminated. The spokesperson said, "We have to take you to the hospital."

I said, "I don't think there's any reason to take me to the hospital. I'm well and I have lectures to give tomorrow, surgical interactions to perform here, and a trip to Beijing at the end of the week, I can't let my hosts down." We went back and forth with this for several minutes.

Finally, I said, "Well ... what if I don't want to go to the hospital?"

They were implacable. They said, "No. You have to come to the hospital."

I said, "Oh, shucks!" (Not exactly the words I said.)

I asked how long I'd have to be there and they told me that it depended on what the test results were. Test results? This is when I learned that they planned to test me for the H_1N_1 virus. Next, they told me that I had ten minutes to pack up my things and they would wait. I contacted my colleagues and told them that I was going to the hospital.

By the time I came back down to the lobby, there were six

people wearing "bunny suits" (Haz-Mat type suits) waiting for me. This image was not encouraging. They escorted me out of the hotel using the service elevator, put me into an ambulance, and drove me to the Infectious Disease Centre at Princess Margaret Hospital, accompanied by sirens and red lights. I entered the hospital through another service entrance and was finally admitted to a double chamber containing a bed with an observation room staffed by nurses. My meals were passed through a sterile corridor. I was examined by the hospital staff who tested me against my will. They took a throat culture and nasal culture where they stuck the swab so far into my nose and down my throat that I almost gagged! I was very upset by this time. Finally, they said, "You appear to be fine but we still have to observe you."

Trying to control my temper, I said, "OK, for how long?" They said they'd let me know based on the results of the tests or within forty-eight hours.

When the tests came back normal, I told them, "It's time for me to go." But they said, "No, even though your test results are normal, you can't go. You may still be in the incubation period. It's important that you realize that the woman who left your plane is very sick in Japan." She apparently had been diagnosed with the H_1N_1 virus. The medical staff told me that they'd had problems with SARS because they had not addressed it quickly or efficiently enough, which lead to a loss of many lives. They didn't want to make the same mistake again.

I called the US Embassy and spoke with someone on the diplomatic staff who told me that it was out of their hands. I asked him what I should do and he said, "whatever they say."

Next, I called my hosts, Dr. Jack Cheng at the University of Hong Kong and Keith Luk at the Duchess of Kent Hospital. Dr. Luk thought he might be able to help with my situation because one of his medical school classmates was the minister of health. For a few moments, I was optimistic. But when he called back, he said, "Alvin, look, his hands are tied, too. I don't know what to tell you. Just do what they tell you to do." So we did another forty-eight hours in this observation chamber—there were others in the group of people with whom I flew from Detroit who were in hospital, too and also under strict isolation. After those forty-eight hours, I thought that I could go.

To my dismay, they weren't finished with me. They said, "You can leave the hospital but you can't go back to the hotel. You may still be in the incubation period."

"How long is that?" I asked.

"Ten days."

Ten days!

So off I was transported to an infectious disease colony, formerly a boys' camp, that was situated on the outskirts of Kowloon. The authorities took strict precautions, maintaining sterility until we got on the compound. Once there, they started me on Tamiflu, an antiviral drug. I met two guys from Cincinnati who were also quarantined, who had planned to do sales meetings in mainland China, but we weren't allowed to congregate. I was given a protective mask and assigned to a bungalow that included a bed that was obviously designed for Chinese boy scouts because it was about a foot shorter in length than I am. So, I got to do a bit of reading, thought about life, and practiced my clarinet.

Finally, they called me and said that they had good news: they had cut the incubation period from ten to seven days. In the meantime, our itinerary was such that we should have been in Beijing. My fellows were already there, having had to travel without me. Finally, the Chinese authorities told me that if I didn't have a temperature between that day and the date I was to travel to Tokyo, they'd let me go. Tokyo was the next city on our schedule. I was finally released, having spent ten days in Hong Kong.

We went to Tokyo for five days and had a delightful visit with Dr. Nobumasa Suzuki who took us to his surgeries, and we spoke to a meeting of the Japanese spine surgeons, and also the university where one of my former fellows, Dr. Katsui Takeshita, was the spine service director. We then went to Dokkyo where Dr. Kenada, now retired but known for his anterior spinal instrumentation, came out of retirement to perform a scoliosis correction and let the group scrub with him. We then went to Singapore.

I'd been to Singapore in 2001 to introduce VATS to the Asian corridor and Australia. Professor Hee Kit Wong was a VATS advocate and performed a scoliosis correction for us. The Singapore group was kind enough to bring out the x-rays on patients I'd operated on ten years ago who, fortunately, had good results. From there, we went to Seoul. In each one of these places, I was tested with a fever gun and passed. Subsequently, I was provided with a quarantine certificate that verified in writing that I had been tested and was certified disease-free. I had the certificate framed and it is now on display in my office.

The rest of the trip was good except that in Seoul, one of our fellows, Jacob Buchowski, flunked the fever gun test. They tested him and we said we'd isolate him if he seemed to be sick. And then we continued on our travels.

Looking back on this experience of traveling during the H1N1 outbreak, I recognize that efficient management of a communicable disease is possible, but sociopolitical nuances interfere and can ultimately cost lives.

In 1990, I was invited to speak before the Mexican Pediatric Orthopaedic Society at their annual meeting held in Acapulco; I gave the Max Luft Lecture. I was a visiting professor for the conference, giving lectures, and collaborating on procedures. I'd been told to be careful about what I ate and drank during my visit, especially at the resort complex, and not to drink the water. While I didn't drink the water-water, (this was when I still consumed alcohol socially), I didn't think about the fact that those lovely pina coladas that I drank on the beach contained ice cubes. Well, when the ice melted, it turned to water! For the first time ever that I could remember, I was in bed for a whole day.

In 1991, I traveled with Vincent Turco, the reigning international authority on clubfoot surgery, to Brazil. We presented lectures on the treatment of clubfoot deformities through the "Turco" and Cincinnati incision to the Brazilian Orthopaedic Society in São Paulo. I then returned twenty years later, in 2011, to lecture at the Napoli Celebration. Dr. Napoli, who pioneered foot surgery in Brazil, was then 91 years old. I also met Osni Salomone and Igigio Carvallo. Osni was the chief of service at the Federalist Hospital of Brazil. We visited Guarana and Pele's birthplace in Três Corações. I've returned to Brazil on many occasions and was last at the Santa Casa de Misericordia Hospital in São Paolo to speak to the spinal deformity group in 2013. The current chief of deformity, spine surgeon at Santa Casa, Robert Nevis, has relatives in Cincinnati and has traveled to the United States on several occasions. In 1991, I was inducted into the Brazilian Orthopaedic Society as an honorary member and spoke at Curitiba, Brazil where one of our visiting fellows was practicing. Dr. Nevis later honored me as a presidential guest speaker to the Brazilian Spine Congress in São Paulo in May 2019.

In 1991, when I attended my first Brazilian Orthopaedic Society meeting, I participated in a tennis match, humorously referred to as the "Doc's Davis Cup," and I won. The return match was set up twenty years later during the time of the Napoli celebration. This time, the organizers brought in Maria Bueno, an internationally ranked tennis player, winner of Wimbledon and other Grand Slam tournaments. This time, I didn't play but I did have a lot of fun meeting her and participating in photo shoots at her tennis club.

In 2019, I was honored to be the presidential speaker for the Brazilian Spine Congress. I have also spoken at the South Latin American Orthopaedic Trauma to Infants Conference on several occasions in Buenos Aires, Argentina and La Serena, Chile, and I visited Santiago to lecture on the spine and clubfoot. While Jeannie and I were there, we also visited the Mistral Valley and the museum site of their Nobel Laureate Gabriela Mistral, as well as the home of the late Salvador Allende, the former president of Chile from 1970 to 1973.

During my first trip to Argentina in the early nineties, I attended a meeting of the Argentinia Pediatric Orthopaedic Society. I met with Hector Malvarez, director of Spine and Pediatric Orthopaedics at the Italian Hospital of Buenos Aires. Hector and I had been Otto Aufranc Fellows at Massachusetts General Hospital in 1968. He had spent the previous year at Toronto Sick Children's Hospital in pediatric orthopaedics under Robert Salter. At that time, his mentor was Dr. Carlos Ottolenghi, who had advised him to study hip arthroplasty in the United States in order to bring the technique to Argentina. Despite the language barrier, Hector and I managed to have many conversations about the spine and about tennis. I only found out twenty years later that he was actually a pediatric orthopaedist and spine surgeon studying adult reconstructive hip surgery. His assistant was Ruben Maenza who visited us in Cincinnati and remains a good friend. Subsequently, I recruited a fellow from Argentina, Eugenia Robles, who is now practicing in Buenos Aires.

In 2013, I traveled to the Caribbean and visited Barbados. There we held a combined meeting of the John Robert Gladden

Orthopaedic Society and the Caribbean Orthopaedic Society. This event is on record as the largest meeting of orthopaedic surgeons of color ever held. There was a significant scientific interchange as the Caribbean and American surgeons and staff presented their research findings.

I have had the chance to visit a number of European nations. During a visit to Spain in 2000, I had the occasion to visit one of my former patients, a young woman who was a daughter of the heirs to an internationally distributed beer company, one akin to the Busch family in the United States. She had been referred to me in Cincinnati, where we operated on her severe neurofibromatosis spinal deformity. Her family had homes in the Philippines and California as well as in Spain. On our visit to Barcelona, her family arranged for us to have prime seats at a bullfight. We also had the opportunity to sample the seaside restaurants in Barcelona, many of which were built when they hosted the Olympics in 1992. The coastal areas had been cleaned up and there were lots of fine restaurants. I spoke at a conference and in attendance was Dr. Ignacio Ponseti, mentioned earlier as world renowned for his club foot procedure. He had a home in Majorca, and also spoke at the conference.

My most recent visit in Spain was to Navarra, a city situated next to Pamplona, where they have the annual running of the bulls. A small group of bulls is let loose on sectioned streets of the city and a group of people try to outrun them. I had no desire to participate! I also returned to Barcelona and visited with Ana Eyee, an orthopaedic surgeon, who came to Cincinnati to visit and work with us. Over the years, I've visited many hospitals in Spain including the St. Joan de Déu Children's Hospital in Barcelona where I scrubbed in surgery on numerous occasions. Their attending surgeons have visited Cincinnati Children's as well, both to observe surgeries and participate in clinics.

In 1990 I visited Verona, Italy. Giovanni DeBastiani had developed the unilateral external fixator used in performing limb lengthening or stretching of the bone. During my visit, I met with some of the staff and participated in the pediatric orthopaedic center there because of my Scoliosis Research Society connections. At Cincinnati Children's, we were the first to use DeBastiani's technique in the Midwest.

In 2001, I assumed the presidency of the Scoliosis Research Society (SRS). Part of the job as president is to attend global spine meetings, and that year Euro Spine was held in Gothenburg, Sweden. I had first visited the Sahlgrenska hospital in Gotheburg in 1984, spending time in Dr. Alf Nachemson's back school. This time, I had the privilege of representing our international (SRS) organization at the conference and gave a presentation. From Sweden, Jeannie and I flew to Paris where the Cotrel Foundation awarded the SRS a $25,000 grant for research. I met with the French minister of finance in Paris to pick up the check. That evening, Jeannie and I dined on a barge cruise along the Seine with Jean Dubosset and his wife, and Yves Cotrel and his daughter, Marie Helene. Other members and spouses of the American delegation included Courtney Brown, Ron Dewald, and Edgar Dawson.

The next morning, September 11 at 10:45 a.m., we left Charles de Gaulle Airport on a direct nonstop flight to New York. For the first few hours, the flight proceeded normally. We were over Greenland when the pilot came on and said, "May I have your undivided attention. The United States is at war. Martial law has been declared and we have to land immediately because no plane can now take off from or land in the United States."

Everyone on the plane wondered: *What is going on*?

Finally, the news came to us that a plane had flown into a building in New York City. But that was all we knew. Our flight was diverted to St. John's, Newfoundland. At least thirty-four planes landed in St. John's that day on a tarmac designed for four planes. Panic-stricken, Jeannie called our son Alvin Jr., who lived in New York City. She couldn't get through to him. Then she called our daughter Carole. Carole told her that she didn't know what was going on, but she did say that a plane had crashed into the World Trade Center. Then she called back and said, "Mom, something's going on. Another plane has crashed into the Trade Center." So, of course, Jeannie got more upset. Finally, Alvin called from New York City. "There's something happening," he said. "I don't know what it is but I can't get home."

Finally, the authorities let us deplane and took us to an arena. Women were permitted to leave with their purses, but men could only take what was in their pockets. In the provincial towns in Canada there are traveling ice hockey exhibition games in the fall. The local hotels were sold out because of these hockey games. But now they had thirty-four planes filled with people and no accommodations. We were taken to the City Auditorium. The teleprompters were on, replaying the news feed of the planes flying into the Twin Towers. The local authorities sectioned us off into groups by airline, provided us with box dinners, and access to restrooms and telephones. They told us that they were trying to get alternative housing. During tragedy, small details sometimes stick with you. I remember I wasn't allowed to bring anything with me from the plane and had to leave behind the book I was reading, John Hope Franklin's *From Slavery to Freedom: A History of American Negroes*.

It was a day-to-day situation. Jeannie and I were taken to St. Mark's Presbyterian Church where we stayed for the next seven days. The church members set up rows of air mattresses on the gym floor. I'm 6'3" so the gym floor is a long distance down for me. When I hit the air mattress, the air went completely out of it! By the time we got there in the evening, the toilets weren't working and there were only two toilets to begin with. Fortunately, there was Gold's Gym down the street and their management made us honorary members so that we could use their showers and facilities. Each day there was a shuttle to Wal-Mart, where we could pick up necessities as well as clothes that doubled as pajamas, shirts, and trousers because we didn't know how long we would be there. I stayed in the gym, reading. At night people would come together and put on talent shows or music events. Anything to distract us from the TV coverage and seeing the planes crashing over and over again into the World Trade Center Towers.

But Jeannie's a very social person so she interacted with more of the people. She got to talking with one of the church volunteers, a retired physical therapist, who'd worked at the local Children's Hospital. Jeannie told her that I was an orthopaedist. The woman got in touch with Bob Dean, the orthopaedic chief of the Janeway Children's Hospital. "There's a Dr. Crawford over here…"

They sent a car for me, and within an hour and a half, I was at the hospital.

"Look, we have a clinic and if you wouldn't mind reviewing some cases…" Did I mind? Of course not! I was happy to have something to do beside watch the news.

We went through all the cases and patients—I loved it! But at 7 p.m., I had to get back to St. Mark's. Bob said, "Our kids aren't home, we've got an extra bedroom upstairs. Would you like to stay with us?"

Trying to be polite, I answered, "We wouldn't want to put you out."

Before I could finish my sentence, Jeannie said, "Yes!"

Bob Dean is a scoliosis surgeon. The next night, the local St. John's Orthopaedic Society convened and held a dinner, which was lovely. Even better, Bob just happened to have a weekly doubles tennis game and invited me to play. Each day, we had to check in at the church. The pilot would update the passengers on the current situation. This went on for about seven days.

Eventually the planes were released. Since our flight was one of the first to get in, it was among the last to leave. Once we claimed our luggage, we realized that airport security had been through everything and didn't put anything back the way we had put it in. On top of that, we had extra items of clothing purchased during our visits to the Wal-Mart in Newfoundland that we had to squeeze in. We finally got on a plane headed for Detroit and then on to Cincinnati.

On the flight to Detroit, there was one passenger who passed out—he hadn't taken his diabetes medication. The flight attendants asked if there was a doctor available and before I could say anything, Jeannie said, "Yes!"

They told me, "You have to make a decision. You need to evaluate him as to whether or not we take him or leave him. If we leave him, we'll be delayed because we'll have to make arrangements for him." So I examined the man and said, "OK, I think he can make it to Detroit." And he did.

The 2001 Scoliosis Research Society meeting was being held on September 19–21 in Cleveland Ohio, and I was to serve as president. Most of the major international meetings had been cancelled because no one knew what was going on with the potential for more danger from 9/11. Several countries would not allow international travel until the situation was made clear. Our meeting was scheduled to be the highest attended ever because of new directions in management and allowing international members to hold office. The meeting went on as scheduled and was one of the more financially successful sessions. Most of the international members who were not allowed to travel donated their prepaid registration fees to the treasury as contributions, also some of the hotels forgave unattended reservations. It was further unique, in that the two principal speakers were African Americans—a first—Augustus White, MD, and Edward Rigaud, executive at Procter & Gamble, as well as a fellow member of the Wannabees band in Cincinnati.

Our visit to Edinburgh in 2003 was the result of my participation in a conference given by the International Trauma Association. Fortunately for us, our visit coincided with the Royal Edinburgh Military Tattoo Festival—an exhibition presented by elite military forces from around the world. The Tattoo is unbelievable. The military companies march in formation with rapidity, juggling bayoneted rifles as they move. One mistake could have been disastrous, resulting in bayoneted or injured soldiers or worse. Fortunately, nothing like this occurred during our visit.

At one point, the city of Edinburgh had eight orthopaedic trauma surgeons. Then the government installed CCTV cameras in urban areas, at the entrance ramps to express ways, and so on. Armed with the ability to identify vehicles, as well as those drivers who were operating their cars recklessly, or were responsible for accidents, the number of trauma center visits was decreased by approximately 40 percent. As a result, local governments decreased the number of sponsored orthopaedic trauma fellowships and released from employment some of the staff traumatologists. This has had some political consequences in Scotland and similar debates about these cameras came up in Cincinnati as well.

In 2004, Jeannie and I visited Dublin and Trinity University in Ireland where I spoke at the National Orthopaedic Hospital Cappagh. I was also honored with an invitation to speak at the Royal College of Surgeons, a famous medical college in London. While in Ireland we visited Iron Age ruins, mounds, and Bronze Age earthworks located outside of Dublin. It's intriguing that many primitive structures located all over the world and built by all ethnicities have many similar features. Nearly all of them were built with functional openings to allow for air, sunlight, and protection from storms. With amazing similarity, cultures establish political and worship areas, food, clothing stores, marriage, policing, confinement, hospitals, and cemeteries.

I have also had the chance to visit a number of nations in Southeast and Western Asia. I was invited in 2003 to Jeddah, Saudi Arabia to participate in a conference presented by the Gulf States Orthopaedic Association. Jeddah is the second largest city in Saudi Arabia. The association is comprised of orthopaedic professionals from five Gulf States: Bahrain, Oman, Qatar, United Arab Emirates, and Saudi Arabia. Jeannie and I stayed at a resort area, and I was assigned a car and driver who would come to the hotel every morning to pick me up and take me to the meetings. Another invited speaker was Jean Paul Métaizeau from Nantes, France. Together, we discussed the progress of his research on the use of flexible intramedullary rods, now a standard for the care of long bone fractures in children.

Saudi Arabia is a very conservative Islamic country, and in some ways, we found the customs inexplicable. I couldn't hold Jeannie's hand or arm to cross the street. On one occasion, I had grabbed her hand to help her across the street, and a warning was given. I had never experienced this level of vigilance before, even though I'd visited other Islamic countries. During the professional conference, the women sat in the upper back corner of the conference room separate from the men, regardless of their professional experience. While I was in the conference, Jeannie visited the homes of some of our hosts and observed that women in their own personal space adopted a different mode of dress than you would see on the streets in the city.

Alcohol isn't available anywhere in Saudi Arabia. So, enterprising person that I am, I decided to stockpile the sample size bottles of liquor that were dispensed in first class on the airplane. I stashed them in my carry-on bag. Every time I asked for another, the flight attendant would bring me one. There was one problem, however. To ensure compliance that no alcohol enters the country, the authorities search all bags on arrival. Ultimately, I had to leave all of my bottles in the pocket on the back of the seat in the plane.

One of the postgraduate fellows eventually hired by our hospital was from Pakistan. During a review of possible venues for international projects, he proposed a visit to his home country and asked if I would consider Pakistan for mission surgery. This was 2007, during the time that Pervez Musharraf was prime minister and political conditions in the country were unsettled, to say the least. Despite that, I decided to go, and Jeannie came with me. During the visit, I operated out of the Doctor's Hospital in Lahore, where our team performed many innovative procedures. I also participated in a pediatric orthopaedic conference of the Lahore orthopaedic surgeons and made several presentations.

Next, we visited a small hospital in Multan, a city located in the Punjab region of Pakistan. Multan is one of the cotton capitals of the world, known specifically for the refinement of its cotton. Unfortunately for us, sometime prior to our visit, there had been some political assassinations in the area. As I worked performing surgeries, the hospital administrator seemed always to be hovering around me, coming in, inquiring how things were going, and asking if we were comfortable. It was distracting, to say the least, and I didn't really understand what was behind these interruptions. One day after I'd finished surgery, I came out of the OR and three men met me, none of them familiar and one of them holding what looked like a Thompson submachine gun. The other two were armed with pistols. I remember saying to myself, "Well, I guess this is where it all ends."

Unbeknownst to me, the hospital administrator was nervous about our security, hence his near constant presence. Prior to my arrival, he hadn't been aware that I was a university professor from the United States. Once he gained this knowledge, he made what turned out to be extraordinary security arrangements. He did not want me to be assassinated on his property! As a result, my posse, consisting of armed men and three vehicles, went with me everywhere that I had to go in Multan. There were three cars, a middle car, front car, and one in the rear, all equipped with sirens. I thought it was all a bit much.

Our host agreed saying that this scenario created more of an atmosphere than was warranted. Because of the motorcade, now even more people could identify me. He added that if I didn't talk much, and just smiled and nodded my head, people would assume that I was Egyptian. Apparently Egyptians were the only people who looked like me, and could be found visiting the area.

Jeannie accompanied me on this visit, and for the most part, she enjoyed the local customs in Pakistan except that she is a "people person." She's accustomed to giving a hug and kiss on the cheek to people she meets, and she enjoys conversation. But in Multan, men didn't talk directly to women. During our time there, we went to a dinner hosted by a man who owned an extensive and very impressive farm. We toured the farm and complimented him on the abundance of his produce and animals. Jeannie especially liked the mangoes. When we were talking about how good the mangoes were, she tried her best to talk to him, to tell him how much she was enjoying them. But she didn't know about the cultural taboo. Our host wouldn't even look at her. This did not make her happy but somehow, we got through dinner.

Later, my postgraduate fellow said, "I think he really likes her," referring to our host. Not convinced, I said, "Well, shoot, she doesn't think so." Apparently, I was wrong. Jeannie recalled,

> We visited the farm and he (the host) spoke about the workers on the farm; he'd built a pool for them to swim in with their families. We saw the beautiful land and there were mango trees, acres of them. So, just like anybody else, I enjoyed the scenery. And let the men talk!
>
> When we got ready to leave, our host said, "I have something for you." I thought but didn't say, "I don't know what he has for us to take. I know my place." He had bushels of mangoes! Because he knew that I liked them! They were packed into the cars, and we had about five cars! I said to Alvin, "What does he think I'm going to do with all these mangoes?"
>
> We had to give them away because we couldn't take them with us. We gave them to everybody at the hospital and at the hotel. I was eating two or three a day! Mangoes are really good but you can't eat ten a day. Someone told Alvin, "He must really have liked your wife because they sent all these mangoes."

Jeannie and I enjoyed ourselves in Pakistan. The country was the subject of many of the conversations that we had with our hosts—this was the sixtieth anniversary of the Gandhi revolution in 1947. In the creation of modern India and modern Pakistan, families were separated. But the subject that we talked about most was 9/11 and Osama bin Laden.

We had the opportunity to stay at the home of a close relative of the future prime minister. Our host was a multibillionaire, having been very successful in the construction industry. He had his own personal zoo connected to his property with lions and tigers inside. We spent the night in a bedroom that overlooked the city and his zoo.

In 2015, I attended a conference in Dubai, United Arab Emirates, hosted by the Arab Health Conference. I was invited by Bill Murrell, an African American, the local host of the conference and head of its orthopaedic group. At the conference, I presented a paper with one of my former fellows, Shital Parikh. While in Dubai, Shital and Bill suggested an extracurricular activity for our free time: to go to the 120th floor of the Burj Khalifa, the world's tallest skyscraper, and rappel down. I was informed that there was safety netting and nothing to worry about. They know that I'll go for almost anything.

"You were in the military, right?" Shital said. "You know how to do this; you just go to a high place, then go down using ropes."

OK.

On the appointed day, a driver picked me up at my hotel and off we went down the expressway. At some point during the ride as I looked out of the window, I realized that the route was unfamiliar and that we were not heading towards the Burj Khalifa. I thought this doesn't look good. My driver was in traditional Arab dress and didn't appear to speak English.

"The Burj Khalifa is back there," I told him, trying to be helpful.

"We go to airport," he responded.

At this point, I debated with myself. Did I just sit here and accept my fate, whatever it was? Or try to escape, exiting a moving car which was traveling in excess of eighty mph on an expressway and make a roll for it?

Eventually, the car arrived at the airport and stopped in front of a hanger where Shital and Bill were standing. I was relieved.

"You made it!" Shital said.

"What am I doing here?" I asked him. "I thought we were going to rappel down the skyscraper."

With obvious delight, my colleagues informed me that they had decided on another fun activity.

"A plane tour?" I asked, assuming what I thought was obvious considering our location. Dubai is famous for the artificial islands where condominiums are built. The aerial pictures are shown all over the world.

"No, we're going to skydive," Shital said.

Shital went on to say that skydiving was something he'd always wanted to do and he had been preparing himself for the experience with changes to his diet, and losing weight. As Bill, Shital, and I queued up to check in, Shital reviewed a few, small "hardly-worth-mentioning" points that needed my attention. First, there was no insurance for skydiving. Next, there was an age requirement: participants had to be less than 60 years old. (Shital reminded me that I had forgotten to bring my passport so proof of age would be fuzzy.) And there was a weight limit. Last, for my part, there was the Jeannie factor as in, I hadn't known that I was going to be skydiving so I hadn't discussed this in advance with her.

As it turned out, Shital didn't make the weight requirement, and neither did Bill. At the end of this exercise, I was the only one who was able to go. And I did go, figuring that if I were to survive, the bragging rights margin would be insurmountable. It was ultimately an exhilarating experience looking down at 13,000 feet to see the world's tallest building appear the size of a toothpick. I am not sure I would do it again, however—actually, *I'm sure that I won't do it again.*

Less far from home, Jeannie visited Canada on several occasions. I had spent about three months in Canada as a traveling fellow in 1972. Many years later, Jeannie and I were attending a dinner party for one of her fellow Cincinnati Opera board members. At the party, we met an Afro-Canadian baritone by the name of Alvin Crawford. Naturally, many of the guests were interested in the fact that the young man and I had the same name. The conversation picked up when someone asked me, "Alvin, weren't you in Canada for a bit?" I said, "Yeah…" They asked, "When were you there?"

I said that I had been there for about three months in 1972. Of course, the guest turned to Alvin the baritone and asked, "When were you born?" He said, "I was born at the end of 1972, but I know who my father is!" This joke went around and around. This Alvin Crawford was of West Indian heritage and is an internationally known singer.

In 1983, I was visiting professor at University of British Columbia in Vancouver. I also gave the Gordon Townsend Lecture that year in Calgary, which is in the province of Alberta. There's an unbelievably fine medical school in Alberta that trains doctors to take care of the people in that area. On my visits to Alberta (specifically the Alberta Children's Hospital), I visited the towns of Banff, Lake Louise, and the Vulture Glacier. Twenty years later in 2003, I was invited to give the Gordon Townsend Lecture again, the first time there had been a return speaker.

These international experiences and relationships were a huge benefit to me personally and professionally. I was able to initiate relationships with leading surgeons from around the world and indirectly promote the quality of spine and pediatric orthopaedics at Cincinnati Children's, ultimately advancing the hospital's international rapport. My exposure to different cultures and practices also made me and my team more perceptive, compassionate doctors in how we understand and relate to our patients every day.

Alvin and Jeannie with Robert and Beverly.

Crawford pictured with Neil Armstrong.

Crawford skydiving in Dubai while on a surgical trip to the United Arab Emirates.

Crawford skydiving in Dubai while on a surgical trip to the United Arab Emirates.

Alvin and Jeannie in formal dress, later into their marriage.

Mr. and Mrs. Crawford after renewing their vows.

The Crawford family: Alvin Jr., Carole, Jeannie, and Alvin.

The Crawford family at the Kappa Alpha Psi Laurel Wreath Award Ceremony.

Dr. Crawford on the cover of *Cincy* magazine in December 2010.

Dr. Crawford in a UC Health coat.

Dr. Crawford receiving an honorary degree from the University of Ioannina in Greece.

Dr. Crawford receiving an honorary degree from the University of Cincinnati.

Dr. Crawford and his former patient Dr. Kelsey Kapolka after her hooding ceremony.

(From left) Derek Kwakye MD, Austin Thompson , Mike Deal, Alvin Crawford MD, and Adam Butler pictured in the Crawley Auditorium at the University of Cincinnati College of Medicine. Kwakye assisted Crawford in creating BMIMC (Black Men In Medicine Cincinnati).

A virtual meeting of members of Black Men in Medicine Cincinnati (BMMC) during the COVID-19 Pandemic.

Dr. Crawford pictured with a group of men that he recruited into orthopaedicis.

Dr. Crawford playing in his band, the Wannabees.

Crawford playing clarinet with musician Eddie Daniels.

OHIO NATIONAL LIFE INSURANCE

Even before my arrival at Cincinnati Children's, I was interested in setting up a comprehensive spinal service. The concept was in the back of my mind, but I knew I had a lot of homework to do. The best spinal unit in the country was the Twin Cities Spine Center in Minneapolis-St. Paul, Minnesota. In 1976, when I was still practicing in Detroit, I negotiated a three-week visit to the Twin Cities and met with a team of influential staff and fellows in the field: Bob Winter, David Bradford, John Lonstein, John Moe, Francis Denis, Bill Carr, and Behrooz Akbarnia. These surgeons knew everything worth knowing about the spine. During my extended visit, they were very kind to me and invited me to their clinics, operating theaters, and even their homes. I was given access to their protocols, patient information brochures, and any other information I needed. Years later in Cincinnati, my team incorporated many of their protocols into the plans for the structure of our own spine center.

Since I wanted to emulate the best in the field, I also visited Dr. Alf Nachemson, mentioned in the previous chapter, at the Sahlgrenska Hospital in Gothenburg, Sweden in 1984. Sweden offered socialized medicine and Dr. Nachemson was considered to have the most objective scientific approach to the treatment of scoliosis in children. In Sweden, patients had more choice in the doctors they saw. I booked a flight to Sweden on the Concorde Supersonic airliner, and on that flight, I was seated behind Jaclyn Smith, a TV actress then starring in *Charlie's Angels*, and a woman named Marguerite Barbera. As the plane began its descent, Mrs. Barbera asked if she could borrow my pen to complete her customs declarations form. During our conversation, she asked what I did for a living, and I gave my usual response—that I was a schoolteacher in Cincinnati. I typically gave this response because 1) it was true, I was a teacher and I saw this as an integral part of my job and, 2) to avoid getting fairly involved medical questions from strangers once they heard I was a doctor. She told me that her husband and someone named Charlie owned a small park in Cincinnati. Further conversation revealed that the small park she referred to was Kings Island Amusement Park. Marguerite's husband was Joseph Barbera of Hanna-Barbera Productions—the creators and owners of animated cartoon characters such as the Flintstones, the Jetsons, and Yogi Bear. And Charlie was Charles Mechem, owner of the Taft Broadcasting Corporation. Needless to say, neither of these men were in my circle of friends! Mrs. Barbera thanked me for the use of the pen and wanted to know if I'd like one of her husband's original off-prints; she said that Ronnie had one. Ronnie was then-President Ronald Reagan. I took her up on her offer and the original print of Yogi Bear, the Jetsons, and the Flintstones that she gave me is currently displayed in the family room of my home. Charlie Mechem and I later became acquainted on the Ohio National Life Insurance board.

The visit with Dr. Nachemson reinforced my desire to focus on the spine in my practice. While I was in Gothenburg, one of my first postgraduate fellows, Stig Jacobsen, who had trained at Denmark Children's before coming to Cincinnati Children's, had arranged for me to visit the Rigshospitalet in Copenhagen, Denmark, and meet with his former chief Georgin Keiberly. Keiberly had written extensively on Legg Perthes Disease, a hip disorder about which I wanted to learn more. While I was there, I spoke at a Danish Orthopaedic Society meeting. Also present in Copenhagen was Kjel Anderrsen who had been a resident with Stig and performed fellowship work on neurofibromatosis at the Chicago Shriner's Hospital with Edward Miller. He was the president of the Danish Orthopaedic Society.

In continuing my education on developing a spine clinic, in 1986, I enrolled in the Program for Chairs of Clinical Services (PCCS) at Harvard Medical School's T. H. Chan School of Public

Health. My project focus was on the "development of a clinical division within a major academic institution." The program was well-run with a world-class faculty. I was given six-weeks leave from Cincinnati Children's to attend this program. In addition to the education I received, the course also stands out in my mind because I was there on January 28, 1986, when the Space Shuttle *Challenger* incident occurred. I remember the participants in my class walking over to the Harvard School of Public Health Library to watch the continuous television coverage of the event. The tragedy vividly illuminated the reality of danger in space flight and the humility and courage of the participants in the US Space Program.

By 1991, I'd realized, too, that in order to prepare myself to excel both in the academic and administrative worlds, I needed to broaden my background. I enrolled at Xavier University in the Physician Leadership and Management Education Program. My place in the program was sponsored by the Choice Care Healthcare Group. It was a competitive selection process because the group would pay for the $6,500 course if the applicant successfully completed it. I had just been chosen as one of the Choice Care Scholars when the Gulf War in Kuwait began. As I was in the active navy reserves, I was recalled to duty with the Navy, and was drafted into Operation Desert Storm, the second phase of the war, on Valentine's Day in 1992. I had to withdraw from the Xavier program and returned to complete it the following year when I had finished my Operation Desert Storm tour.

I flew to Joshua Tree, California and joined the reconstituted 5th Marine Corps Division in Twentynine Palms, home to the Marine Corps Air Ground Combat Center. There we were trained in desert warfare, and then were sent to Oceanside for nuclear, biological, and chemical training. Not long after, our unit was lined up on the tarmac to be shipped out to the Gulf. But on the same day, President George HW Bush declared the United States' objective in Kuwait was "mission accomplished." We did a Marine Corps stand-down, meaning training or troop movement was halted, but we were not discharged or released to regular military or civilian life. Not all of the Marine Corps generals agreed with President Bush that the mission was accomplished and as such, our stand-down lasted six months. I was stationed (stuck) at Camp Pendleton until June of 1992.

At Camp Pendleton, I had little to do except report to sick bay twice a day. Luckily, however, years earlier I had set up the Pediatric Orthopaedic service at San Diego Naval Hospital, and a few of my former residents were still there and now in charge. I was given temporary additional duty with attending privileges at the San Diego Naval Hospital.

While I was gone, my office in Cincinnati received a call from an insurance company. That didn't really grab my attention at first. Usually, the only calls my office received directly from insurance companies were those notifying us that the company intended to deny reimbursement for one of our procedures. But this call was different: an inquiry from the Ohio National Life Insurance Company. The nominating committee was interviewing candidates and they wanted to know if I was interested in serving on the board.

Ohio National Life Insurance Company was under the umbrella of Ohio National Financial Services. It was, until recently, a mutual company, not a stock company. In a mutual company, every policyholder is a shareholder. Ohio National maintains its shareholder meetings once a year. With a stock company, shareholders, especially institutional shareholders, attend the meetings. But with a mutual company, the policyholders generally do not attend, and instead sign a proxy for the vote of their shares. As a result, there may only be a few people other than the board of directors actually present at the shareholder meeting.

I found out later that prior to this phone call, Ohio National had held its shareholder meetings at their corporate office in Cincinnati, which happened to be about three blocks from Christ Hospital, where I frequently saw patients as a consult. The CEO at that time had just convened the meeting when three middle-aged African American women walked in and took seats in the back of the room. He glanced over at the sergeant-at-arms to confirm their eligibility to be in attendance and the man nodded his head in affirmation. After the meeting was adjourned, the CEO greeted the trio personally and invited them to sit down and talk with him.

One of the ladies, informally acting as a spokesperson, said, "Yes, we would be happy to talk with you."

He asked, "Why are you here?"

The woman answered, "We've been getting proxy statements for years, inviting us to the annual meeting. But until now, we never took the time to do it."

As it turned out, one of the ladies was a registered nurse and the other two were unit clerks who worked at Christ Hospital and were insured by Ohio National. On their days off, they usually played cards. But this time, having received notice of the Ohio National annual meeting, one of them said, "Why don't we go to this meeting? We've been invited to come but never do." The other women agreed. They said that they had really enjoyed the meeting. This exchange was an epiphany to the CEO. He shared with me that he'd never even considered that African Americans could be policyholders. The possibility had not occurred to him.

Historically, insurance company underwriting standards often excluded many Black people because their actuarial tables favored middle-class, white lifestyles. The actuarial statistics inferred that diseases like hypertension, type 2 diabetes, obesity, and more, were risks that would disincline the insurance sales agent from pursuing Black people as clients. Insurance companies pursue healthy patients and make many assumptions about Black people that limited their ability to secure good insurance. The CEO told me later, "We do have Black people as clients and there's nobody representing them. Maybe we should have somebody on the board." That was the beginning. To me, this was a "Lyndon Johnson, Great Society" statement. He took the next step to consider having a Black person on the board.

I participated in several interviews and at the end of the vetting process, I was still standing. There was only one woman on the board at that time, so it was still predominantly an "old white boys' club." But for me, it was the beginning of some positive relationships. The company was good to me and I benefitted from the networking opportunities, which were vital to developing my leadership and management skills for the spine clinic.

Some of the board members said to me later, in private conversations, "You don't realize it, but the meetings are conducted much differently now and that's probably because you're here." By that I assume that some of the jokes and other sidebar discussions that had taken place at earlier meetings didn't occur now because

I was present in the room. Over the years, I was assigned to the audit and budget committee, the proxy committee, and the governance and nominating committee. I was updated on the company's financial performance and marketing activities. I commented often that there was never anyone who looked like me represented on our marketing materials and that the company should address that problem. Subsequently, there was a large billboard installed in the arrival concourse at the Greater Cincinnati-Northern Kentucky International Airport (CVG) that included images of people of color. I was proud of that and like to think that I had something to do with it. It was the beginning of many diverse images on the company's marketing ventures.

I participated on the board through the tenures of three CEOs and became friends with them all. The company was well run, and they all took the company to higher levels of diversity and inclusiveness in hiring practices and sales. As I write this, the current president and CEO is Barbara Turner, the first woman and person of color to hold the position. The company is converting from a mutual to a stock-traded business.

The other part that I played in the company was directly related to African American policyholders. In the early 2000s, companies like Lincoln National, Equitable, and Metropolitan were investigated by the US Securities and Exchange Commission and other government regulatory agencies, and subsequently were sued because of discriminatory practices. Such practices including billing Black clients for the full premium of a life insurance policy, but Black clients typically received a dividend paid out at 73 percent or less than dividends paid out to white policyholders. This was a common practice in the industry at that time.

Ohio National's then-general counsel asked to set up a meeting, explaining there was some good news—that Ohio National didn't have a lot of lawsuits because they didn't have as much "skin (pun intended) in the game at all," unlike the Equitable and Metropolitan—and some bad news—that the company had never proactively set out to insure Black people. The only cases with Black individuals they held in their books were those associated with small insurance companies that Ohio National acquired throughout the Midwest. The general counsel then walked me through a variety of scenarios, demonstrating that the company had all of its ducks in a row in regard to compensating those individuals who may have been negatively impacted. The company subsequently reached out to those beneficiaries who were still alive and made them whole: paying those amounts that should have been compensated at the time the dividends were paid. I thought that was the most positive gesture that the company could offer. As a result, Ohio National publicly reported its position in these situations. There were several weeks of coverage on this subject in media outlets including *The Cincinnati Enquirer*. The preemptive actions that Ohio National took prevented negative publicity for the company.

I'm grateful for the financial and corporate knowledge I've acquired regarding the way corporate leaders deal with issues: I've used them as best practices in my orthopaedic department. During my visits to Minneapolis and Sweden, I learned the best protocols for developing a spine clinic; my work with Ohio National also taught me valuable lessons about leadership and business management. I've also made personal friends with many members of the board and employees of the company, in some cases having treated their children. The company's support of Cincinnati Children's Hospital Orthopaedics Division, especially in the development and support of our teleconferencing room and gait laboratory, has been a benefit to the hospital and the community, and contributed to our hospital's rise to number three orthopaedic division in the United States.

IT IS WHAT IT IS AND OTHER TRUTHS

When it comes to working with patients, I owe a lot of my success to three actions: the ability to adjust and understand failure, honesty in communication with patients, and acknowledging my colleagues' contributions.

Failure itself provides the incentive to succeed. Scientific research hinges on quality data collection and complete assessment. It's imperative to document complications; they often reflect the factors that can't be controlled—surgical infections, for example. Despite the implementation of sterile techniques and the adoption of environmental modifications to prevent contamination, the chances of developing a surgical site infection are 1 to 3 percent.[8] Honest communication—informing patients of both the possible successes and failures of a procedure—empowers them and helps them understand the complications that might arise. Consent is paramount—the family and patient should be encouraged to ask questions in a calm environment. With any surgery, but especially a spinal surgery, there are many risks. All parties involved need to know what complications can arise from surgery, in order to make an educated decision. Consent is essential in doctor-patient communication. In conversations with patients and their families, I would often ask: "What did you hear from this conversation?" This would allow me to gauge their understanding and ensure that they truly had a grasp of the procedure or treatment I was proposing.

As I wrote earlier, my colleagues have contributed significantly to the success of our orthopaedic clinic and should be acknowledged. The following excerpts are from colleagues, residents, and fellows, some have already been named in this book, who helped tremendously in the development of our quality orthopaedic division. I include this collection of retrospections to give a fuller picture of both myself and the orthopaedic division at Cincinnati Children's.

Tal Laor arrived at Cincinnati Children's from Boston. She was charged with the task of improving relationships between radiology and orthopaedics, which historically had not been very good at Children's, with a lot of headbutting and clashing of personalities. It was a bit like entering a war zone. I appreciated that Tal pushed me to reconsider using some new technology in the practice, like MRI. She recalled,

> I tried to bring peace to both parties so that we could have a mutually beneficial relationship. It wasn't easy in the beginning. I never butted heads with him [Dr. Crawford] but I disagreed with him. I think, despite the gruff exterior, he, too, was looking for good relationships with radiology. He felt that people weren't listening to him in our department and not meeting his needs. Sometimes, his needs and requests were not feasible or even acceptable. Sometimes they just weren't appropriate. And this particularly came to light when our department moved from having general old radiography that you could hold in your hand to being computerized and using the picture archiving and communication system or PACS. He wasn't happy about that at all. He fought it tooth and nail. Orthopaedics and radiology actually had to go to an outside arbitration so that we could move forward with the computerized system. Eventually (it took a lot of work), he came to the realization that times are changing. My main area of work is MRI, and it took a fair amount of time to get him on board. I'd say, "Dr. Crawford, we can do an MRI on this child and give you more information."

> He would respond, "I don't need information! I can tell clinically!"
>
> Well, yes, he's got a lot of clinical experience. But, sometimes, there are things that we may see better than he can recognize. And it took a little while to realize that you don't do an MRI on everybody but a lot of times it is more useful. There's no radiation.
>
> It was obvious early on that Crawford knows what he's talking about. There were times when I'd look at a radiograph and I'd have no idea what I was looking at. I'd show it to him and he was as good a radiologist as some of us were, if not better. He became an educational plus for me. It got to a point where we actually wrote a paper together which, to this day, people refer to. Dr. Crawford is one of the pioneers of surgical therapy for idiopathic chondrolysis of the hip in children. The importance being that, if you diagnose this early, some children will benefit quite dramatically from Dr. Crawford's surgical intervention. Historically, the child would just be watched, and could end up having loss of joint cartilage, and a horrible disorder with bad degenerative changes. We've been able to diagnose this disorder earlier than was previously recognized. This was one paper that, hopefully, made a difference.

Blaise Jones was a radiology fellow at the University of Cincinnati College of Medicine in 1989. He returned to Cincinnati in 1999 and took over as the neuroradiology consultant for me. He is now the chief of neuroradiology and associate director of clinical operations at Cincinnati Children's. He recalled,

> When I returned to Cincinnati in 1999, at least once a week, he [Dr. Crawford] would come down with the complex spine cases. Typically, there were cases that were referred to him from across the country or around the world because no one else was willing to take on their difficulties. He would sit down with me, his fellow, and our radiology fellow, and review the

cases and talk about how the imaging would impact the medical management. This was when my relationship with Dr. Crawford changed. While he was still intimidating, it was very flattering that he would value my input on these cases and I appreciated that.

The main focus of the consultations was for me to point out to him some of the anatomic details that we could see on the imaging, yet at least two-thirds of the time I was learning from him the important aspects of the surgical approach as opposed to what we might think was more important on the imaging. As time went on, these consultations became much more helpful on both sides. I had a better understanding of what he needed to know, and he had a clear understanding of how I was describing things and how they were relevant.

Our relationship became more teasing, that sort of joking back and forth. He would come down [to our department] and say things like, "I wanted to review this case with you yesterday but you had gone home already. It must be nice to be a radiologist." I would come back with a comment like, "You don't need to tell me about your poor career choice, Al. You could've been a radiologist if you'd wanted to instead of putting up with this orthopaedic stuff!"

Angie Strader has already been introduced in this book. Before she worked as a nurse in the spine clinic, she was my patient. She recalled,

> The first time I met him, a nurse named Ginny, his nurse for years, came out and told me to put on this outfit—it was horrendous—it was a halter top with shorts. Here I am, a 14-year-old girl, putting this horrible outfit on. We wait, again, and then here walks in this man whose voice sounds like Darth Vader (I used to call AHC "Darth Vader") with all of these residents, young handsome men, like fifteen of them! I was mortified! He said, "Do you know why you're

here?" He would always talk to the patient, but he was terrifying! He wasn't mean, he was just scary! That was my first encounter with him.

He said, "We're going to wait and see." My spine was at a point where, if it continued to get worse, I would need surgery. But they just needed to wait and see (what developed). We had appointments with him every three to six months over the next two years until I was 16 and my curve had finally reached the point where he said, "OK. It is now time to have surgery."

At 16 years old, it hit me, I still said, "Hmmm. It'll be OK." But, I was in high school, just learned how to drive, and had a boyfriend. I was more concerned about it [the surgery] ruining my life.

I said, "Wait a minute." He turned around and looked at me. (Because I never talked to him.) I said, "I want to do this after homecoming but before prom so that I can be ready for prom. I am not missing my prom." He chuckled. We had a connection at that moment. I think he respected me because I spoke up to him and most kids didn't. So he said, "OK. We'll schedule the surgery for February."

The surgery went well. I was in the ICU for two days, in the hospital for about a week. I was out of school for six weeks. I was in a brace that was riveted on—so you couldn't take it off—for a month after the surgery. Now? Everything has changed about this surgery. It's so much better. That's what gave me the desire to help the kids who were going through it. I just felt that the surgeons had no understanding about what the patients, most of them girls, were going through emotionally.

I did make it to the prom and the dress was a horrible peach color!

Angie then joined the spine clinic as a nurse in the early 2000s. She recalled,

> One day we went into a patient's room to tell this patient that she needed spine surgery, the same surgery that I'd had. I looked at the patient, who was an adolescent female, and she was tearing up. Everything came flooding back ... I told Dr. Crawford, "I'm not doing this anymore unless you allow me to develop something to teach these families and the children what's going to happen." And he said, "All right, do it."
>
> When a child is about to have major spine surgery, you are talking to two difference audiences with difference sets of fear: parents who are afraid that their child will become paralyzed, and teens worried about going to prom and fitting in, being able to wear a bathing suit, things like that. I had a unique position because I was that child and then I grew up and worked for the man who had done my surgery. I was able to relate to parents, families, and the children.

Angie laid the groundwork for one of the most comprehensive spinal surgery handouts given to families for pre- to post-treatment, and it is all inclusive of the three "Os" of spinal deformity treatment: observation (assessing activity), orthotics (bracing,) and operation (surgery.) Her perspective as a patient and a nurse taught me a lot about the importance of listening when it came to communication with patients. As a patient, her prom dress was incredibly important to her, and as her doctor, she was a person first and my patient second. If I needed to adapt her treatment so she could enjoy prom, I did my best to make that work.

Kathie Hays joined my practice in 1993 as an OR nurse. She recalled,

> I think he's always on the cutting edge, ready to try new things. We did a back surgery on a young lady from Italy that the doctors in Europe had refused to do. Basically, they told her parents to take her home because there was nothing they could do for her. And when he [Dr. Crawford] told us that he was

going to do it, we said, "Oh, my gosh! What have you gotten us into?" The best thing was seeing her in the cafeteria about three months later, sitting very straight and eating her lunch.

I believe we did a sixteen- or eighteen-hour surgery. You get to be a sort of camel! Most of the time, I was "scrub" so that was what I did. He [Dr. Crawford] was always calm, cool, and collected. He would take an outcome that wasn't very good and turn it around. He was always very caring when I saw him with his patients; the "tough guy" lowered his guard.

Because we were such a tight team: we would stay with no lunch and finish the case because that's the kind of team we were. There was a core group—your first line of team, your second line of team. The first line would pick the case they wanted to do. The second line would take the next one—that's how we ran it. We didn't worry about eating: he [Dr. Crawford] is worse than a camel! Not only does he not drink but he does not eat! So he expects his team to do the same thing! We always laughed at him and asked, "Do you eat?" And he'd say, "Sometimes!"

Gert Whitaker worked as a nurse in my clinic from 2007–2008. She recalled,

We put in a long day. I usually would be here mornings between 6:30 and 7:00 especially on Monday mornings because we had Monday meetings between 7:30 and 8:00, depending on what time he got done with "Boot Camp."[9]

His nurse managed his practice and schedule: surgical schedule and clinical schedule. We saw the patient in clinic, I'd coordinate their care, pre- and post-op, explain the goals before surgery, and then determine when the patient would have surgery. He [Dr. Crawford] would tell me what kind of case it was going to be—what day it would be and the time-

> frame it would take. When the patient was on the floor, he would expect us (nurses) to round with him. He knew that it could impact them sometime down the line in their postop care, (because that was a part of what we took care of), then when they came back for the clinic visits.
>
> He's [Dr. Crawford] very much about facts. He keeps you focused. If I start venting, he'll shake his head at me and that's my cue: "I don't want to hear about all that. Tell me what the facts are."

Alan Oestreich was a pediatric radiologist with whom I started working in the eighties. Although I don't have a quote from him, his contributions were significant to the success of our orthopaedic training program and clinic. He and I coauthored the textbook *Atlas of Pediatric Orthopaedic Radiology*, which incorporated our collective experience at that time.[10] We met each Sunday for over a year to develop this book. He has also published numerous articles and the *Pediatric Radiology Medical Outline Series*.[11]

I have also become known among my colleagues and fellows for some of my "Crawford truths." Perhaps my most well-known adage is "it is what it is." I live by this adage and it serves as a reminder that one has a choice in life—it is what it is so make what you can of it. Many of my residents and fellows have taken these truths and carried them to their own practices. I consider the continuation of the phrase as part of my legacy.

Samarjit "Sam" Jaglan was my fellow in 1989 and is now chief of orthopaedics at the Marshfield Clinic in Cumberland, Wisconsin. He recalled,

> There are all these sayings, I'm sure you've heard: "It is what it is." And he used to say, sometimes, when people needed him right away, "Well, you know I can't be in two places at one time. When we figure that out then we can have two of us." I don't think we want two of him!

Lance Bolin, who earlier recalled my infamous "spine-maker" chant, was my lead physician's assistant at Cincinnati in 1996. He remembered:

> He [Dr. Crawford] actually published an article entitled "It Is What It Is." It's how he's practiced. He didn't sugarcoat stuff. The words came out of his mouth, sometimes they weren't very pleasant. He was honest with you, he told you like it is. And that's what you want from a friend, from a colleague, someone who's going to be honest with you and tell you exactly, good, bad, indifferent. At the end of the day, it is what it is.

Venkat Perumal is a former fellow who is now at the Department of Orthopaedic Surgery, Foot and Ankle Division, at the University of Virginia. He uses the adage with his residents, telling them, "It is what it is!" and reminding them, "I learned that from Alvin Crawford!"

Sandy Singleton, now Director of the Orthopaedic Division at Cincinnati Children's recalled the "it is what it is" adage usage in a less fond memory. She recalled,

> You know when he's angry with you. I don't think I've ever made him as angry as that day when I missed a deadline for abstracts for their annual Scoliosis Research Society meeting. He had just won an award from the SRS. You had to have your abstracts in by a certain date, and then you went to the meeting and presented them. Well, I realized that I missed the deadline. Before I went to tell him [Dr. Crawford], I called the president of the SRS. And I thought, they know Dr. Crawford. They've got to have some pity on me and let me turn these in late. They said, "No. A deadline is a deadline." I had to go in and tell him. I was scared to death.

I said, "I'm so, so, so sorry. We missed the SRS deadline." He looked up at me and said, "Well, it is what it is." After that, I had all kinds of systems to remind me of everything!

Rasesh Desai was my fellow in 2007, and is now an assistant professor at the University of Kentucky, who also recalls using the adage frequently,

> There is not a day that passes by when I encounter any kind of situation that I always think about "It is what it is." That helps me not to worry.

Of course, "it is what it is," was not my only famous/infamous adage. As I said, I had a bit of a reputation for my truths and others carried them on.

"Come, come, hurry, hurry. You don't have to be slow to be good."

Viral Jain, a spinal surgeon and an associate professor at Cincinnati Children's, remembers my advice on the importance of speed in the operation room,

> That's my favorite. When I joined here, I considered myself a pretty good surgeon. But I wasn't on par with his expectations. So he said, "You're good, but you can be speedier." In my first case, after I was done with my fellowship, a simple thoracic fusion scoliosis, getting to the OR room at 8:30 a.m. or 9 a.m. and leaving at 3 p.m., the surgical time for me was about four-and-a-half to five hours. Afterward, same situation, we finished the surgery in two hours and one minute.
>
> The advantage? The patient is exposed to less anesthetic agents and medicine, less exposure of tissue to bacteria, and less blood loss.

Bruce Honsaker, an orthopaedic registed nurse (RN) at Cincinnati Children's, had a slightly altered version of my adage: "Come, come, hurry, hurry. Anybody can be slow."

Charles T. Mehlman, my fellow in 1995 with whom I traveled to Shanghai, also recalled the adage:

> Speed does not kill. You don't have to be slow to be good. These are ways to teach residents that there

are certain skills that you should learn how to do smoothly, efficiently, and safely. And there are other times when you should slow down and devote your time appropriately.

"I've got good news."[12]
Shital Parikh, who as I previously recounted, missed out on a skydiving opportunity and was my fellow from 2002–2003, is now a professor of pediatric orthopaedics. He remembers this particular punchline:

> What would happen was, if a resident or fellow had not shaved, Crawford would say to him, "I have some good news." Which means that he either has a razor or a place where you can shave. He won't tell you that you haven't shaved or that you don't look like a professional. He would just say, "I have some good news," which means that you're in trouble!

Lawrence Wells, my fellow in 1990 and now an assistant professor at the Children's Hospital of Philadelphia, also received "good news."

> My first/favorite Crawfordism is "Good news." He gave me "good news" when I first met him. I came to rounds one day and had not shaved. So I had some hair on my face that wasn't supposed to be there, according to him. And so, he gave me some good news, he gave me a Gillette razor. And he said, "Dr. Wells, I think you need to go take care of some things. And I'm going to give you some good news. Here it is." In full regalia. With everybody there. That was another thing that I've never forgotten. And it's amazing that it's served me so well over these years, decades now.

"The answer is, 'I don't know.'"
This Crawfordism comes directly from being a fellow with Dr. Aufranc at Massachusetts General Hospital in Boston. One day,

at the Mass General White Building, we'd met the fellow from the Baker Building to check on the x-rays from the previous day's cases. When we did a wound check the patient asked if we had seen their x-rays. Dr. Aufranc said, "No, I haven't but if you want I will take a look." We took the stairs down seven flights, looked at the x-rays, and walked back up seven flights for him to tell the patient the x-rays looked good. Dr. Aufranc had not seen the x-rays and while it would have been easy enough to say they were fine or inquire with the fellow, he simply said he didn't know and would go check, even if it meant walking seven flights of stairs. I made the decision right then and there to never let my pride get in the way of making sure I had all the right information. Patients deserve honest doctors and it is always a better choice to say "I don't know but I will find out right now."

Kelly Wenning, an RN at the Cincinnati Children's West Chester Campus, recalled,

> He always said, if you don't know something, I would rather that you say you don't know than say, "Well, I think it's [this or that]." I had to catch myself several times after I'd worked for him for awhile. I would say, "I don't know but I will find out." Or "I will find someone who can give me the answer" as opposed to going on with some long dissertation. People would joke about that. He'd say, "Let me stop you right there. You don't know right?" And you would have to say, "No, I don't."

Angie, who has been mentioned several times, also used the Crawfordism.

> He wants the truth. An example would be, "Did you call [such-and-such patient]?" It would be very normal for someone like me or somebody else to say, "Well, I was going to but I didn't have time." And he would interrupt and say, "Excuse me. I don't think you understood my question. Did you call [such-and-such]?" He didn't want to hear anything else, just a yes or no answer. And I've taken on that trait myself.

> I've found myself doing that with my own children. I've taken on a Crawfordism!

Michael O'Brien, who is now at St. Elizabeth's Medical Center in Edgewood, Kentucky, whose daughter trained here in orthopaedics, was my resident in 1977. He recalls,

> He was demanding. If you didn't know the answer to the question, the answer was "I don't know." Then you'd better know it the next day, go find out.

Fellow Charles Mehlman says:

> The classic situation at the hospital would be: he'd ask a junior resident, "Is the patient in room 602 discharged?" And they'd say, "I wrote the discharge order and [I did this and I did that...]." There is an answer there. The person is trying to make it clear that they aren't a deadbeat; that they've been thinking. And he'd say, "Maybe you didn't understand what I asked you. My question was, "Is the patient in room 602 discharged?" "Well, we checked the dressings and we did [these things...]." And he would press and the answer was, "I don't know but I will find out. I will go to room 602 and I will report right back to you." We are so conditioned to never be wrong as physicians that dysfunctional ways of answering questions come into play.

"We're talking about human beings."
Keith R. Gabriel, my fellow in 1986, and a proponent of my Crawfordisms, says,

> I have several [Crawfordisms] that pop out of me. My own residents, of course, recognize them as such. One is when a resident is a bit pressed on the basic issues or basic pathology, Dr. Crawford would often say, "Well, this is human anatomy we're talking about." That little phrase, inserted into a discussion

at the right time, is absolutely devastating to someone who hasn't studied or hasn't read properly.

Rasesh Desai, who is now at the University of Kentucky, remembered the adage:

> Whenever a resident or fellow talks about something nonscientific without any medical evidence, he would say, "Let's talk about humans." It is in the sense that whatever you are saying is not something based on medical evidence.

"Every article can find a home."

It is important for surgeons to contribute to the growth of the field and one of the ways to do that is submitting articles for academic journals. I encouraged my resident and fellows to publish often, leading to my adage "every article has a home," as long as they get written. Viral Jain recalled, "At the end of my fellowship, he was not satisfied. He said that we should have written twenty papers. Even today, he will tell me, "Write! Write! I want to see your name in the journals."

Venkat Perumal, who is now a foot specialist at the University of Virginia, echoed the sentiment, "Whatever article you write, there's a journal for it. So keep writing what you are writing, there will be a journal that will be happy to take it. All articles have a home."

"I've never met anyone who has died from not eating lunch that I know of."

My eating habits were clearly well remembered. Gert Whitaker recalled,

> On Tuesdays we had clinic all day, 8 a.m. until 4:30 p.m. typically. Dr. Crawford doesn't believe in eating, so we didn't have a lunch period scheduled. You caught lunch when you could!

And Venkat Perumal remembered,

> Sometimes for scoliosis surgery, you scrub and the surgery lasts ten, fifteen hours. Dr. Crawford never leaves. The thoracic surgeon does his part, leaves, and as a fellow, you are there for the entire case. You are helping the surgeon. It's hard. You don't even have time to take a break to go to the bathroom or get a drink of water. And he [Dr. Crawford] keeps going and going and going. One of the nurses said, "Dr. Crawford, do you think Dr. [_____] needs a break? To go to the bathroom or something?" And he would say, "Oh! I thought he had a catheter!" He [Dr. Crawford] says, "Oh, I'm used to it." We found out that he was kidding.

So limited was my eating schedule that Shital Parikh recalled, "One of my co-fellows and I actually took a picture of him eating. That was an achievement because you never see him eating!"

"I never think in the operating room."
Preparation is key, especially in the operating room. I wanted my residents and fellows to understand and know there is no room for cockiness there. Surgeons should be so prepared that they can do each procedure by rote because of the work they have done beforehand to be ready. A part of preparation is to also familiarize potential anatomical variations and complicating factors as a result of the "Seven Ps": Proper prior planning prevents piss poor performance. My residents took the guidance with them as they embarked on their own careers.

Lawrence Wells:

> I know you've heard this one: the Seven Ps, that's a military one. It's interesting that, for me, I took those principles in 1991, not having heard it that way before. It's guided my practice and my life. I live by those principles. I try to pass it on to my fellows and they look at me as if to say, "Hmmm." There's a PC version and there's the regular version. (One word

can make a lot of difference.) It's amazing that I've lived by that, championed that, and it has served me well. And more importantly, it's served my patients well.

Viral Jain:

> He wanted us to be prepared, to read about the cases or the patients, read about the instrumentation systems, which are complex so you need to know everything. Most of my fellows would read about the case but they would not read about what you would use as instrumentation for example. Crawford wanted us to be prepared in case something happened and he had to leave the OR, so that we could finish the case. That's how prepared he wanted us to be.

Venkat Perumal:

> In the operating room, he'd always tell me, "You need to be prepared for surgery. You need to look into the anatomy. You need to read about these cases the day before." If you're not prepared for surgery, you should not be in the OR. When he's doing surgery, he'll ask questions. If the fellow doesn't know the answer or if they don't know what they're doing, he'll tell them to go to "the library." At that time, the library was next to the OR and it wasn't exactly a library but a converted broom closet in a sterile area that had all the relevant articles for the cases we were doing.

Rasesh Desai:

> He had his own disciplines that he wanted everybody to follow. And none of those were out of this world. He wanted fellows and residents to be prepared for the case; they had to do their own homework before surgery—to know the implant sizes and the stats—it was good to start that thinking process.

Charles Mehlman:

> That is his short and sweet way of saying that he's thought through his plan A and plan B, maybe a little plan C. That was his way of being more prepared than anybody else—the roots of his own brand of meritocracy that he brought to the table for anybody that he dealt with.
>
> If Alvin was doing a case that was an unusual case, no one in that room showed up more prepared than he did. To the point of having his enumerated surgical plan written in his own hand and placed in a sterile cassette drape. You could look through the clear plastic and see "step one, step two, and step three."

"The enemy of good is better."

In medicine, as in many areas, the enemy of good work is the desire for better. It is so easy to keep adjusting something because of some unattainable goal of perfection, but often this can just make things worse. Do good work and then take a step back, hands off.

Bruce Honsaker:

> That's one that I heard quite often, especially when I would be a bit overzealous in some of my casting. I modified my Risser cast technique once but was actually choking people with it. Dr. Crawford sat down with me very calmly and discussed exactly what was going on and the variations of casting we'd done over the years. And I told him about the modification that I was putting on to allow the cast to fit better around the neck. And he said, "Wait a minute." Some of the kids had a Risser/Cotrel cast in which we pulled upward against a kyphosis, straining the back. So when I did that, I was pulling against the neck strap. I didn't realize this until Dr. Crawford helped me dissect the technique. He said, "I'm sorry,

Bruce, it's OK. Calm down. This is something we'll figure out." And we did.

Other Crawfordisms:
- "The barristers would have a field day with that answer."
- "It's amazing what you can see by looking."
- "It's amazing what you can hear by listening, but it's hard to listen if your lips are moving."
- "The issues above are resolved in creation as the holy father gave us only one mouth but two ears."
- "When all else fails, tell the truth. (Then you won't have to remember the lie!)"
- "It's in the literature."
- "The strength of silence is amazing."

"It is what it is." Again.
This is my favorite mantra but it has, at times, caused confusion. In 2004, I was invited to give the presidential address at the American Academy of Orthopaedic Surgeons (AAOS) conference in San Francisco. It is an organization of over 19,000 participants and at some point, as the date of the conference approached and printing deadlines loomed, the society secretaries and admins called me for the title of my speech. I responded, "it is what it is." After several rounds of this conversation, the AAOS admins were, understandably, annoyed with me. Jim Herndon, a friend of mine and then president of the AAOS, said to one of the admins, "I'll call Crawford and get this straightened out." So he called me.

"Alvin, we've got to get the conference materials printed. Don't be difficult with this. What is the name of your presentation?"

"It is what it is," I responded. Which is what it was.[13]

THE SINK TEST

It's my firm belief that the surgeon in charge should know as much or more about the case than anyone else. There is no room for cockiness. In an effort to encourage this mode of thinking in the operating room, I implemented the sink test. In the first stage, the doctor-in-training—my assistant, typically a fellow or resident—would walk/talk me through the entire procedure, from beginning to closure, while we were scrubbing at the sink. If the doctor-in-training knew all of the steps for the entire procedure, then, I would allow them to lead. I would be the best first assistant they ever had. If they didn't know the whole procedure, then they would assist me and lose the opportunity to be lead on a surgery.

I made clear to my fellows that I, literally, reviewed every case I ever operated on, even if I'd done that kind of case a thousand times. It's amazing how many times after reading an article at least eight or ten times, I'd find something new in it. It became intriguing to me to figure out what I'd missed, and it made me a better surgeon. I began doing that in the midstage of my career and encouraged my fellows to do the same.

In reviewing cases with my fellows, if we got to a part of the case where the assisting doctor (resident or fellow) didn't precisely know the procedural anatomy, I gave them the opportunity to think about it. If they still couldn't come up with the right answers, then I felt that it was unfair for me to deprive them of their learning by simply telling them the answer. I wanted to make that material available to them.

There were rooms that exited directly from the main operating room. These were utility prep rooms or closets for supplies and instruments. There were lots of miscellaneous items in them. I converted the closet into a library by installing shelves for documents and case articles.

In the mid-nineties, one of my residents complained to the dean of the College of Medicine that it was dehumanizing to be told to "go to the closet." The dean at the time, a psychiatrist, said, "Alvin, that's not right. You've got to think of feelings."

So we renamed the closet and it became the learning center, and, subsequently, it morphed into the resource center. I felt that was the right thing to do. The residents began referring to it as the library, while others called it the outback. Regardless of the name, it was an important part of the educational process and allowed those in training, and me, to be as up to date on the procedure in order to render the best possible care, without the added risk of leaving the sterilized operating room.

I selected the classic and lead articles of the procedures that we were doing and made those available in the resource center. At the time, there were only two ranked orthopaedic textbooks out and both of those were also available. This was before the electronic age, so the center actually had printouts of all the articles. In the early years, that meant making mimeographed copies. All the articles were catalogued and made readily available.

If the resident or fellow did know some information, while the patient was being prepped they were able to go into the resource center and pull the appropriate document. Then they could sit and read it. I let them know that if they found the answer and came back, then they could complete the case and I would continue to assist them. If they felt uncomfortable doing any of this, then they could assist on the case or, maybe, they could take off for the day. It was an option. Everybody in the room—and the room was a team—needed to be as knowledgeable as possible about the case and procedure.

It got to the point where the questions were so uniform and consistent that, sometimes, the OR nurses participated. Diane Schneider, surgical tech, one of my favorite associates, was known for setting up the operating table with a platform that she could stand on so that she appeared taller than the surgeons, or so I was told. I never believed it. We were together long enough that she knew the questions asked of any surgery we were doing. It was clear if she liked a resident or fellow because she would school them in advance as to what the question was going to be and what the correct answer was before I even got into the room. If the trainee didn't have the correct answer to the question, they were allowed to step into the closet and review the technique. And this was all done with the goal of giving the best care to and using the best knowledge for the benefit of the patient who was on the OR table, anesthetized. In the end, that's what it's all about.

A number of my former fellows and RNs recall the library and the importance of continual education.

Kathie Hays, RN,

> I saw him teach residents that I work with now, who are excellent orthopaedic surgeons, and I believe it's the way they were trained. Very tough, very military. I believe that some of the residents didn't like that. But he always made sure that they were prepared and if they weren't prepared, he'd make them leave the operating room and find the answers.

Mohammad Alfawareh, my fellow in 2006,

> Sometimes he asked me about something in the operating room, and my answer started with the phrase, "I think." He kept telling me, "Don't think in the OR. Think at your office and execute at the OR." That was one of the guidelines of my practice thereafter, in which I planned my surgery earlier at my office, and then I came to the OR with a clear plan and performed my surgery as planned.

Hongbo Liu, my fellow from 2007–2009,

> He always challenged us, asked us questions. He had his own rules, if you did not answer the question correctly, sometimes, he'd ask the resident or fellow to go to the library, go there and come back to the OR. If you do not know the answer, you had to stop!

> Fortunately, I worked with him for two years and I never got asked to elaborate. It doesn't mean that I was very good; it's just that I knew the answers to those questions. I was prepared!

Lance Bolin, Physician's Assistant (PA),

> It was the biggest thing that I took away from him, that you can learn every day, don't think that you know everything because you don't. There's plenty of opportunity to learn and better yourself on a daily basis.

Both of these methods of education, the sink test and resource center, were ways to ensure that my trainees never let their egos get in the way of doing the necessary preparation. Patients deserve doctors who have learned as much as they possibly can on the procedure. Especially with spine surgeries, where the risk is so high, patients are putting their lives in our hands and it is not enough for doctors to assume they know the material. If they can't pass the sink test, then they need to take a step back and learn from the experience so they can be better prepared the next time.

THE FOURTH ACT: SABBATICAL

I stepped down as chief of the pediatric orthopaedic division in 2005, and Eric Wall succeeded me. This proved to be the opportune time for a sabbatical.

The purpose of the sabbatical was to accomplish three endeavors. First, I wanted to get out of Eric's way for at least three months as he took the reins of the division. I thought that it would be better for my replacement if I disappeared for a while and relieved some of the pressure of having me there.

The second was to spend at least part of the allotted time in association with a minority institution. The only full-fledged orthopaedic residency at a predominately minority institution was at Howard University. I had not been a part of Howard and wanted to get involved there if possible. Another plus: my daughter, Carole, was living in Washington, DC at that time and a stint at Howard would give me the opportunity to spend some time with her.

The third thing that I wanted to do was retrace certain steps in terms of my own development. I wanted to go back to Boston Children's and San Diego Naval Hospital and see what was new.

One of the people that I'd mentored at San Diego in 1971 was Jeff Cassidy. He had trained at Texas Scottish Rite and had returned to San Diego as a pediatric orthopaedist and spine surgeon. So as the second step in my sabbatical plan, I made arrangements to go back to San Diego, communicating to Jeff that I was open to giving lectures but would not be doing any surgery. He asked me if I would apply for credentials anyway, just in case. I should have picked up on that clue, but I didn't. The day I arrived in San Diego, I was scheduled for a complicated neurological spine surgery which, fortunately, went very well. From that point on, I spent most of my time between performing surgery in the operating room and giving lectures. Somehow, we managed to squeeze in a little tennis. It was good to be back in San Diego. I visited the practitioners in town, some of whom were my old residents that had elected to set up practice in San Diego after they finished their residencies. It was great to relive old times.

Howard University was a delight. Terry Thompson, the chief of orthopaedics there, and I had communicated on what I would be able to do. I was interested in putting together some teaching material and felt it would be an excellent opportunity. The trainees there were excellent. I had a fixed set of lectures in pediatric orthopaedics for the three or four weeks while I was there. Their program was pretty tough, starting at 6 a.m. I was used to playing my clarinet at 6:30 a.m. but I hadn't participated in a teaching program that began at 6 a.m. before! I spent time not only at Howard but also at the National Children's Hospital in Washington, DC. I knew Laurel Blakemore, the director of the program there, so I gave lectures, participated in clinical care conferences, and was involved in developing a formal pediatric elective with Howard.

I also taught freshman gross anatomy. A surgeon depends on the knowledge of anatomy and surgical skills throughout their professional life. I even stayed in one of the student dormitories during that time, meeting with some of the medical students who'd started an orthopaedic interest group. One of the students I met, MaCalus Hogan, was in charge of that group and is now a professor at the University of Pittsburgh. On leaving, they made me an honorary faculty member of the Department of Orthopaedic Surgery. The Howard visit, an academic-in-residence professorship, was funded through a grant from the John Robert Gladden Society. In addition, there was partial sponsorship from implant companies seeking to expand their academic outreach into the African American community. Most important, though, was the opportunity to visit with my daughter.

While at Howard, I visited the university's Medical Museum and came across two interesting historical artifacts, which I photographed for my collection. The first was a telegram sent in 1943 to the chief of hematology and oncology at Howard by a professional organization for internal medicine and blood diseases. It communicated the acceptance of a paper submitted to the organization. The telegram welcomed the Howard team, inviting them to the meeting (presumably to present the paper in person) and provided the logistical details. The second item was another telegram, delivered about ten days later which said that the association, unfortunately, had to rescind the paper and regretted having invited the Howard team, adding that they would not be able to present at the meeting. The scenario unfolded simply because the association found out that Howard University was a Black institution, and they (the association) did not allow Black people to present at scientific meetings.

The museum also displays posters of Dr. Charles Drew, the founder of the blood-banking process in this country. There is a tale surrounding the demise of Dr. Drew. The myth is that he (Drew) was in an automobile accident in North Carolina and the hospital there would not take him as a patient. They subsequently found out that the blood-banking process that he had invented would have saved his life. What actually happened was that Drew was badly injured in an automobile accident and was taken to a hospital but died almost immediately before anything could be done for his injuries. It's my opinion that Dr. Drew, as an African American, is not as widely credited for developing blood-banking as he should be.

From Howard, I went back to Boston Children's Hospital to review some of the procedures that I'd been interested in and visit with my friend, John Emans, the current director of spine surgery, who (with his wife) were medical students when I was there in the early seventies.

My next stop was Dallas. Tony Herring, one of my former associates and a junior resident of mine at Boston Children's, was director of orthopaedic surgery at the Texas Scottish Rite Hospital for Children there. I kiddingly call Tony my "first fellow" at San Diego Naval Hospital and also my tennis nemesis. (The ball was in.) Texas Scottish Rite is very well-supported, which allows them to be ahead of the curve in medical research and development. I spent about three weeks in Dallas, mostly in the clinics, and lecturing to residents. I also scrubbed in surgery cases involving the spine and complex hip disorders. Dr. Dan Sucato had begun performing Ganz Pelvic osteotomies and invited me into his operating room. Needless to say, Tony and I got in some tennis, as well, during this visit.

In the nineties there were few minority orthopaedic surgeons within the overall American Academy of Orthopaedic Surgeons community. Their annual meeting provided an opportunity for orthopaedists from all over the country/world to network with each other. Many of them were from major programs. There were break-out sessions and affinity alumni group meetings during the conference but since there were so few of us who were Black, we'd meet in the hallway, or go out together for a drink. This changed because of a fellow named Charles H. Epps Jr., professor and chair of orthopaedics at Howard University

Charlie was, for many years, director of the only African American orthopaedic surgical program in the United States, which was at Howard University. He formed an ad hoc group of minority orthopaedists and residents, informally referred to as the Meharry-Howard Club, so-named because, at that time, the majority of Black orthopaedists practicing in the country were educated at either Meharry or Howard medical college. Charlie's plan was to have a luncheon for all these residents. He created a sign-up sheet as part of the AAOS registration process in the early seventies that included the notification: "the Meharry-Howard Club is having a luncheon," with the time and location. But this approach didn't work well at that conference because few people actually signed up. One year, he took a leap of faith (based on the number of Black attendees at the conference) and ordered thirty lunches. He worried, "how am I going to eat thirty lunches?" Fortune was with him, thankfully. At every meeting, there ended up being more attendees than he had ordered lunches for!

Charlie recalled our relationship,

> I did my medical training and residency in Washington DC during an era when the medical profes-

sion and the rest of society were segregated. It wasn't always easy. There were opportunities to join professional organizations and, in doing so, I became the first African American in several areas. It happened to be more of a coincidence than something I planned to do consciously. Even in our Washington, DC medical society, we (African Americans) were not welcomed in the early 1960s, but because of the civil rights initiatives, the majority could no longer deny us membership or opportunities. As a result of being the "first," I became a leader in those organizations: the first African American on the American Board of Orthopaedic Surgery, the first to chair a national committee for ortho surgery, the first African American president of a national orthopaedic organization, the American Orthopaedic Association. Sometimes, you just happen to be the right person and at the right time.

I've had the pleasure of knowing Alvin since he was a resident in training in Boston and came through Washington, DC on a couple of occasions. Our careers were parallel, but I was a little ahead of him. Once, he stopped by my office on his way to the DuPont Institute. I was particularly impressed with the original work that he did in the treatment of congenital clubfoot, arthrogryposis, and scoliosis.

As time went on, there were more Black doctors joining the AAOS who had not trained at Meharry or Howard, which led to a discussion of a new name that better reflected the makeup of the group. One idea was to rename the group the John Robert Gladden Society, named after John Robert Gladden, a graduate of Howard University College of Medicine and the first doctor of color to pass the American Board of Orthopaedic Surgery, which was a prerequisite for membership in the AAOS. The members agreed unanimously, and the John Robert Gladden Society was officially established in 1998. I was honored to be elected president of the society in 2009.

At the urging of Gus White, and since many of the doctors in the society were serving underrepresented populations, we defined the society as a multicultural organization. It was not solely for Black doctors but it was focused on supporting and furthering Black orthopaedic surgeons. In the first two to three years of its existence, a sizeable number of its members were not people of color. Through attrition and, perhaps, because the Society has a more sociopolitical focus as opposed to a scientific one, many of the Eurocentric individuals left the organization, but it still stands strong today.

The primary focus of my term as president of the Gladden Society was on launching efforts to invigorate the organization. Again, a telephone conversation that I had with Gus White over the Christmas holidays was the catalyst. Gus asked if I would consider leading the Society with a goal of redefining its purpose to make it more relevant. The Society's meetings were held at the annual Orthopaedic Academy conference, but it wasn't an alumni club for a particular school. Many of our members, including me, were graduates of programs besides Meharry and Howard. So, what was the Gladden Society's purpose? I was tasked with redirecting focus of the group to give it a more pragmatic and useful role as we moved through the beginning of the twenty-first century.

For a start, we took a close look at the structure of our medical student scholarships—programs that were in place before I became president in 2009—and developed a strategy to promote them to another level. In one instance, we teamed up with an organization called "Nth Dimension." Nth Dimension was founded by Bonnie Mason in 2004 with a mission of addressing the lack of women and underrepresented minorities in the orthopaedic surgery field. Bonnie was an unbelievable organizer and, with the help of Verona Brewton, was able to secure financing through Zimmer Implant Corporation for research externships. Participating medical students were invited to the Gladden Society luncheon and provided with passes to academic lectures and other programs that were part of the American Academy of Orthopaedic Surgery meetings. Next, she created a day-long experience just for the students that included immersion in test-taking skills (such as the licensing exam), financial literacy, and business management related to setting up a medical practice and initiating research. Our goal was to provide exposure to programs that had a practical application. The Gladden society also assisted in supporting a program of Cultural Competency at Harvard University.

We also actively encouraged members of the Gladden Society to become more involved with mentoring medical students in their local communities. My involvement in mentoring precipitated the society's creation and funding of the Alvin H. Crawford Mentoring Award, which involves a national competition to honor a surgeon who has supported and guided an individual. Bonnie was ineligible because of her company's involvement, but was personally responsible for those medical students under her tutelage having an 80 percent match rate to orthopaedic programs. Fortunately, we were able to change the eligibly requirement and in 2017, Dr. Bonnie Mason received the Alvin H. Crawford Mentoring Award because of her unwavering commitment to preparing medical students and graduates for positions that are competitive for matching into orthopaedic surgical residencies.

The Gladden Society also assisted in providing support for two pipeline programs, designed to reach kids from Black and Hispanic neighborhoods. These programs, one in Florida and one in Los Angeles, are set up to reach out to young people as early as elementary and middle school, with scientific activities. The kids earn points for having good grades and being good citizens. Their mentors then provide progress reports back to the Gladden Society.

On yet another level, the Gladden Society set up mock oral exams for graduating residents to address challenges they'd experienced over the years with the American Orthopaedic Surgery boards. We developed a pre-exam based on questions from previous examinations, and recruited Gladden Society members who had been examiners and/or sat for the American Board of Orthopaedic Surgery to set up the mock exam trial runs in Atlanta; Washington, DC; and Los Angeles. I am incredibly proud of the work the Gladden Society has done and continues to do. I am honored that I was able to be involved from its inception.

FOURTH ACT: CLINIC

The transition clinic for pediatric orthopaedic disorders, a concept developed over several years, was designed to learn about the ultimate outcome of surgical and rehabilitation interventions to acquired, traumatic, or congenital conditions that had occurred before skeletal maturity. The only way to do this was by revisiting these patients as adults. Beginning with a database of over 27,000 interventions in 2011, I thought that this would give me a unique opportunity to look back at some of the patients, many treated when they were very young children, and learn what the muscular-skeletal outcome was once they had achieved maturity.

My team set up the parameters and wrote a grant specifying that we would see patients with non-neurologic disorders only and who received intervention to their muscular-skeletal system prior to becoming skeletally mature—from newborn to 35 years old. The primary study group contained ages 16 to 35 years old, though we continued to consult more broadly. We convened a cadre of adult orthopaedic specialists to serve as consultants and to comprise the surgical arm of the transition clinic. We applied for the Arthur H. Huene Memorial Award through the Pediatric Orthopaedic Society of North America. While we didn't succeed in getting it, the proposal was eventually funded with a start-up grant from the University of Cincinnati Orthopaedic group.

We now have a comprehensive database and can evaluate individuals by whatever occupation or disabilities they may or may not have as a result of the orthopaedic disorders encountered as a child. Individual conditions run the gamut from scoliosis to developmental hip conditions, including slipped capital femoral epiphysis and Legg Perthes disease, to clubfoot deformities, or other deformities of the lower extremity. It was a rewarding experience to see patients treated many years ago. Fortunately, the majority of them are doing well.

In 2001, I joined the Harms Study Group, a consortium of international spine surgeons formed in 1994, named after Jürgen Harms, renowned German scoliosis surgeon. The group is a multicenter database consisting of over three thousand patients about whom there have been over 125 peer-reviewed scientific publications and nearly 550 scientific meeting presentations. At this writing the group had completed the manuscript of a textbook on neurological scoliosis that is based on their research, and they asked me to write the foreword. Their research in this area is on-going and includes some of my own former patients.

My ultimate goal for the transition clinic was to promote its integration into general pediatric and pediatric orthopaedic fellowships. The way the pediatric orthopaedic profession is evolving, it will be invaluable to know the outcome of muscular-skeletal disorders on patients as they grow into adulthood. It will be helpful for physicians to observe firsthand the adult manifestations of some of these pediatric conditions. Strategically, I had hoped that the clinic would become self-sufficient, evolving into an integral part of pediatric orthopaedic surgery and providing a longitudinal follow-up on nearly every condition in the pediatric realm.

While I was still practicing at Cincinnati Children's, we were referred a child with a severe scoliosis along with intractable pediatric cardiology disease. It's my recollection that he received his first pacemaker at three or four years of age. The child had such significant cardiac abnormalities that his doctors didn't think that he would survive an operation to fix his spine. At about this same time, we were investigating minimally invasive surgery to correct adolescent idiopathic scoliosis and thought that this child was an ideal candidate. It was one of the most unusual surgeries that we've ever done. It was the first and only case that I've scrubbed where there was an interventional cardiologist in surgical scrubs in the operating room, standing by the anesthesiologist ready to provide service if we needed them because the boy's heart was so precarious. Because we'd been told that the child might not survive the procedure, we had pallets on him, which are the protective covers required when surgeons anticipate that electronic cardiac (shock) resuscitation might be needed to return cardiac function.

We set up the case, performed the minimally invasive technique and, just as we were preparing to close the wound, the neuro-evoked potential monitoring went out. We were concerned that it was a spinal cord injury, but realized he actually was having a cardiac arrest. It was very fortunate to have a cardiologist scrubbed in the surgery who immediately took over. Since we were at the point of closing the wound, we performed chest massage and electronic stimulation of his heart to revive him. His heart literally stopped beating for a number of minutes, and we were concerned that he might have sustained brain anoxia and, possibly, some mental deterioration post-surgery. Thankfully, he didn't. We were able to resuscitate him and closed the wound.

Five years later in May 2016, I saw this young man at our new university orthopaedic facility at Holmes Hospital. We talked about that experience, about how unusual it was: surgery with pallets for electrical shock for resuscitation and having a cardiologist scrubbed and present in the room. We also talked about our good fortune—really his good fortune. He has since undergone a cardiac transplant, is 21 years of age now, and doing well, attending college at Wright State University. I spent about an hour with him, his mother, grandmother, and grandfather. It was a great visit.

I fully retired from Cincinnati Children's Hospital in 2013. After which, I was offered the position of professor emeritus in the College of Medicine. This provided me with opportunities to pursue projects that I'd considered many years prior—cognitive approaches to clinical decision making, physical diagnostic and clinical application in gross anatomy—but had never had the time. I'd always been interested in exposing young physicians and surgeons to a more global and comprehensive practice of medicine. Now, with a less structured schedule, I could explore other aspects of medicine. One idea that I developed was a boot camp. Boot camp is a military term for in-depth training that prepares trainees to react reflexively and appropriately to all circumstances. I conduct the boot camp session with the residents and fellows at Children's Hospital on Mondays at 6:30 a.m. We go through all of the pediatric orthopaedic basic conditions, reinforcing the functional elements that an active pediatric orthopaedist should know. It's not a lecture format structured like a PowerPoint presentation, but it does include the ancillary steps and peculiarities involved in the musculoskeletal diagnostic groups, including the contributions of radiology, genetics, cardiothoracic surgery, urology, and pediatric general surgery. We lump it all together and call it boot camp. The session is designed to be interactive, separated into thirty minutes of didactic lectures and 30 minutes of x-ray assessment of subtleties of the traumatic pathology.

Boot camp also includes simulation to teach physical diagnosis. When I was a medical student, the skill of physical diagnosis was pretty basic, and for practice, medical students used to examine each other. Students reviewed the physical exam, the blood pressure checks, and all of the factors relating to patient interaction.

Today, UC is one of the pioneers in the use of simulation. The course Physical Diagnosis through Simulation begins freshman year by using professional patients. The students attend lectures about a particular condition, then go in and examine the patient. Their behavior is observed and evaluated. They are graded by the professional patient as well as by the professors. The instructor sits in a monitoring room where there are video feeds into the exam room and reviews how the student physician enters the room, washes their hands, introduces themselves to the patient, and if they address the patient appropriately and with respect. Instructors want to make sure there is a humanizing effect in the exam room.

The professional patients are unique. There were some who have done it for a long time; they enjoy the experience and are paid for doing it. Others are students at the College Conservatory of Music (CCM) in theater arts. These individuals take simulation to another level with their acting skills. You've never seen a heart attack like one of these simulators can do a heart attack! The student is graded on assessing and developing a treatment plan. I think the experience solidifies the information much more than when medical students just examined one another, like when I was in medical school.

The better surgeon is the one who knows their anatomy. I've participated in and taught freshman anatomy courses since residency in Boston. I was able to participate in the Vesalius course sponsored by Sandy Joffe at UC in 2021. Robust knowledge of anatomy is essential for surgical treatment of common orthopaedic disorders. I continue to assist in the gross anatomical dissection of the upper extremities, the lower extremities, and the back. I also continue to teach anatomy because I firmly believe it is the foundation of a good surgeon.

IT AIN'T OVER UNTIL THE TALL MAN IN THE WHITE COAT PLAYS SAXOPHONE

The other thing that I've really been able to explore more in my fourth act is music. My career choice started with music, and it looks like it will end in music. In 2015, I decided to stretch myself musically by applying to the College Conservatory of Music. CCM is the second finest public conservatory in the United States. I elected to take their jazz improvisation class. In order to enroll in the class, I had to take prerequisites. CCM looked at my prerequisites from 1957, 1958, and 1959, and said, "Well, there have been a few changes since then!" I was allowed to be a guest in the jazz improvisation class.

The experience was unbelievable! There are so many great young musicians out there and they know so much more than I did at their age. I revisited all of the modes of western music that I had forgotten so long ago, like the seven modes of a modal scale. At CCM, the students are incredibly well taught, and they can play every tune in twelve keys! The instructor explained it to me this way: A musician might be playing at a particular club. The owner has connections, and a diva comes in. The diva is a Grammy winner and wants the musician to play "All the Things You Are" for her, but in the key of C, her favorite key. Or another key if she changes her mind again at the last minute. The musicians need to be ready to adapt to the key the singer is singing in without any preparation. I thought this training was amazing.

In addition to studying at CCM, I also took lessons from the bass clarinetist at the Cincinnati Symphony Orchestra for several years. I've been involved with the UC Alumni Summer Band and with the Queen City Concert Band. Both bands play tradition classics, modern popular John Williams compositions, and marches, including some by John Philip Sousa. I've enjoyed all of the challenges of practicing for the summer and winter concerts.

For years, I've played with a jazz group called The Wannabees + Two, so named because there are three of us who have worked outside of music (the Wannabees)—Ed Rigaud, former P&G executive and one of the founders of the National Underground Railroad Freedom Center; Dr. Wendell O'Neal, who at one time was the vice president of laboratory services for the Health Alliance of greater Cincinnati; and myself. Then we included two professional musicians (bass and drums, the + Two) to our group: Walter Cash (holder of several patents while an employee at P&G) most often on bass, and various hired drummers, in addition to singers LaVieena Campbell and Melvin Williams. We were probably one of the best bands in the city, which is perhaps easy to be when our primary audience is nonprofit events, and we don't charge. We got all sorts of compliments!

In 2015, the Cincinnati Symphony Orchestra did outreach to community bands and orchestras via the ROAM initiative, (Reaching Out to Amateur Musicians). John Morris Russell, the music director of the Cincinnati Pops, attended one of our rehearsals and prepared the Queen City Concert Band for our upcoming concert. During the intermission, he mentored the brass section, while Ron Aufmann, the Symphony's bass clarinetist and my CCM instructor, mentored the woodwinds. John (he is usually referred to as JMR) really is the most wonderful man—high energy and very amiable. It was unbelievable to have orchestral professionals mentoring amateurs. After that coaching, our rehearsal performance was probably the best we ever played.

My son and I participated in a workshop led by jazz saxophonist and teacher Jamey Aebersold, known for his music education books, play-a-longs, and workshops. Aebersold's course included an intensive experience of music-making beyond playing scales. It was also neat to hang out and live in the student dormitory with my son.

I also participate in the Undercover Band: a big band formerly headed by the late Larry Hawkins, a retired P&G lawyer.

P&G is a large multinational organization that sponsors many extracurricular group activities for its associates, including bands and orchestras. The nucleus of the Undercover Band was already in place when somebody asked me if I'd be interested in being a part of it. We've performed annually at Union Terminal during the Christmas holidays. Once again, it's a band well-liked by the nonprofits because of our charges or lack thereof.

I had an interesting experience at Union Terminal during the Christmas holiday. The Museum Center has all kinds of goodies and activities for kids during the season, including music. The Undercover Band was playing, and as I was stopped near my music stand, a little kid came up to me. I recognized him as one of my former surgical patients. Solemnly, he put two quarters on my music stand. He was tipping me for playing in the band! I thought that was the cutest thing! I spoke with his dad after the concert and the dad told me, "He must think a lot of you, Doc. I'll tell you, he doesn't give up money much at all!"

Dr. Armando Torres, an orthopaedic surgeon, musician, and composer in Mexico City composed *Eh'ecatl, for solo B flat clarinet Opus 13*. The piece was dedicated to me by himself and Dr. Jorge Mijares, the then president of the Mexican Orthopedic Society. The piece was based on the motif of Mozart's clarinet concerto and the divertimenti. I've been fortunate enough to perform the piece on many occasions. Performing a piece dedicated to you is a humbling experience I will be forever thankful for.

I've had the opportunity to play clarinet in the UC alumni community band. We play a summer schedule in several public parks. Another great side benefit is to substitute for the band at university basketball games if the university band is away for a postseason tournament football game. We sit in the cheap seats behind the baskets, but the joy is that the cameras are focused there for free throws and it's amazing the number of times my young patients have told me they saw me playing when the free throws were being shot at our end.

THOSE I'VE MET (AND ALMOST MET) ALONG THE WAY...

Over the years, I have had a number of brushes with fame, and just as many that I narrowly missed. As a surgeon, and especially as a director of a surgical division, it can be easy to become focused solely on the job and forget about life outside the operating room. Looking back on my own experiences, I encourage medical students and new surgeons to remember to make sure that even as they are pursuing their academic and professional goals, they are expanding their worlds beyond/outside the operating room. The experiences and relationships they can build there will make them more empathetic, connected doctors.

I was in the operating room. Someone said, "Dr. Crawford, the hospital operator is trying to find you. They want you to escort some VIPs around the hospital." I told them I was in the operating room but could come when I finished up. I went to the surgical control desk afterward and realized everyone seemed to be very excited there, but I didn't know why.

Apparently Oscar Robertson (professional basketball hall of famer and University of Cincinnati legend) was there and had a friend with him on his visit.

And I asked, "Who is the friend?"

They said, "It's Brian McKnight."

I said, "I don't think I know him. Is he from Cincinnati?"

They said, "Dr. Crawford. You've been in the operating room too long." This was not the first or last time I've heard this comment. Brian McKnight was a famous soul singer, a balladeer. I admit here that I truly did not know who Brian McKnight was even though he had two or three of the top ten records on the charts at that time. But I ended up going down with some of the staff to get autographs. He and Oscar Robertson spent the day at Cincinnati Children's. Oscar was the local chair of the sickle cell fundraiser and Brian was the national chairman. At a party for them that night, they asked McKnight to sing. He started playing the piano and I knew every one of those tunes! I'd heard them on the radio in my car. So, I was more familiar with him than I thought. In 2000 there was a feature about Brian, his home, and family in *Ebony* magazine. I told myself, *Crawford, you should get out of the clinics and operating room more and get with the program! Figure out what's going on in the world!*

On a visit to the Bay area while working at the Henry Ford Hospital, I attended a party in Oakland with one of my former fellows, the late Don Townsend. I'll never forget the date because Jeannie had called from Michigan that evening to tell me that our house had been partially destroyed by a tornado. At some point during the evening, Don said, "There's Danny Glover." I looked around and asked, "Who is Danny Glover?"

Don was incredulous. "Danny Glover! The movie star!"

I still didn't know who he was.

I think Don chose to ignore that and, instead, took me over to meet the actor. "Let me introduce you to him." Don told Danny, "This is the guy I've been talking to you about." Glover was very pleasant and said, "Dr. Crawford? I'm coming to Cincinnati. I'm the national chairman for the National Association of Sickle Cell Disease. Would you be willing to show me around your hospital?" I told him that I would and asked him to let me know when he planned to come.

When Danny Glover visited Cincinnati, I arranged to meet up with him and showed him around Cincinnati Children's. A short time into the tour, PR sent somebody down to intercept him.

"Dr. Schubert, our CEO and chief of pediatrics, found out that you were going to be here, Mr. Glover, and he'd like to meet you."

I said that we'd go by Schubert's office first. Glover said, "OK, good. After that, you'll have to tell me about the hospital. I have some questions." We went to Dr. Schubert's office and Schubert's face lit up. He was a real fan.

He said, "Mr. Glover, I watched you on *Lonesome Dove*!"[14]

I thought, but didn't say, *Shoot, I've never heard of Lonesome Dove!*

The two of them bonded and Bill Schubert "stole" Danny Glover from me! Once the nurses and other staff members learned that Danny Glover was in the hospital, we ended up with an entourage of people who wanted to "help" me show him around!

In 1989, as a fiftieth birthday present to myself, I signed up for a tennis fantasy camp with the "Legends" held at Newk's Ranch (John Newcombe) in New Braunfels, Texas, which is just outside San Antonio. An advanced camp for adult tennis enthusiasts, tennis legends in addition to Newcombe included Owen Davidson, Mal Graham, Cliff Drysdale, Roy Emerson, and others. They led a crew of amateur tennis fans, some of whom were celebrities like actor-comedian Alan King and billionaire business mogul Les Wexner. The attendees were grouped into teams based on skill level and then we prepared for Davis Cup–level play. During the week we practiced hard and drank a fair amount of Foster's Lager, a favorite of Grand Slam doubles winner Owen Davidson. By midweek, I had abdominal and abductor cramps. The experience gave me a real appreciation for what professional tennis players go through both in front of and away from the net. I ended up winning the Most Improved Player award based on my performance in my pseudo-Davis Cup matches.

In 2008, I was the recipient of the International Trumpet Award, which is described as "celebrating the best in African American excellence and achievement." Prior to this, I had operated on the granddaughter of a well-known executive. The father of the child was involved in a corporation in Kentucky. The girl had previously been treated at another children's hospital, but her father was not pleased with the treatment. He contacted the CEO at Cincinnati Children's at the time to see if he could meet with me.

The meeting was set up and the man asked me many questions: "What do you do? What do you know about orthopaedics?" We did this question and answer for a bit and when it was over, I thought, *well, that's interesting* and forgot about it.

About a week later, the CEO reached out and said that the father of this child wanted to meet with me again. We met and, this time, he went into more detail about more specific medical conditions. I finally asked, "Well, what's this all about?" He said, "I have a granddaughter…"

The third time, the CEO called and said the father was bringing in his child and wanted me to perform surgery on her, which I did. About six months later, I was informed that I was a recipient of the Trumpet Award. The awards are given every year with the ceremonies broadcast on Black Entertainment Television (BET) across 177 countries. The year I was awarded it, other honorees were Magic Johnson; Lisa Leslie, the WNBA champion; Ian Smith, MD, a diet and sports guru from New York; Tracy Morgan, the comedian; Anthony Anderson, actor; and Raven-Symone, actor.

For the awards, we spent an entire day at the Martin Luther King Center in Atlanta. There were advisors to help us gear up to go to the "big show." I was asked to write a five-minute speech, in which I included the line, "Not only was it important that a child who looked like me could be a chief of orthopaedics but, as of this week, I can say that a child who looks like me can be president of the United States."

It was a huge production, like the Academy Awards! I was interviewed on the red carpet outside, ("Who are you? What have you done? Where are you from?"), and once I accepted my award and walked off the stage, I was taken to a backstage room with a wall embellished with trumpets. That was a neat thing. I also learned about "seat fillers" at these events. I saw people standing in the hallway as we entered and I asked the woman next to me, "Who are all of these people?" She told me that they were waiting for seats—there can never be an empty seat so when someone goes up to accept an award, someone comes from the hallway to sit in their seat. That way, when the camera pans the audience, the room always looks full.

As a high school student and Ford Foundation scholar, I had qualified for early college entrance to Morehouse College, often referred to as the Harvard for Black males. But Morehouse had a hefty tuition, and I had a brother and sister in college, so I didn't end up attending. The truth be known, I wanted no part of science, technology, engineering, and mathematics, (STEM) because I was going to be a musician.

In 2009, I was selected to receive the Candle Award as a part of Morehouse's Candle in the Dark Gala. Each year, Morehouse College selects a Black individual who has made some contribution to science or the humanities. There are two categories for the award: the Benny Award, named in honor of the college's former president, Dr. Benjamin Mays (whose reputation is such that some people think he lives on the right or left side of God) is only awarded to Morehouse graduates; the Candle Award goes to someone who contributed to society but wasn't a Morehouse graduate. One of the Benny Awards that year went to a fellow by the name of Max Roach, who was the nephew of Hank Aaron's current wife, and when he attended college at Morehouse, he stayed with them. Now, he lives and works in San Francisco and is an oncologist who constructed a sweeping research project about prostate cancer in African American men. At the event, I got the chance to meet Henry Aaron and his wife, as well as the president of Morehouse.

I was interviewed by CNN commentator Tony Harris and realized that sitting next to me was Smokey Robinson. Smokey and I got to talking and he asked me where I was from. I told him, Memphis, Tennessee. He said, "You know, I used to spend summers in Memphis. I stayed with my aunt in Orange Mound."

I said, "Shoot, man, I'm from Orange Mound."

Apparently he lived down the street and around the corner, about four houses from me!

Smokey told me, "My mother sent me down to Orange Mound in the summers so that I wouldn't get shot in Detroit. I did that for about three or four years when I was a kid."

We connected, talking about Orange Mound and other things; it was just so unbelievable because we'd done some of the same things growing up. Smokey said, "When I'm in Cincinnati, why don't you call."

While working at Chelsea Naval Hospital in Massachusetts, a Marine, who had been injured by a grenade came in. One of his lower extremities was pretty mangled. During this time, the military had implemented a rapid reentry protocol from Vietnam—flying the wounded over to the United States—rather than stopping at a regional facility. Like we do with rounds, we convened a strategy, and the patient was set up for amputation. I told my chief, "We can't amputate this guy." He said, 'What do you mean? He's only got skin and bones left and the bones are all broken."

I explained that his neurovascular system is intact, which meant there was a possibility of salvaging the limb. My chief said "Alvin, I think you're wasting your time. If you want to do that, go ahead. But we're not going to let him get septic or die from the complications just because you want to do that."

We did a debridement (cleaning out) of the wound. The limb had good blood supply, and good neurological function following debridement. We kept watch over him and when he didn't get infected, we did a bone graft, stabilized the limb, and rehabilitated him, which ultimately saved his leg. After that, I never knew what happened to him.

Thirty years later, almost to the day, his wife called me. She said, "I want to do something special for my husband. My husband has talked about you pretty much every month of our life for the last thirty years. He's talked to his sons and everybody. We wanted to find out where you were. We didn't know where you were or what you were doing. I want to bring him to see you. And that will be a birthday gift for him." It was his sixtieth birthday.

The hospital contacted *The Cincinnati Enquirer* when he came to see me. It was a wonderful visit. We met and talked and went to dinner. He had a son at the Citadel in South Carolina. He told me that he was still in touch with some of the guys who were on the military ward with him. It's amazing to reconnect with patients years after I have treated them.

I met James Moody, a world-renowned saxophonist, in an airport in San Diego. James was a tremendous jazz saxophone player, a true jazz master. He's been recognized as such by the National Academy for the Arts. We talked about music, of course, and I wanted to ask him for an autograph. I was a bit reluctant, but, as usual, Jeannie (who is more socially inclined that I am) encouraged me to get his signature! Moody played a saxophone solo on a recording of the song, "I'm in the Mood for Love." His solo has been transcribed, interpreted, and improvised by vocalist Eddie Jefferson and King Pleasure (born Clarence Beek). All jazz buffs are familiar with this version. I learned it and committed it to memory when I was in high school. Meeting and talking with Mr. Moody was a tremendous experience for me. The plane was delayed, usually a nuisance but not this time. It gave me the opportunity to talk more with James Moody.

George Coleman is a tenor saxophone player from Memphis, Tennessee who had attended Manassas High School and was my jazz mentor in high school. Coleman was anointed as a Jazz Master by the National Endowment for the Arts (NEA) in 2015. We met and went over Charlie Parker transcriptions that he had written out. He helped me enormously with my sight reading of musical scores, giving me complex parts to play. George Coleman was one of the first side men (a supporting musician) that Miles Davis picked when he began recording. He continues to play today.

∾

Charles Lloyd is also a preeminent saxophone player and NEA jazz master still active today, and like me, he's a product of Orange Mound but attended Manassas High School. I've known Charles since we were in junior high school. His father was the first, if not the only, Black pharmacist in Orange Mound when I was young. Since his family lived almost directly across the street from the swimming pool (one of my favorite places), I'd see Charles almost every day during summers in the pool. We were both drawn to music and once we got together and he comped chords for me, meaning he accompanied me on chords. He wanted to learn to play the piano and to be more skilled on the saxophone. Charles subsequently went to the University of Southern California and earned bachelor's and master's degrees in performing arts. One of his recordings from the Monterey Jazz Festival in 1966, "Forest Flower," is a classic. It was popular with the flower children who were at the forefront of popular culture at that time and became one of their anthems.

Neil Armstrong was a corporate director colleague of mine on the Ohio National Financial Insurance Company/Financial Services board. Neil was known internationally because he was an astronaut but, by training, he was a physicist and academician. We had many conversations during 1999 because of the widespread fear that the start of a new millennium would crash all the computers, and any device that was technology-dependent would have to be reprogrammed. Neil took it upon himself to explain the scenario to me one day because, I admit, I was a bit in the dark about the Y2K problem.

The insurance company contracted with two IT people to take us through the process if there was a tech shut down. We had coordination drills and systems failure drills. The preparation protocols were unbelievable and costly. As the date approached, the board met more often. The "millennium twins," as we facetiously nicknamed the consultants, attended every meeting, giving hour-

and-a-half presentations to review the detailed operations of off-site backup facilities, emphasizing how imperative it was that the insurance company avoided gaps in service processing. We're very fortunate that nothing happened.

Neil talked about visiting high schools internationally, telling students about his adventures. Often during the question-and-answer period, one of the first questions would be, "Mr. Armstrong, we've read so much about your father who walked on the moon. What kind of man was he? How well did you get along?" Confused, Neil would say, "What?"

"Your father. He walked on the moon! What was he like?" Neil thought that was hilarious. It had not occurred to any of these kids that the first man to walk on the moon was still alive!

James Blake is a professional tennis player, now retired. James has scoliosis and, as a child, he was in a brace. Since that's my area of interest and expertise, I asked Paul Flory, director of the Association of Tennis Professionals Western and Southern Open in Cincinnati, if he could arrange a meeting. James, along with several other tennis professionals, visited our scoliosis clinic, met the children, and distributed marketing materials including t-shirts and ball caps, all of which the children really enjoyed.

At that time, we were doing video-assisted, minimally invasive arthroscopic surgery for scoliosis. In fact, we may have been the only hospital using those techniques then. James looked at some of the x-rays and asked, "Would my x-rays look like this?" Then I showed him the x-rays of the patient post-surgery, with the rods in place. James said, "I want one of those! As soon as I'm done with my tennis career, I'll come to Cincinnati and let you do that to me."

In September 2015, James was working as a commentator at the US Open. James happened to be standing outside his hotel in New York waiting for his limo to go the tournament. Right there, in front of the hotel, he was brutally assaulted by a policeman who threw him down to the ground and handcuffed him without saying a word to him. The scene was all over the media. The officer mistook James for a rip-off artist who was allegedly staying at the same high-end hotel. The policeman didn't take the time to interview James to find out who he was, or learn that he was a world-class tennis player who had attended Harvard University on an academic scholarship, or that he was a sports announcer for a major network. The officer just wrestled James to the ground. The scenario, while traumatic for James, who fortunately wasn't seriously injured, was horrifying in its familiarity to Black men. James has recently written a book about this, and other experiences Black athletes have encountered entitled *Ways of Grace*.

I had a young scoliosis patient with neurofibromatosis who had undergone several surgeries with what was called a growing rod. We inserted this type of rod because her curve was severe, but we could not fuse her spine because she was so young. With these rods, surgeons can incrementally lengthen them, allowing the rod to grow with the patient. She won a contest sponsored by a local radio station that allowed her to fly to New York and meet a celebrity. She made the expense-paid trip with her mother, and when she came back, she showed me her pictures from the trip. In one picture, she was standing next to a beautiful woman and I remarked, "Oh, this is really neat! That's a beautiful woman. Is that your aunt or someone?" She looked at me in disbelief and said, "Dr. Crawford. I think you've got to get out of the operating room a bit."

I said, "What do you mean by that?"

She said, "Dr. Crawford, you don't know J-Lo?"

I said, "Who is J-Lo?"

She turned to her mother and said, "Mom, we've got to free Dr. Crawford up! Give him some time to live his life! He doesn't know who J-Lo is. If he thinks that she's my aunt, then he's definitely not getting out enough!"

She said, "Dr. Crawford, Jennifer Lopez. Now please don't say that you don't know who Jennifer Lopez is!" *So I didn't...*

In 2016, I agreed to participate in a fundraiser for the Cincinnati Arts Association. In this case, my donation was my participation in an event patterned after *Dancing with the Stars*.

In typical fashion, I asked, "*What's Dancing with the Stars?*"

Jane Klumb, my administrative assistant, who is used to my significant underwhelming knowledge of all things current, alerted me by phone one evening when the program was on TV. I watched it and agreed to participate. After that, everyone I spoke to about this said, "No way are you going to do that!" And it was a rigorous workout. I was assigned a professional dancer, who choreographed a routine to fit my skill level. I rehearsed twice a week for two hours with the dancer, then daily for an hour on my own. It was all ego. People said I couldn't do it, that I had three left feet instead of two, so obviously I wanted to prove them wrong. My team didn't win but it was good show. The video is on YouTube.[15] (Even *I* know what YouTube is.)

Sometime after the fundraiser took place, I received a phone call. I had been putting together a scholarship endowment and there were insurance requirements. The arbitrator said that there was a problem with my test results from the required physical that I had undergone. The laboratory tests were repeated and the results were the same. The arbitrator advised that the problem was that I had lost fifteen pounds over a period of six months. As a doctor, I am aware that losing that much weight over a short period of time is a concern.

I told Jeannie and she admitted that she, too, had noticed that I had lost some weight. Later, when we spoke of the situation again, Jeannie, who had given it some thought, mentioned the fact that in the past few months, I had been exercising more than usual: two intensive dance rehearsals every week plus an hour per night. I hadn't put the two together!

I informed the insurance arbitrator and sent her a copy of the YouTube video of my performance. She sent it on to the underwriter and within a week, I received an email informing me of approval for the insurance.

With many scoliosis patients, I see them over quite a bit of time. They are usually in a brace while we are considering surgery, or they might be just under observation. As their doctor, I got to know them well because I see them every four to six months and can build a good rapport. One time a little girl and her mother came into my office and she had earplugs on. I looked at her (earplugs in) and said, "Hmm. What's so important about whatever you're listening to that you have to have those earphones in while I'm talking with your mom?"

She told me, "It's my new MP3 player."

"An MP3 player. What do you do with it?"

She said, "Dr. Crawford, you have no idea." She was right, I didn't. "It can store so many CDs on it."

I said, intrigued, "Really?"

She said, "Yes. I have, like, 2,300 songs."

I said, "Jesus! 2,300 songs! What are you going to do with 2,300 songs? You'd never have any time to even listen to them. When can you get the time to listen to 2,300 songs?"

She looked at me and said, curtly, "While I'm sitting in your office waiting for you to come into my examining room!"

At this my fellows and residents—and at that time I had a coterie of international and domestic residents and postgraduate fellows following me through rounds—pretty much lost it right there! That made the rounds of the orthopaedic department and the entire hospital. I consider that I struck out and she hit a grand slam on that play!

EPILOGUE

In a 1984 article in *Cincinnati Magazine*, I was asked how my friends and colleagues would describe me. I replied, "an aggressive, obnoxious son-of-a bitch."[16] Looking back, I see that some of my teaching methods were harsh, and some students felt they were learning by fear in a scorched-earth environment, especially when they failed to reach the right answer. I was outwardly a chief-of-survival service, achieving high quality results in extremely complicated surgeries, and conducting successful clinical research. But so much of this was built on a certain amount of intimidation, creating fear for family, friends, trainees, and associate staff—essentially anyone associated with me who wasn't my patient.

I had to grapple with the question of what created this anger and led to this overwhelming desire to be the best. Was it my upbringing that led to this aggressiveness? The need to excel has always been a part of me, rooted by my mother. Though I always knew she loved me, she was incredibly hard on me and my siblings to succeed. She herself had a difficult harsh upbringing, and an element of the saying "hurt people hurt people" played out in my relationship with her. Her desire for me to be successful was a foundation for my education and career but I also recognize the consequences of such a staunch drive for excellence and perfection. Of course, my aggressiveness and anger were not solely a result of my upbringing, but exactly what led to it I am not sure. I do know that somewhere along the way, my attempts to imitate and emulate traditional, classical chiefs of surgical services was losing me my family, children, and friends.

I was in the military and in many ways, saw my efforts and hard work rewarded. I was concerned, however, that racism would prevent me from getting a leadership position in the civilian world. I initially thought success in the military could be transferrable but instead found a well-paid civilian job was not easy to come by for someone who looked like me. My goal of becoming an orthopaedic chief at a major pediatric hospital seemed increasingly unattainable. I didn't have any examples—anyone who looked like me—to look up to and the isolation I felt seeded a lot of anger. While I ultimately earned the position at Cincinnati, it was still a tenuous welcome and many of the community and attending staff did not make their response to my arrival subtle.

I developed an aggressive practice but lost direction in my personal life. An attempt at counseling was unsuccessful until a domestic disturbance brought reality abruptly to my attention. I was forced to recognize that all was not good. It so happened that at this time I had been accepted to a Harvard postgraduate clinical service course. Part of the course involved techniques for listening and conflict resolution—techniques that were foreign to aggressive surgical department heads. The time away from my practice gave me an opportunity for reflection and to assess my situation. Did I want to maintain this harmful trajectory I was on or did I want to put the work in to mend the relationships with my friends and family? I subsequently enrolled in a leadership/management course in healthcare at Xavier University. The program served as a continuation of my education at Harvard and was designed to develop administrative qualities in physicians, another skillset that I lacked. Both programs gave me tools to recognize how I handled conflict and served as reminders that leadership is not about physical or dominating strength. I needed to avoid the victim personality—which I was using to justify my actions and avoid learning how to handle issues more effectively.

Around this time, I was called to active duty at Operation Desert Storm and spent six months with a lot of time to consider and reflect. With the aforementioned realities, my approach to humans at all levels has dramatically changed. My grandchildren will grow up knowing this me, not the "obnoxious son of a bitch" they may have heard about in stories.

This change has allowed an equilibrium to return to my life, and my family and friends are now pleasantly supportive. I have begun, and plan to continue, my focus on giving back through teaching, mentorship, and financial assistance. With limited time, I feel this is best accomplished by serving on their boards. My experiences include vice president of the American Orthopaedic Association, where I was eventually awarded the 2022 Pillar Award sponsored by Dr Keith Gavriel and Dr. Bill Hennrikus. I was one of the first two African American board members of the American Academy of Orthopaedic Surgeons, and president of Scoliosis Research Society, where I was subsequently awarded the Lifetime Achievement Award. I was also the past president of the John Robert Gladden Orthopaedic Society, and reviewer of the *Journal of Pediatric Orthopaedic Surgery*, *Journal of Spinal Deformity*, and guest reviewer for many other journals within my sphere of experience. Recently, I have been selected as the chairman of the Montague Cobb Institute.

Similarly, I am deeply committed to and active in many aspects of the medical colleges that have most impacted my career, as I hope to continue to influence tomorrow's surgeons and doctors. I am fortunate enough to participate in both philanthropic and academic stewardship as a member of Cincinnati Children's Hospital Medical Center Foundation; University of Cincinnati Foundation, Dean's Advisory Committee, UC College Conservatory of Music; member of the Tennessee State University Foundation; and founder and executive chairman of Black Men in Medicine at UC College of Medicine. I am keenly aware of the diminishing pool of Black males entering the medical field and work with the diversity and inclusion community to promote culturally competent care among medical students and faculty. My African American colleague, Anthony Rankins, MD, clinical professor at Howard University College of Medicine, became the first African American president of the American Academy of Orthopaedic Surgeons and continues to contribute to medical education in the form of supporting a scholarship for underrepresented medical students through the Society of Military Orthopaedic Surgeons (SOMOS).

Many years ago, I joined the local chapter of Sigma Phi Pi fraternity. Started in 1904 by a small group of professional Black men of achievement in Philadelphia, Sigma Phi Pi is unlike other Greek letter organizations in that members must have already received college and professional degrees at the time of their induction. Called the Boulé, members are Archons, spouses are Archousai: a concept derived from and patterned on ancient Greek government. The goal of the society resonates so well with me—to foster a fraternal union in which Black men of distinction could thrive in social interaction, in an atmosphere of mutual respect as individuals, and together as an organization, to fill a cultural void caused by a pattern of exclusion of peoples of color from the mainstream of American life. The fraternity is the oldest Greek letter organization among Black Americans. Over time, I took a turn as president, or Sire.

I have never left my love of tennis and indeed found a way to mix tennis and medicine through my membership on the board of Cincinnati Tennis for Charity, the sponsoring facility for the Western & Southern Open Tennis Tournament, to raise funds to support inner city youth tennis, UC's Barrett Cancer Center, and Cincinnati Children's Hospital. And perhaps my most unique role, I am a member of the African American Capital Enterprise (AACE), started in 2018 by Cincinnati Reds owner Bob Castellini and Ed Rigaud as Major League Baseball's first African American ownership group.

As the time of this writing in 2022, our country continues to be in turmoil with deadly encounters between Black males and the police frequently in the news. In the face of this tragedy, compounded by the COVID-19 pandemic, unfortunately the platitudes of expected resolutions to these issues are suspect to me. As the saying goes, "I've played this tune and seen the movie before ... with little change in hearts and minds." I draw encouragement from the diverse participants in the protests and marches, such as the Black Lives Matter efforts.

Yet while life and opportunities for Black individuals have improved, certain situations in our country lead me to believe that a return to conditions I encountered growing up could be just a vote away in any election. I plan to dedicate my energies to help Black medical students navigate the roadblocks that may hinder them as they pursue healthcare professions.

Legacy as a concept can be complex. Looking back, I see my legacy as multifaceted—a legacy with the pediatric orthopaedic division; with my team of administrators, nursing staff, residents, and fellows; with my patients and their families. One layer of my legacy I am particularly proud of is my approach to interacting with children. I encourage them to express themselves freely and share their thoughts and opinions about their diagnosis and treatment, working to make sure I engaged with them directly, not just through their parents. Many of my former patients are now adults and several have let me know that they remember me as the first doctor that spoke to them, all others communicated with their parents.

In my approach, I focused on getting the child involved in what I was doing to make them better. With adult patients, it's not always clear what their motivation is, but kids have one goal: getting back to playing with their friends. I made an effort to ensure that my fellows and residents were trained that way as well.

As for the parents, I felt that the most important issue was ensuring consistent, educated, consenting discussions. They needed to know that the treatment of their child was a group effort and as the doctor, it was my responsibility to make clear that we were all working together. I tried to explain the steps thoroughly, making sure to clarify the points at which medical and/or even legal situations could arise, even though this phase of the conversation could be uncomfortable or even frightening. If there were complications, the parent would feel that they had been informed. At that point, together, we could discuss how to resolve any untoward situation.

I came to Cincinnati Children's in 1977. At that time, I wasn't able to secure a director position at any other children's hospital in the United States. To develop an academic practice, I needed doctors, fellows, residents, and researchers. The best of the best were more inclined to consider Philadelphia, Boston, Los Angeles, or Chicago. But the University of Cincinnati was able to provide visas for international residents and fellows. Based on my previous experience at the duPont Institute, we also accepted osteopaths as qualified physicians. Both actions expanded the reach and allowed Cincinnati to garner a high-quality, rigorous workforce. Now some doctors of osteopathic medicine (DO) training programs even select Cincinnati Children's as a fixed element in their training pathway.

The pediatric orthopaedic division was focused on utilizing innovative approaches. For example, doctors Eric Wall and Donita Bylski-Austrow pursued a technique of modulating the growth of the thoracic spine to prevent the progression of scoliosis deformity without a spinal fusion. The biomechanics of the activity of the thoracic growth plates was documented by this team and continues to be cited in our literature. There were no obstacles to being creative. I have included quotes from so many of my colleagues and peers because it's hard to mention any without mentioning all, and I am acutely aware of the importance of giving credit where credit is due.

Our nurses and administrators were an essential part of the practice and while the work was demanding, it also afforded a lot of opportunity for autonomy with patients and family. Respect—among the doctors and nurses and behind the patients and staff—was a foundational quality of the division.

I've been honored with accolades that I never thought possible; among them, two eponymous chairs at the UC Medical School, one in pediatric orthopaedic surgery and the other in spine surgery, and a center named after me, the Alvin H. Crawford Spine Center. One of the most cherished of my honors was to give the commencement address to the 2016 graduating class at the UC

College of Medicine and to "hood" (place the hood from her graduation gown over her head) a former patient of mine: a young woman whom I had operated on and who had succeeded despite physical difficulties.

An acquaintance of mine, formerly the president of a Kentucky university, recounted a conversation that he had with a public official who commented that, instead of a retirement, he planned a "re-wire-ment." My acquaintance thought that was noteworthy and so do I.

So rather than be fully retired, I am instead being rewired. I've begun an orthopaedic transitional clinic, examining former patients (aged 16 and older) who underwent care and/or intervention for pediatric orthopaedic issues to assess the impact of the process. I appreciate Peter Stern, former chair of the Department of Orthopaedic Surgery, and Michael Archdeacon, the current chief of orthopaedics at UC, for allowing me to actively practice as a Professor Emeritus and continue my research in my "re-wire-ment." Ferhan Asghar kindly assisted me in surgical management of cases as well as shared his OR time at UC Westchester.

The purpose of the Alvin H. Crawford Spine Center was to expand the boundaries of treatment of certain disorders. Peter Sturm, director of the Crawford Spine Center, and Viral Jain have taken this mandate to a higher level by including management of early-onset spine conditions found in very young children and soon Alvin Jones, a former pediatric orthopaedic surgical fellow will be joining them.

James McCarthy, now the director of the division, who holds the Alvin Crawford Chair in Pediatric Orthopaedics, has been a leader in our field. His special interest is neurological orthopaedic disorders. With support from Ohio National Life Insurance, he has developed one of the finest gait laboratories for children in the United States. He is a former president of the Pediatric Orthopaedic Society of North America (POSNA), and has consistently led the department to a respectable ranking (in 2022, Cincinnati Children's was ranked number three in the nation) among children's hospitals, as reported in *US News & World Report*.

The University of Tennessee Health Science Center established four learning communities to help students navigate medical school. One is the Alvin H. Crawford House. These are virtual houses and provide a much-needed connection point for these students. There are advisors who meet within the community, providing advice, support, and encouragement. I see the Crawford House as a virtual community that provides the student with resources and useful staff to improve the medical school experience. I'm delighted at having the House named after me.

At the 2018 University of Cincinnati graduation exercises, I was awarded an honorary doctor of science in recognition of "brilliance and benevolence in his profession; passion as a change agent for inclusion and community impact."

At the 2019 Pediatric Orthopaedic Society of North America (POSNA) meeting, in recognition of significant contributions of articles based on clinical research regarding the management of hip, knee, and spine conditions, I was named to its inaugural Hall of Fame.

In February 2019 the University of Cincinnati Department of Orthopaedic Surgery presented "The Journey: Experiences of Three Generations of (African American) Academic Orthopaedic Surgeons" in celebration of the inaugural Alvin H. and Alva Jean Crawford Eminent Visiting Scholar Professorship. African Americans comprise only 1.7 percent of orthopaedic surgeons, the whitest surgical specialty and less than five have been professors and/or directors of their departments in majority US medical schools. Drs. Augustus White (mentioned many times in this book) and George Russell also participated. A monograph of this historical event is in progress.

Upon Jeannie's retirement from teaching, she decided to fund the aspirations of children who had dreams of going into the arts. Jeannie may seem extremely gentle and soft spoken, but she is actually very tough and tenacious. In 2017, we created the Alvin H. and Alva Jean Crawford Scholarship with the purpose of supporting both underrepresented minority UC medical students and underrepresented students entering the College-Conservatory of Music, and lastly, we sponsor a diversity scholarship for Northern Kentucky University College of Informatics. In February 2019, Jeannie was deservedly recognized as one of that year's four "Great Living Cincinnatians."

I began this book with the story of my upbringing in Orange Mound in Memphis, Tennessee. At that time, there were no Black students at the University of Tennessee College of Medicine, now known as the University of Tennessee Health Science Center (UTHSC), where I would eventually earn my degree. Now that is no longer the case. Having my name on one of the learning communities at UTHSC serves as a reminder of how far the medical field has come, yet how much further there is still to go, so more students who look like me have access to leadership medical careers. I hope this memoir will serve as a reminder to any young reader, regardless of what they look like and what circumstances they come from, that their dreams and aspirations are important and valid. A career built on treating people with dignity and respect is always one worth pursuing.

It is what it is…

ACKNOWLEDGMENTS

Acknowledgments are always difficult when you've lived as long as I have, had a career as wonderful as mine, and received help from so many fellow humans. "My God, what if I fail to mention someone."

Starting off with thanks to your mom, family, wife, and kids is never a bad start. I've been blessed to have been supported by my wife, Alva Jean, and my children, Carole and Alvin Jr., his wife Charlotte, and the next generation of grandkids, Mia, Elle, and Uma. They bear witness to the struggles their father/grandpa encountered in a journey that continues even as the print of this book is drying. They have been resilient through multiple relocations and focuses on my part.

My wife assumed that I would be a studio musician when we started dating, and she has stayed through this wild ride that led me to become an academic pediatric orthopaedic surgeon, knowing that until my sophomore year in college I wanted nothing to do with science and/or academics so long as I could play my horn.

My mother, the center of my universe growing up, a divorced, single, Black woman with three children underfoot, was destined to be a domestic worker with little financial support, yet successfully raised Gwen, Robert, and myself to become college graduates with successful careers. Her life was made better in a second marriage while she pursued nursing when her first three children were transitioning to adulthood and leaving the nest. She produced another younger sister Clarice, and brother, Michael. My mother was, for the time of my youth, not necessarily sweet and gentle, but she loved me, and I knew her desire was for all of us to be successful.

Through a journey outlined with tremendous sociopolitical changes, in addition to medical-educational transformations, I started my orthopaedic career in the military, having set up the first full-service pediatric orthopaedic department at Naval Hospital San Diego (for which I was awarded the first of many medals). Being in the Elmo Zumwalt Navy, where there was true equal opportunity and incentive, my efforts continued to be rewarded. At the time a mentor commented that many felt I could be successful in the civilian community, so perhaps I should leave the military. I initially thought success could be transferrable and looked for a civilian job, although I was concerned that racism would prevent me from getting a leadership position in that world. A military friend, Dennis Lynne, invited me to join him at Henry Ford Hospital and all was well. Professional life couldn't have been better at Henry Ford, and my associate was the ultimate caring pediatric orthopaedic who was not interested in complex surgical challenges, so we became the perfect combination. Yet I was anxious at the end of the day. My anxiety was that I felt I could develop an elite freestanding pediatric orthopaedic program in a children's hospital if given the chance; however no one would give me a job.

Ed Miller in Cincinnati was developing an orthopaedic department separate from a surgical subdivision. I interviewed and became the chief of orthopaedics at Cincinnati Children's Hospital. I'm not sure the community and attending staff were eager for this change and their response was not subtle. In addition, my family was less than comfortable with our move to the "most segregated city in the United States." Aaron Perlman, my predecessor at Cincinnati, was my biggest fan, and made every effort to assist me in any way he could.

Fast forward to the time of this publication, and we now have a respected children's orthopaedic center with eponymically endowed chairs in pediatric orthopaedics, pediatric spine surgery, as well as the Crawford Spine Center dedicated in my name. You'll have to read the book for the details of getting from there to here.

A friend recently quoted "if you see a turtle sitting on a fence post, you know it surely didn't get there on its own." This book shares with you both the amazing journey and details those who helped steer the wheels. I hereby apologize if for any reason someone is left out.

There is a potential sea change in race relations in our country at this time based on continuing, if not worsening, encounters between African American males, police, and other authority figures. The brutal killing of George Floyd streamed live to the entire world allowed the majority community to see in living color the atrocities prevalent against African Americans, which are not uncommon in many communities. Unfortunately, the platitudes of expected predicted resolutions to this brutal slaying and other similar situations are suspect. I've seen this movie and played this tune before with little substantive change in hearts and minds. I'm encouraged by majority populations taking part in protests and marches. Their personal commitments and involvement across Black racial lines are dramatically different than kids on the sidelines who threw objects and spat on my generation of protestors. While life and opportunities for this group have improved, certain situations in our country lead me to believe that it's a precarious situation at best.

I plan to dedicate my remaining energies to helping Black males and females navigate the roadblocks as they pursue this wonderful healthcare field of orthopaedic surgery. Our university division has not been able to attract a full-time African American male in the 45 years I've been here in spite of my personal successes. Three African American males and one female are in the current resident staff.

Recognition of several humans in my orthopaedic career path is paramount. Dr. Otto Aufranc, once recognized as the world's finest arthroplasty surgeon, befriended and mentored me as his fellow on compassionate treatment of humans at Massachusetts General Hospital. My life was dramatically changed in 1967–68 when the new orthopaedic chief at Boston Naval Hospital, John Howard, convinced Arthur Pappas and others to accept me into the Harvard University training program. With those introductions, a singularly unique opportunity allowed me to be trained by John Hall and G. Dean MacEwen, and mentored by Mihran O. Tachdjian, the reigning premiere practitioners, as well as many others in the emerging specialty of pediatric orthopaedic surgery.

I have identified in the book numerous staff, residents, and colleagues who have helped me along the way. My special relationship of over 50 years with John Anthony "Tony" Herring, during which time we have agreed and disagreed agreeably, but always with tremendous respect and care, has been remarkable and is further detailed in the book, as is a relationship with his wife Kathie and my wife, Jeannie.

While the racial statistics in the field of orthopaedics determined that the majority of my professional friends and colleagues would be white, the orthopaedic divisions I oversaw were always mixed race and genders. I'm particularly pleased to have mentored a testosterone-free spinal surgical team.

I hold high hopes for several of my mentees of color who are destined for leadership in our respective fields, including Jaysson Brooks, Tonya Dixon, Macalus Hogan, Viral Jain, Wayne Johnson, Alvin Jones, Shital Parikh, George Russell, and Larry Wells. Thank you to mentors of color Charlie Epps, Cato Laurencin, and Randall Morgan to mention only a few.

A sincere thanks to Bob Anning, Angelo Dean, Lester Duplechen, Clyde Henderson, Bill Hennrikus, Chris Lewis, Francesca Mangano, Elsie Mason, Cedric Ricks, Dick Schwartz, Dr. Wilbur Suesberry, Michael Thomas, James O. Bolden, David O'Malley, Amos "Sco" Otis, Jim Anderson, Robert Luke, and many others who've helped along the way.

Starting our mentoring program, Black Men in Medicine Cincinnati (BMIMC) infused me with learners Adam Butler; Mike Deal, MD; Derek Dwayne, MD; and Austin Thompson for our beginning group, and more participants continue to follow in their footsteps. Developing this group would not be possible without Dolores Dodson, Dean Andrew Filak and his assistant Karen Christian, Lisa Johnson, Mia Mallory, Bleuzette Marshall, and kind lodging facilities from Michael A. Lieberman, PhD. My sanity (music rehabilitation) started with former dean, Peter Landgren, continued with Craig Bailey, who is possibly one of the world's finest jazz saxophonists, and jazz professor, Scott Belck.

My appreciation is extended to Mike Archdeacon, Angela Koenig, James McCarthy, Peter Stern, and Peter Sturm for allowing this emeritus professor to continue to educate our training staff. My journey in writing this book took many years and several iterations. I am delighted to publish my memoir here, at the University of Cincinnati Press. It's here I met many, many times over the last few years with Elizabeth Scarpelli, founding director of the Press; Sarah Muncy, my developmental editor; and undergraduate production coordinator and my fellow UC Alumni Band member Jared Brancatelli. Last, but certainly not least, Ms. Jane Klumb, my invaluable administrative assistant, always makes the best efforts to bring me into the world of communicative electronic technology.

ENDNOTES

1. Jim Farber, "A Burst of Light, Even in Dark Times," New York Times, July 30, 2016. https://www.nytimes.com/2016/07/30/arts/music/sharon-jones-documentary-interview.html (accessed December 20, 2022).

2. Dr. Augustus White worked as a surgical technician at E.H. Crump Hospital while a college senior at Brown University. He is the coauthor of the most extensive book on clinical biomechanics of the spine, became professor of orthopaedics at Yale and Harvard Medical Schools, and retired as professor of orthopaedics at Harvard, and was the master of the Oliver Wendell Holmes Society of the Harvard Medical School.

3. Alyson Ma, Alison Sanchez, and Mindy Ma, "The Impact of Patient-Provider Race/Ethnicity Concordance on Provider Visits: Updated Evidence from the Medical Expenditure Panel Survey," *Journal of Racial and Ethnic Health Disparities* 6, no. 5 (October 2019): 1011–20. doi: 10.1007/s40615-019-00602-y.

4. "Honors and Recognitions," University of Tennessee Health Science Center. https://catalog.uthsc.edu/content.php?catoid=29&navoid=2758 (accessed December 12, 2022).

5. Ralph Ellison, *Invisible Man*, 3.

6. Joseph Heller, *Catch-22* (New York: Simon and Schuster, 2011).

7. Alvin H. Crawford, J. L. Marxen, and D. L. Osterfeld. "The Cincinnati Incision: A Comprehensive Approach for Surgical Procedures of the Foot and Ankle in Childhood." *Journal of Bone and Joint Surgery* 64, no. 9 (1982): 1355–8.

8   "Surgical Site Infections," Johns Hopkins Medicine, https://www.hopkinsmedicine.org/health/conditions-and-diseases/surgical-site-infections (accessed December 17, 2022).

9   Boot Camp is where we teach the basic techniques of diagnosing and treating various conditions. There are two segments, a didactic lecture on a condition followed by a clinical and radiological review of actual cases that have presented in the past two to three weeks, mostly trauma. We go through identification, observation, and management. The focus is on organizing a sequence: sex, age, medical record number, side of extremity, location of injury, bone density, diagnosis, and treatment options.

10 Oestreich, Alan and Alvin H. Crawford, *Atlas of Pediatric Orthopaedic Radiology* (New York: Thieme Publishing, 1985).

11 Oestreich, Alan, *Pediatric Radiology Medical Outline Series* (Doylestown, PA: Medical Examination Pub. Co, 1984).

12 Good News was the commercial name of a disposable shaving razor. I kept a supply at the nursing station in the clinic.

13 Alvin Crawford, "It Is What It Is." *Journal of Bone and Joint Surgery* 64, no. 10 (2004): 2332-4.

14 *Lonesome Dove* was a cowboy series that aired in 1989. The miniseries was adapted from the novel of the same name written by Larry McMurtry. When it aired, it was the number one program on television.

15 "Dr. Crawford Rehearsal for Cincinnati Dancing for the Stars 2017." https://www.youtube.com/watch?v=ZzggNGOsO3c (accessed December 18, 2022).

16 *Cincinnati Magazine*, "Dr. Alvin Crawford, a Man on Top with Just One Big Worry: That It Will End." December 1984, vol. 18, no. 3. https://books.google.com/books?id=WR4DAAAAMBAJ&pg=PA110&dq=alvin+crawford+1984+article+in+Cincinnati+Magazine&hl=en&sa=X&ved=2ahUKEwj4q8OK7678AhU5jokEHRSSACoQ6AF6BAgDEAI#v=onepage&q=alvin%20crawford%201984%20article%20in%20Cincinnati%20Magazine&f=false (accessed December 18, 2022).

BIBLIOGRAPHY

Crawford, Alvin H., J. L. Marxen, and D. L. Osterfeld. "The Cincinnati Incision: A Comprehensive Approach for Surgical Procedures of the Foot and Ankle in Childhood." *Journal of Bone and Joint Surgery* 64, no. 9 (1982):1355–8.

Crawford, Alvin. "It Is What It Is." *Journal of Bone and Joint Surgery* 64, no. 10 (2004): 2332–4.

"Dr. Crawford Rehearsal for Cincinnati Dancing for the Stars 2017." https://www.youtube.com/watch?v=ZzggNGOsO3c.

Ellison, Ralph. *Invisible Man*. New York: Vintage Books, 1995.

Farber, Jim. "A Burst of Light, Even in Dark Times," *New York Times*, July 30, 2016. https://www.nytimes.com/2016/07/30/arts/music/sharon-jones-documentary-interview.html.

Heller, Joseph. *Catch-22*. New York: Simon and Schuster, 2011.

"Honors and Recognitions," University of Tennessee Health Science Center. https://catalog.uthsc.edu/content.php?catoid=29&navoid=2758.

Keiger, Dale. "Competition and Dr. Crawford: His Only Fear Is That It Will All End, Just as He's Hitting His Stride." *Cincinnati Magazine* 18, no. 3, (December 1984): 109-1110.

Ma, Alyson, Alison Sanchez, and Mindy Ma. "The Impact of Patient-Provider Race/Ethnicity Concordance on Provider Visits: Updated Evidence from the Medical Expenditure Panel Survey," *Journal of Racial and Ethnic Health Disparities* 6, no. 5 (October 2019): 1011–20. doi: 10.1007/s40615-019-00602-y.

Oestreich, Alan, *Pediatric Radiology Medical Outline Series* (Doylestown, PA: Medical Examination Pub. Co, 1984).

Oestreich, Alan and Alvin H. Crawford, *Atlas of Pediatric Orthopaedic Radiology* (New York: Thieme Publishing, 1985).

"Surgical Site Infections," Johns Hopkins Medicine. https://www.hopkinsmedicine.org/health/conditions-and-diseases/surgical-site-infections.

ABOUT THE AUTHOR

Dr. Alvin H. Crawford grew up in the segregated suburb of Orange Mound in Memphis, Tennessee, one of the first planned African American communities post-slavery. He graduated cum laude from Tennessee State University in 1960, earning degrees in Chemistry and Music. After some convincing from his brother, Crawford steered away from a profession in music and began exploring medicine. He started at Meharry Medical College in the fall of 1960 and subsequently transferred to University of Tennessee College of Medicine (UTCOM) with the support of his community. Crawford became the first African American to attend UTCOM and became the first African American in Tennessee to attend and graduate from a southern non-HBCU medical school, finishing well in the upper third of his class in 1964.

Dr. Crawford then entered the Navy and completed his internship at the U.S. Naval Hospital Chelsea and served two years in Southeast Asia. He then returned to Boston to complete his residency in the Harvard Combined Orthopaedic Residency Program, winning the Boston Orthopaedic Club Outstanding Resident Award, while still as an active member of the Navy, and became the first African American to complete the Harvard residency program. He performed the prestigious Otto E. Aufranc Fellowship in Adult Reconstructive Surgery and then a fellowship in pediatric orthopaedics at Boston Children's Hospital. Upon completing training, Dr. Crawford organized the first pediatric orthopedics and scoliosis service based at the San Diego Naval

Hospital, where he served as Chief from 1971-1975. At the end of his military service, Dr. Crawford was selected for the OREF Carl Berg Traveling Fellowship and then did a six-month research fellowship at the Alfred I. duPont Institute.

His first academic job outside of the military was at Henry Ford Hospital in Detroit. He was then recruited to Cincinnati to start an academic pediatric orthopaedic program there. He became the Director of Orthopaedic Surgery at Cincinnati Children's Hospital Medical Center (CCHMC) in 1977 and remained chief for 29 years. The program grew to become one of the largest and most highly ranked pediatric orthopaedic programs in the country. At Cincinnati, he developed minimally invasive approaches to scoliosis correction and became one of the nation's foremost authorities on video-assisted thoracoscopic surgery. He has been a prolific academic surgeon, authoring more than 200 publications, 60 book chapters, and authored/co-authored six books. Upon retirement, he was honored with Chairs in his name in Pediatric Orthopaedics and Pediatric Spine Surgery. Additionally, CCHMC named their scoliosis center in his honor—the Crawford Spine Center.

Dr. Crawford has had a longstanding commitment to inclusive orthopaedic education, both domestically and abroad. He has been committed to advancing pediatric and scoliosis surgery

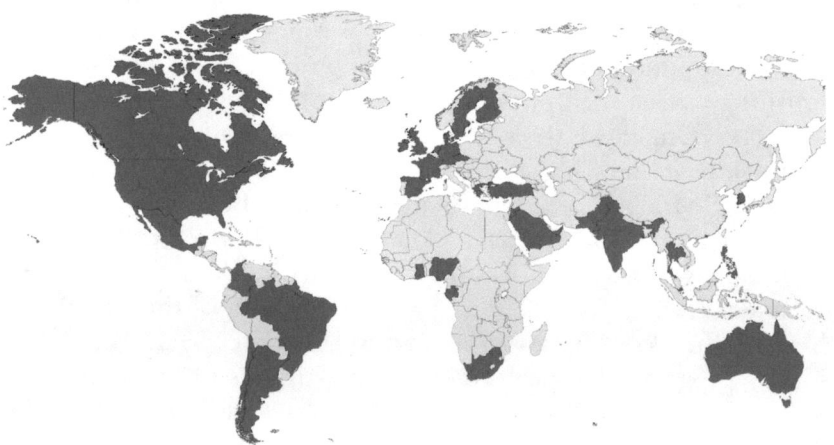

Locations of Crawford's international activities.

around the world and has taught and/or operated in 43 countries. Dr. Crawford started Black Men in Medicine Cincinnati (BMIMC), a mentoring program for African American male medical students, a diminishing, underrepresented and at-risk group.

He has been the recipient of an array of awards and accolades. He is most proud of Honoris Causa awards from the University of Ioannina Greece and the University of Cincinnati College of Medicine for his contributions to the advancement of medical science.

His passion for music has continued throughout his life. He started playing the clarinet in seventh grade, started college as a music major, and has continued to play in classical and jazz bands. He believes that his love of surgery and music have been mutually beneficial and helped him become better in both areas.

Dr. Crawford has been married to his wife Alva Jean (Jeannie) for 58 years and together they have two children, Alvin (Charlotte) and Carole, and he is the proud grandfather to Mia, Elle, and Uma.

Crawford and his granddaughters.